W9-AKC-973

The Essential
Moral Handbook

Old Testament Trinity
Andrei Rublev

The Essential Moral Handbook

A GUIDE TO CATHOLIC LIVING

KEVIN O'NEIL, C.SS.R., AND PETER BLACK, C.SS.R.

Liguori
LIGUORI, MISSOURI

Imprimi Potest:
Richard Thibodeau, C.Ss.R.
Provincial, Denver Province
The Redemptorists

Published by Liguori Publications
Liguori, Missouri
www.liguori.org
www.catholicbooksonline.com

All rights reserved. No part of this publication may be reproduced, stored in a retrieval system, or transmitted in any form or by any means—electronic, mechanical, photocopy, recording, or any other—except for brief quotations in printed reviews, without the prior permission of the publisher.

Library of Congress Cataloging-in-Publication Data

O'Neil, Kevin, 1955–
    The essential moral handbook : a guide to Catholic living / Kevin O'Neil and Peter Black.
        p.   cm.
    Includes bibliographical references and index.
    ISBN 0–7648–0922–9 (pbk.)
    1. Christian ethics—Catholic authors. 2. Catholic Church—Doctrines. I. Black, Peter, 1954– II. Title.

BJ1249 .O64 2003
241'.042—dc21   2002016145

Scripture citations are taken from the *New Revised Standard Version of the Bible*, copyright 1989 by the Division of Christian Education of the National Council of the Churches of Christ in the USA. All rights reserved. Used with permission.

Excerpts from the English translation of the *Catechism of the Catholic Church* for the United States of America, copyright © 1994, United States Catholic Conference, Inc.—Libreria Editrice Vaticana; English translation of the *Catechism of the Catholic Church: Modifications from the Editio Typica,* copyright © 1997, United States Catholic Conference, Inc.—Libreria Editrice Vaticana. Used with permission.

Excerpts from *Vatican II: The Conciliar and Post Conciliar Documents, New Revised Edition* edited by Austin Flannery, O.P., © 1996, Costello Publishing Company, Inc., Northport, N.Y., are used by permission of the publisher, all rights reserved. No part of these excerpts may be reproduced, stored in a retrieval system, or transmitted in any form or by any means—electronic, mechanical, photocopying, recording, or otherwise, without express permission of Costello Publishing Company.

Copyright 2003 by Kevin O'Neil and Peter Black
Printed in the United States of America
07 06 05 04 03   5 4 3 2 1
First edition

Contents

Contents

Contents

Introduction

O ur experience as priests and teachers of moral theology is that people often have a view of moral theology that is incomplete, that does not capture the fullness of moral theology nor the moral life. Many consider moral theology primarily as a field of theology which tells people right from wrong and offers moral guidance on specific moral issues. With all the developments in technology, particularly biomedical advances, people are daily reminded of the importance of reflection on the rightness or wrongness of action and, perhaps, as a consequence, have a heightened awareness of the field of ethics and moral theology. While it is true that the moral life is about right and wrong action, it is about much more than that. The very terms we use, that is, "theology," "moral," and "ethics," can help us to comprehend moral theology more completely.

Saint Anselm described theology as "faith seeking understanding." Although it is possible for an unbeliever to study the various disciplines of theology, the whole purpose of theology is for people to delve more deeply into their faith in an attempt to understand it more fully and to write down in a systematic way what they have learned. For example, we believe that Jesus is both divine and human. That statement of our belief has been mulled over through the centuries by theologians who have spoken to us of Jesus' divinity and humanity. Using terms from philosophy, theologians have tried to express a bit more clearly *what* we believe and write it down so that it could be passed on to future generations. Our theological tradition develops as theologians over the centuries draw from, and build on, the thought of believers and thinkers who have preceded them. Thus, the task of theology is never completed, because we will never fully understand God nor, consequently, our faith. Still, the study of theology is an effort to penetrate the mystery of God and the mysteries of our faith more deeply and to pass those insights on to the whole community of faith, present and future.

When we speak of *moral* theology, then, we are getting more specific about what we are trying to understand—in this case, faith seeking understanding about moral matters. Ordinarily, the word "moral" refers to behavior, so, in its narrowest sense, moral theology is faith seeking understanding about behavior that is consistent with our beliefs. This definition represents a less expansive understanding of moral theology. If we go further, a brief look at the word "ethics" will help us to fill out our understanding of what moral theology is all about.

The Greek word *ethos* is the root of our English word "ethics." In Greek, however, there are different spellings of this word and, consequently, different meanings. One meaning of *ethos* is related to the idea of "morals," so the word *ethos* can refer to a particular custom or way of doing things. Another meaning of the word *ethos*, however, refers to the character of a person. We call a person "honest" if he or she consistently tells the truth. In that example, *ethos,* or ethics, includes both the right action of telling the truth and the character of the person as truthful. Thus, an examination of the Greek term *ethos* helps us to grasp more fully what moral theology is all about.

Before we complete this brief analysis of the words themselves, we might look at one more obscure meaning of the word *ethos* as a way to understand moral theology. *Ethos* also means "a residence," or "a home." At first blush, this definition may seem to have nothing to do with moral theology or the moral life. What does a residence or a home have to do with moral character and action? Granting that we all have had different experiences of home life, many people typically see "home" as the place where we belong, where we are ourselves.

Might we not think of the moral life as a journey on which we are finding our way home to where we belong? Surely none of us has arrived at this point, nor are we totally consistent in our moral lives. The words of Saint Paul in his letter to the Romans could be ours, we are sure, as well. "I do not do what I want, but I do the very thing I hate" (Rom 7:15). We envision where we should or would like to be, aware that we are not yet there. A graphic image, then, of the moral life is one of a journey home to where we belong. The story of the Prodigal Son (Lk 15:10–32) fits this image well. The moral life and moral theology are about finding the way home to our true selves.

All of this examination of words can help us understand better, we hope, why we speak of moral theology as faith seeking understanding about the type of people we become (moral character) and what actions are consistent with that identity. Put another way, moral theology is about finding the way home to our true selves as believers in the God revealed to us in Jesus Christ. As we will see, "being home" is marked by right relationships with God, with others, with ourselves, and with Creation. This book will spell out in greater detail the Roman Catholic Tradition of moral theology that follows from this vision of moral theology and the moral life.

Section One of this book focuses on the foundations of the moral life. Our faith speaks to us of a God who created us in his own image, a Triune God. The first chapter examines the significance of the image of God at work in moral theology and its implications for the way we understand who we are called to be and what the moral life is all about. Our Triune God, who is community, invites us into relationship with him and with one another. In the second chapter, we examine our response to God in the moral life through our responsible use of freedom, a life of virtue, and well-ordered loves in our lives. Our response to our Triune God entails our own attention to our relationships. When thinking of the human person in moral theology, we must keep in mind our fourfold relationship: relationship with God, with others, with self, and with all Creation. The responsible use of freedom fosters "right relationships" in all of these areas. Chapter Three looks at the formation and exercise of conscience, making moral judgments which foster these right relationships. Failures in our responses break relationships. Chapter Four presents a biblical vision of sin within the context of relationship. Section One concludes with the theme of conversion, a focus on the journey home.

In Section Two, we move to a more theoretical area of moral theology, but an area with very practical implications for who we are and what we do. Entitled "Avenues to Moral Truth," this section examines some of the resources that the Roman Catholic Tradition uses to discover the truth about ourselves and right and wrong action. We begin with an explanation of Tradition itself. Chapter Six looks at Sacred Scripture, the "soul of all theology," according to the Second Vatican Council. With a particular focus on the beatitudes and the commandments, we examine how Scripture influences both our moral behavior and who we are called to be. Next, we look at the natural law tradition which has served as a very important source of moral wisdom within Roman Catholicism. In the eighth chapter, we consider the role of the teaching of the Church as a source of moral wisdom. The teaching office of the Church stands within the Roman Catholic Tradition and uses resources we will study as roads to moral truth to guide itself in offering sound teaching to the faith community.

Section Three of this work offers a brief overview of the various subdivisions of moral theology. In these chapters, you will find, outlined in broad strokes, the teaching of the Church gleaned from the resources studied in Section Two of this book and applied to specific areas of morality. We will summarize contemporary Roman Catholic teaching on social ethics, sexual ethics, bioethics, and environmental ethics.

John's Gospel concludes by stating that all the books in the world could not contain everything that could be said about Jesus and his ministry. With no intention of comparing in significance the life and ministry of Jesus with the Roman Catholic Tradition of moral theology, the same could be said of the discipline of moral theology. We believe, however, that this book will provide readers with the essentials for grasping the Roman Catholic Tradition of moral theology and applying them to their own lives. Saint Irenaeus said that the glory of God is the human person fully alive. Our hope is that this work will contribute to a greater understanding of the fullness of life and bear fruit in the lives of readers so that God may be given glory.

We are grateful to many people for their support while we were working on this book. Some provided us with warm hospitality and a place to work. We are most thankful in this regard to the Redemptorists of Holy Redeemer College in Washington, D.C., Msgr. Don Zimmerman, the Secchia Family, the Oblates of Oblate School of Theology in San Antonio, and the Redemptorists and staff of San Alfonso Retreat House, West End, New Jersey. We thank our guides at Liguori Publications: Judy Bauer, managing editor, and Cecelia Portlock, production editor.

We also received helpful feedback on drafts of chapters from friends and colleagues. We are grateful to Rev. James Dowds, C.Ss.R.; Dr. Richard Gaillardetz; Rev. Kenneth Himes, OFM; Msgr. Jeremiah McCarthy; Rev. Francis Moloney, SDB; Michael and Susan O'Neil; and Sr. Katarina Schuth, OSF.

Our gratitude runs deeper to those who formed us in the faith and blessed us with their lives. We acknowledge our parents and dedicate this work to them: Margaret O'Neil, the late Bernard O'Neil, Ernest Black, and Iris Black.

SECTION ONE

Foundations of a Moral Life

CHAPTER ONE

Created by Love for Love

W hy begin a work on the essentials of Roman Catholic morality with a chapter on God? Some might think it more appropriate to start with humanity and human freedom since morality
concerns our choices for moral character and good and evil actions.
Yet, Pope John Paul II describes the moral life as a response "due to
the many gratuitous initiatives taken by God out of love" for us (*The
Splendor of Truth,* §10). This description of the moral life seems more
accurate for two reasons. First, God always acts first and thus the
moral life begins with God's grace. Second, we respond in freedom
in the moral life to something that happens. It may be an unkind
word, a violent act, a smile, a compliment. All these occur, and we
respond in some way. As we will discuss later, the way we interpret
what happens in our lives, the way we judge good and evil, precedes
our action in freedom. This dynamic marks the moral life.

From our faith perspective, the moral life does not begin with us,
but rather with God. Pascal once wrote that "we would not seek you,
Lord, if you had not first found us." God acts first in our lives. Consequently, an authentic image of God is crucial for moral theology
for two principal reasons. First, we must know to whom we are responding and what the nature of the response should be. Second,
focusing on truthful images of God moves us to a clearer understanding of ourselves and our purpose in life. Our Creation story
and theology tell us that we have been made in the image and likeness of God (Gen 1:26). No other creature can make this claim. So,

truthful images of God will yield a more authentic response in the moral life that will, in turn, shape us truthfully in the image and likeness of God.

We are immediately confronted with a difficulty when speaking of God, however. Because God is mystery, it is impossible to fully comprehend God (CCC §§39–43). Our only way to attempt to understand God is by analogy, through reflection on our own human experience. That is what theologians have done for centuries. Our approach will be no different.

Our faith confesses a God who is Trinity and who has revealed himself throughout salvation history. The mystery of the Holy Trinity is the most fundamental and deepest mystery of our Christian faith (CCC §234). We will reflect briefly on God as Trinity and on one particular image of God presented by Jesus in the Gospel according to Saint Luke. We also draw out the implications of the image of God for the moral life.

1. Trinity: A Communion of Love

One of the most beloved icons in both the eastern and western world is the renowned *The Old Testament Trinity* or simply *Trinity* by the Russian painter Andrei Rublev (1360–1430). A reproduction of this painting serves as the frontispiece of this book (p. ii). This image is based on the Genesis story of three visitors at Mamre, three angels who surprised Abraham and Sarah with a visit (Gen 18:1–8). This scene from Scripture has been the occasion for artistic reflection on the Trinity for centuries.

Rublev's *Trinity* presents three haloed angels seated around a small table with a chalice in the center. True to the purpose of an icon, *Trinity* draws the viewer into itself in at least two ways. First, we are caught up in a subtle circular movement within the icon. The posture of each angel draws our attention from one to the other. The angel on the right appears to be leaning toward the angel in the middle, who, in turn, looks toward the angel on the left. The angel on the left inclines its head toward the one on the right, thus bringing us back to the beginning. So, viewers would find themselves caught up in the movement of the glances of the angels from one to the other. We are also drawn into the painting by an open space at its base, where viewers would be standing. It is as if we are invited to a place at the table with the three angels.

Rublev's image provides a wonderful entry point into the mystery of the Trinity, to the God who created us, redeems us, and sanctifies us, while, at the same time, it invites a reflective response from each one of us.

First, the icon suggests our understanding of the relationship among the persons of the Trinity. They are coequal persons. In Rublev's image, it is unclear which angel represents which person of the Trinity. This observation is made more to indicate the equality of the persons in the Trinity than to suggest that the persons are one and the same. Each angel, in fact, is distinct: Father (Creator), Son (Revealer and Redeemer), and Spirit (Sanctifier). The life of the Trinity, conveyed in the image, is a union of love: the Father loving the Son, receiving the love of the Son, the Spirit as that love personified.

The first thing to say about the Trinity, then, is that it is a communion of love, an eternal giving, receiving and exchanging of love among the inseparable persons of the Trinity—Father, Son, and Holy Spirit (CCC §221). This is the inner life of our Triune God, the way that the persons relate to one another. Some suggest that the position of the lateral angels in Rublev's icon forms something of a chalice, symbolic of the internal life of the Trinity as a chalice of love.

We believe, however, that God does not contain his love within the confines of the Trinity. It is God's desire to share love not only among the persons of the Trinity but to go out from their communion. This quality is caught in the icon at the point where the chalice of love, representing the inner life of the Trinity, is offered through the open space at the base of the icon; a real chalice is offered to the viewer who has taken the observer's "place" at the table. Another interpretation of the significance of the open space is that it is the place where Trinitarian life flows over into a creative love.

The Creation of the world, and humanity in particular, is an expression, a manifestation, of God's love and reaching out to humanity. It is the original and universal testament to God's all-encompassing love (CCC §288). Thomas Aquinas says beautifully, "Creatures came into existence when the key of love opened his hand" (see CCC §293). Throughout salvation history, God continually reached out to humanity. The stories of our salvation recount these events, particularly through the prophets (CCC §§54–64). The fullness of the revelation of God, however, comes through the human face of Jesus of Nazareth. "Long ago God spoke to our ancestors in many and various ways by the prophets, but in these last days he has spoken to us by a Son" (Heb 1:1–2). Jesus is the concrete expression of God's love for us. John 3:16 says that "God so loved the world that he gave his only Son." The Spirit, also gift to us, moves us to know and to love Jesus and to seek union with the Father through him.

2. Implications of a Triune God for Humanity

What are the implications of this Trinitarian God for humanity made in his image and likeness? Created in God's image, humanity is destined to a life of love with the Trinity. Just as the Trinity is characterized by giving and receiving love, so too are we to be people of love, offering and receiving love in our own lives. This understanding of ourselves is fundamental and what we are about as God's creatures. In his encyclical, *The Gospel of Life*, Pope John Paul II writes: "The meaning of life is found in giving and receiving love" (*The Gospel of Life*, §81, *Origins*, 24/42 [April 6, 1995]). This claim is rooted in our understanding of the Trinity as a communion of love. Created by Love, we are destined to live in community, in relationships of love.

Our becoming the image and likeness of God entails likening ourselves to the persons of the Trinity in their distinctiveness as well. The Father is the source and fullness of love and truth; we have been created in his image, made with a desire for God, a longing for love, for truth, for goodness, and for beauty. So, God the Creator has imprinted himself on us in this way. Our lifelong goal is to become who we in fact are, this image and likeness of God. Our insight into who the Father is has come to us chiefly through his Son, Jesus. The love and truth of the Father is manifest in Jesus and inspired by the Holy Spirit. Jesus reveals to humanity most clearly who we are called to be, since he is the fullest revelation of God. "In reality it is only in the mystery of the Word made flesh that the mystery of humanity truly becomes clear" (*Pastoral Constitution on the Church in the Modern World*, §22; CCC §359).

Through reflection on, and conformity to, the person of Jesus, we approach our true selves. We come to perfection and true stature in Christ. At the same time, like Jesus, we become the human face of God in the world, expressions of God's love in the world.

The love between Father and Son is personified in the Spirit, the third Person of the Trinity. The Spirit, given to us at baptism, is at work first in our lives, prompting our desire for God and moving us to believe in and accept Jesus (CCC §§683–684). We are conformed to the Spirit through lives of love that bear witness to Jesus and move others to belief in him and to union with God the Father. We also image the Spirit who is the personified love of the Trinity in the loving relationships in which we participate.

Ultimately, Trinitarian life marks our moral lives by the communion of love in all our relationships, that is, our relationship with God, with ourselves, with others, and with all of Creation. The meaning of life is found in giving and receiving love. Trinitarian life is the model for this exchange of love, and it is the same Trinity which graces us to live it.

3. The Human Face of God

We have said that Jesus is the fullness of the revelation of God. Jesus' whole life and ministry show us the Father. Jesus rarely simply explained who his Father was; rather, he used images and stories to encourage the imagination of his listeners. His parables and actions throughout his public ministry consistently called people to think bigger than they had before. The parable of the Good Samaritan, for example, encouraged listeners to broaden their care for their neighbor, even to the enemy. When an adulterous woman was brought before Jesus by a group of men who were confident that she should be stoned to death for her sin, Jesus made a simple statement after some moments of reflection: "Let him who is without sin cast the first stone." All the men walked away; he had invited them to move beyond self-righteousness to self-examination about their own sin. We still find these stories and actions of Jesus stimulating today because, despite the witness of centuries of saints, we continue to live in small, often self-absorbed worlds; and these stories draw us into a struggle to understand Jesus and ourselves more fully and to follow him with integrity. His words and actions challenge us to be more, to be, actually, our true selves.

Jesus' parables moved people both in his own day and move people even now to see themselves differently and more truthfully. Jesus' words and parables that reveal God also challenge us to see him more faithfully and to abandon images of God which are small and untrue. A glance through the gospels offers images of God as a shepherd, a fisherman hauling in his net, a lawgiver, a mother hen protecting her chicks, a just judge, a woman delighted upon finding a coin, and many, many more.

THE GOD OF THE PARABLE OF THE PRODIGAL SON

One of the most captivating images of God presented to us in the Bible is the father in the very familiar story commonly called the Prodigal Son (Lk 15:11–32). Luke is the only evangelist to tell the story that has become the subject of works of painting, sculpture, music, ballet, and countless sermons and homilies over the centuries of Christianity. Its appeal is drawn primarily from our identification with the sons in the story; but we are also attracted to a father as good and as forgiving as this one. We focus on this image because we believe that it captures the God of the moral life in a unique way.

Then Jesus said, "There was a man who had two sons. The younger of them said to his father, 'Father, give me the share of the property that will belong to me.' So he divided his property between them. A few days later the younger son gathered all he had and traveled to a distant country, and there he squandered his property in dissolute living. When he had spent everything, a severe famine took place throughout that country, and he began to be in need. So he went and hired himself out to one of the citizens of that country, who sent him to his fields to feed the pigs. He would gladly have filled himself with the pods that the pigs were eating; and no one gave him anything. But when he came to himself, he said, 'How many of my father's hired hands have bread enough and to spare, but here I am dying of hunger! I will get up and go to my father, and I will say to him, "Father, I have sinned against heaven and before you; I am no longer worthy to be called your son; treat me like one of your hired hands."' So he set off and went to his father. But while he was still far off, his father saw him and was filled with compassion; he ran and put his arms around him and kissed him. Then the son said to him, 'Father, I have sinned

8

against heaven and before you; I am no longer worthy to be called your son.' But the father said to his slaves, 'Quickly, bring out a robe—the best one—and put it on him; put a ring on his finger and sandals on his feet. And get the fatted calf and kill it, and let us eat and celebrate; for this son of mine was dead and is alive again; he was lost and is found!' And they began to celebrate.

"Now his elder son was in the field; and when he came and approached the house, he heard music and dancing. He called one of the slaves and asked what was going on. He replied, 'Your brother has come, and your father has killed the fatted calf, because he has got him back safe and sound.' Then he became angry and refused to go in. His father came out and began to plead with him. But he answered his father, 'Listen! For all these years I have been working like a slave for you, and I have never disobeyed your command; yet you have never given me even a young goat so that I might celebrate with my friends. But when this son of yours came back, who has devoured your property with prostitutes, you killed the fatted calf for him!' Then the father said to him, 'Son you are always with me, and all that is mine is yours. But we had to celebrate and rejoice, because this brother of yours was dead and has come to life; he was lost and has been found.'"

What does this story tell us of God, understanding that God is always more mysterious than comprehensible? Perhaps it is important to know that this story follows two other short parables of a "lost and found" nature. In the first, a shepherd loses a sheep, leaving ninety-nine on their own to find the lost one. We are told that "there will be more joy in heaven over one sinner who repents than over ninety-nine righteous persons who need no repentance" (Lk 15:7). In the second parable (Lk 15:8–10), a woman loses a coin and scours her house in search of it. Finding a coin which even to Luke's listeners would be insignificant, equivalent to one cent or a pence, the woman throws a party for her friends to celebrate her find. Both stories end with the characters rejoicing over what was lost and now found. Both stories offer images of God.

The Prodigal Son is a lost-and-found tale as well, to some extent, but it is more explicitly a story of love. Our attention might go immediately to the sons, but, as in the previous parables, the focus is really on the one who has lost something, the father. What can we say of the father? He loves his two sons. His love is unconditional. This does not mean that the Father does not care or is not concerned about what his sons do, but his love for them does not depend on their actions; it is not in response to their good behavior. It is the father's free gift to his sons.

Neither son seems to understand his father's love. The younger believes that he is unworthy to receive a welcome in his father's home because he has abused his father's generosity. "I am no longer worthy to be called your son." We could spend more time on the younger son to understand the significance of his actions in the culture of his day. As in our own day, an inheritance is usually received upon the death of the benefactor. Suffice it to say, the son's request for his inheritance before his father's death was the equivalent of wishing his father dead. Surprise after surprise would overtake the listeners of this parable as they hear first that the father grants the inheritance to a son and, second, that he receives this same son back with open heart and arms, lavishing gifts upon him after the son "squandered his inheritance." The younger son was mistaken to think that he had lost a home because of his behavior.

However, the elder son also fails to understand his father. He appears to think that his father's love is in response to his faithful work, his constancy in his labors at home. The elder son has a *quid pro quo* approach to life, it seems. "For all these years I have been working like a slave for you, and I have never disobeyed your command; yet you have never given me even a young goat so that I might celebrate with my friends." Since he has worked so hard for his father, the father should have given him at least a goat to eat with his friends. Love is more like a contract in the elder son's mind, it appears. Love is earned. So, failing to understand his father's love, the elder son apparently cannot love his brother in a similar way, nor is he capable of calling him brother. In the text of the parable, the elder son says "your son" to his father, not "my brother." This son, unfortunately, remains lost at the end of the parable.

GOD'S LOVE NEVER FAILS

As are all parables, this one is rich in symbolism and could be the subject of a book itself. Our purpose is simply to ask how this image of God impacts our understanding of the moral life as a response to God.

First, the Prodigal Son reminds us that, contrary to what we may believe and even consider just, God's love for us does not depend on our behavior. We are welcome in the house of God despite our behavior; the image of God portrayed by the prophet Hosea illustrates this fact. Hosea's wife, Gomer, was unfaithful. Yet, as many times as she returned, Hosea took her back. The prophet tells the story of his personal life to speak to the Israelites of God's relationship to them. When they come back, aware of their sin, God receives them; just as the father received his "prodigal son" in Luke's parable.

One could argue that both the prophet Hosea and the father of the prodigal son demanded repentance before welcome was offered. But this is not true. Rather, Gomer and the younger son repented before "going home"; it was not a condition placed upon them by Hosea or the father in Luke's story. While it may be necessary, and we believe it is, for Gomer and the younger son to reach this awareness and acknowledgment of their wrongdoing, it is critical to note that this acknowledgment of wrongdoing is not a condition for acceptance. The father of the younger son does not wait for his son's "confession" to finish. The son's words of sorrow are lost in the hugs and blessings of the father.

We might wonder, then, whether we lose God's love for us through our sins? Does God cease to love us if we sin mortally and consequently withhold eternal life from us? God's love is all-inclusive. As Matthew 18:14 says: "It is not the will of your Father in heaven that one of these little ones should be lost." In these instances, it is not God, our loving Father, who says "no" to us. Rather, we say "no" to God. Does God cease to love us and withhold eternal happiness from us? No, *we refuse* to accept the invitation, much as did the elder son in the parable of the Prodigal Son. He refused to enter the banquet and to celebrate his brother's return. He refused to love in that way. As unreasonable as it sounds, we might well choose to stay out of the banquet of heaven, choosing sin instead of God's life. God so respects our freedom that he does not force even eternal life on us. We accept or reject it by the way we live the moral life. Subsequent chapters will explain these thoughts further.

IMPLICATIONS FOR THE MORAL LIFE

What are the consequences of these reflections for our understanding of the moral life? First, it puts the responsibility for our abiding with God squarely on our shoulders while always graced by God. Second, as we shall see shortly, the ideas about the moral life considered previously caution us against painting a false or incomplete image of God which one might believe effective in bringing about proper moral behavior but which would ultimately be unfaithful to God. "God's going to get you" might provoke fear in a child and even keep the child from doing something wrong. However, it comes at the expense of an authentic image of the God revealed by Jesus. Accepting the father of the prodigal son as a manifestation of God challenges images which are incomplete or only partially true.

Skeptics might argue that this image of God is too much, that it makes God too good. As human beings, we frequently put limits on our love for one another. Children are given ultimatums, as are parents. But is not our incredulity at such a good God rather an indication of our human limits on love rather than truthful descriptions of love? Consequently is it not possible that God's love continues where any "reasonable" human love would cease? Saint Alphonsus Liguori referred to God's "craziness" precisely on this point: that God's love fell outside the bounds of what most human beings would consider reasonable. God loves when we might think the limit is reached; God welcomes when we might close doors; God forgives when we might think we have been merciful enough.

Summarizing this first section, we focused on the central belief of our faith, God as Trinity. God is known to us as a communion of love which enjoys communion among the three Persons whose love overflows in creative love. Made in God's image we are invited into a communion of love with God and with one another. The chief way we understand God and move toward the fullness of life is through the person of Jesus who reveals the Father to us and the Spirit who moves us to know and accept Jesus. Confident in the truthfulness of Jesus' revelation of the Father, we looked at the Prodigal Son parable as a particularly significant revelation of who God is for us in our moral lives.

4. False and Incomplete Images of God

Before moving to the human response to the God who created us out of love for love, we examine false and incomplete images of God which have, at one time or another, figured too prominently in the moral life of believers. We do so to call attention to the inadequacy of such images in the interest of shaping a more authentic relationship with God. Many images could be addressed here, but we focus on three which particularly distort who God is and what the moral life entails.

GOD AS DISTANT FROM THE CONCERNS OF THE WORLD:
SEPARATING SPIRITUALITY AND MORALITY

Few people would suggest outright that God is not concerned about Creation, about what goes on in the world. Yet, we may subtly express this idea when we fail to link our spiritual and moral lives. The author of the First Letter of John writes: "Those who say, 'I love God,' and hate their brothers or sisters, are liars; for those who do not love a brother or sister whom they have seen, cannot love God whom they have not seen. The commandment we have from him is this: those who love God must love their brothers and sisters also" (1 Jn 4:20–21).

A sixth-century Christian writer, Dorotheos of Gaza, offered an image that is helpful in keeping the unity of love of God and love of neighbor together, as well as focusing on the things of the spiritual realm. He asks his readers and listeners to imagine a compass whose point is planted on a piece of paper and then visualize a circle being drawn around it. The point in the middle, he says, is God; the outer circle is the world. He imagines lines, like spokes on a wheel, running from the outer circle toward the center. He writes:

> The closer they are to God, the closer they become to one another; and the closer they are to one another, the closer they become to God. Now consider in the same context the question of separation; for when they stand away from God and turn to external things, it is clear that the more they recede and become distant from God, the more they become distant from one another (Dorotheos of Gaza, Discourse 6; in *Dorotheos of Gaza. Discourses and Sayings*. Cistercian Studies Series, number 33; trans. by Eric Wheeler, 1977, 139).

A false image of God and the moral life presumes that we can love God and hate our neighbor; that we can be caught up in the inner life of God, as if seated at the table with the three angels in Rublev's *Trinity*, and not be part as well in the overflowing love of the Trinity into the world, through Jesus and the Spirit. In fact, as we hope earlier sections in this chapter have shown, we cannot be in full communion with God if we do not reflect the Trinity in our own lives, particularly if our lives are not conformed to Christ.

Several years ago, one of us met with a couple who was engaged to be married. After some conversation about the wedding itself, he asked them about their membership and participation in a parish community. The groom-to-be was quick to remark that he and his fiancée did not go to church because "all those hypocrites go and sit in the front benches but go out and do whatever they want to afterwards. They're not good people." The young man avoided the question, actually, but there was wisdom in his response. He expected people who believe in God to be good moral people, to treat others well. Seeing the apparent contradiction between the faith life of some people and their moral lives, this young couple mistakenly, we believe, opted out of a common faith life. The young man also judged others without knowing where they were on their path of conversion; he presumed that they were content with where they were, even arrogant. Still his comments touched on a truth.

Any notion of a God being in relationship with someone yet not caring whether or not that person was engaged in building up the kingdom of God creates a false image of God, not just an incomplete one. It is inconsistent with our understanding of the Trinity and of Jesus' life and ministry.

Scripture tells the story of a God who is caught up in the lives of his Creation. God tells the Israelites and us that we are his people. Time and again in the Scriptures, God calls people back to relationship with himself. God is concerned about the treatment of the widow, the orphan, and the stranger in Israel. In Jesus' ministry, God's concern for the sinner, the sick, and the suffering is most evident. The Scriptures do not reveal a God who is disconnected from his Creation. Rather, God created the world out of love and sustains it in love.

Saint Thomas Aquinas says that to love God is to make God's love one's own. Moral lives that do not contribute to the goodness of the world do not, then, reflect an authentic relationship with God. In fact, spirituality, our life with God, and morality, our conformity to God's image through the responsible exercise of freedom, go hand in hand. No image of God which separates the two is faithful to the God revealed in Scriptures and the Tradition. Nor is the pursuit of the good separate from the pursuit of God. John Paul II writes that "to ask about the good, in fact, ultimately means to turn towards God, the fullness of goodness" (*The Splendor of Truth*, §9). An authentic image of our Triune God and the God revealed by Jesus in the parable of the Prodigal Son reflects a God passionately concerned about his Creation and about the building up of his kingdom.

GOD AS LAWGIVER

No image of God seems more prevalent in the history of moral theology than God as the Divine Lawgiver. We suggest, however, that God as lawgiver is an incomplete depiction of God and should not be the dominant image operative in the moral life.

References to law are abundant in Sacred Scripture. Apart from the texts of the Books of Deuteronomy and Leviticus about the Ten Commandments given to Moses, many other books speak of the law. In Matthew's Gospel, in particular, Jesus refers again and again to the law of Moses and the prophets, indicating that Jesus has come to fulfill the law, not to abrogate it. Jesus gives "commands" to his disciples as well. When the Church wrote a catechism after the Council of Trent in the sixteenth century, the part dealing with the moral life was structured around the Ten Commandments. Law dominated the view of morality with the presumption that these laws or commands originated from the Divine Lawgiver. The Trent *Catechism* wrote: "Now among all the motives which induce men to obey this law the strongest is that God is its author" ("Introduction to Part III, the Decalogue"). Later in the same paragraph, this *Catechism* refers to God as the "Legislator Himself." The image of God presented is certainly the one of lawgiver, and the reason given that one would obey these commands is because God is their author.

The *New Catechism of the Catholic Church* entitles its section on morality "Life in Christ" (CCC §1691 and following), indicating that the goal of the moral life is primarily and precisely life in Christ, not the observation of law. These two ideas are not mutually exclusive, of course. Life in Christ presumes observation of the law, but the opposite may not be presumed. Regarding the Decalogue, the *Catechism of the Catholic Church* places the observance of the commandments in the context of our covenant, our relationship with God (CCC §§2060–2063). The commandments "express the implications of belonging to God through the establishment of the covenant. Moral existence is a *response* to the Lord's loving initiative" (CCC §2062). Fidelity to the covenant with God is the starting point in the new *Catechism*; this presumes or expects conformity with the commandments. God has acted first, and our response of following the commandments fits the nature of our relationship with God. The image of God is different here, however, from the dominant one in the Council of Trent *Catechism*. We return again to the initial image of God as the loving Creator, Redeemer, and Sanctifier.

Rather than seeing God primarily as a legislator, the truer image is the self-giving Trinity which loves us first and invites a response in love. The commandments are articulations of how that covenant with God should be lived in terms of our relationship with God and with others; they guide us. Far from being a law imposed on us restricting our freedom, they are rather commandments to help us channel our freedom so as to be conformed more faithfully to Trinitarian life and love.

In addition, the Divine Lawgiver image can fail to capture the love that God has for his people and his desire for their happiness and union with him. This image could suggest that God is simply the one who orders the world and has set up certain laws to keep everything functioning well. The Council of Trent *Catechism* does not immediately give the impression that the commandments flow from God's love for humanity. Rather, the idea of covenant so well captured in the new *Catechism* serves as a better context for understanding the law and commandments. The image of God accompanying this idea of a covenant is not that of a lawgiver but of one who has created us out of love and invites our free response in love.

Presenting God primarily as Divine Lawgiver can also falsify the nature of the moral life entirely. As we will see, the moral life is a free response to God's initiatives. If the moral life consists solely in obeying the laws of a Divine Lawgiver, the whole inner movement of the moral life might well be missed. A lawgiver does not care if citizens love him or her nor does a citizen who obeys a law necessarily even consider the lawgiver as somehow benefitting from adherence to the law. The legislator simply wants the law followed for good order and the protection of citizens. Even though the first of the two great commandments is often phrased as "Thou shalt love the Lord your God..." who can really *command* someone to love them? The image of God as lawgiver can promote a legalistic response in the moral life where the moral agent is chiefly concerned with prescriptions and prohibitions and less with shaping his or her life according to Christ, the fullest revelation of God.

An image of God, such as this one, which fails to capture the "loving initiatives" of God as primary, and a moral life which does not suggest union with God as its goal above all else misses the true identity of God, thus distorting who God is and what the moral life is all about.

GOD AS JUDGE

A story is told of a bishop in the United States who was giving a homily at a confirmation ceremony. In his homily, he asked the people in the congregation to look at a one dollar bill. On the back of the American dollar bill is a pyramid with what appears to symbolize the eye of God at the top of the pyramid. The bishop asked the congregation to look at the eye. He said that when he was growing up, the predominant image of God that he had was that God was watching him like a hawk, waiting for him to trip up and to sin. No matter where the boy was, God could see him. God kept a book which contained all the bad things that the boy had done and would hold that evidence against the boy when they met on the day of judgment. The bishop said that he lived always fearful of the watchful eye of God.

While some might praise this approach, believing that such an image of God probably kept the young boy out of trouble, it presents an incomplete and nearly false image of God. Interestingly, the bishop continued his homily to say that, as he grew older, he came to see the eye on the dollar bill in a new way. Rather than seeing the glare of an angry God waiting to catch him in sin, the bishop saw the loving gaze of a God who was so crazily in love with him that he could not keep his eyes off him. What a transformation in image!

To see God and prefer God as Judge makes sense for some. Some may prefer an inadequate notion of justice as the overriding character or description of God rather than a God of mercy and love, insisting that God must be vigilant and strict regarding right or wrong since, otherwise, sinners will get away with evil and not pay for it. This view sounds close to the reasoning of the elder son in Luke's parable of the Prodigal Son. Angry and resentful that his father could love and bestow lavish gifts on a son who practically disavowed him, the elder son wants the judgment from the Father, not mercy or love.

When God as Judge is the primary image in the moral life, the prevailing motive for being a good person and for doing what is right is to avoid harsh judgment from God. Most surely, one can find scriptural references to support an image of God as Judge—more often in the Old Testament than in the New Testament (see Mt 7:1–2; Lk 19:11–27). Consider the story of the unmerciful servant in Matthew's Gospel, 18:23–35. In this parable, a servant was forgiven a large debt by his master, thus avoiding prison for himself and for his family. This servant, treated mercifully, encounters a fellow servant who owes him a mere pittance and the unmerciful servant refuses to forgive his fellow servant and has him thrown into prison until he pays his debt. Astonished at the lack of compassion shown by one servant to the other, the unmerciful servant's fellow slaves report the story to the master who then punishes the unmerciful servant. The parable from Jesus concludes: "So my heavenly Father will also do to every one of you, if you do not forgive your brother or sister from your heart."

Clearly, the image of God here is a judge. One can imagine the parable instilling fear in Jesus' listeners, prompting them to examine their own lives in light of the lesson of the unmerciful servant. This fearful response could be quite effective. However, God as Judge is simply an incomplete image of God. As mentioned regarding God as Lawgiver—and as human experience attests—a judge is not necessarily engaged in the lives of the people whom he or she judges. The relationship is in the public forum, presuming no particular relationship or bond beyond the courtroom. Although the judge is concerned with right and wrong, the interpersonal dimension of the relationship between God and humanity is missing.

In fact, how judgment will take place is unknown to us. What is known is God's mercy and love for his people. Consequently, no image of God can contradict one which appears more truthful. So, if an image of God as judge were to negate the truth of the image of the God as merciful in the Prodigal Son parable, we would have to hold for the truth of the image that seems to reflect more faithfully the Trinitarian love of God rather than the limited love of humanity.

5. Conclusion

The moral life is a response to God. This chapter examined who our God is. To whom do we respond in the moral life? The importance of getting this image right is twofold: we must know to whom we respond and why we do so. What is there about God that invites a response? Second, our understanding of God affects our understanding of ourselves. Drawing on the beauty of Rublev's icon of the Trinity, we focused on God as Trinity, as a communion of love enjoying the giving and receiving of love among the persons of the Trinity first, and then in creative love with the whole world. Next, we looked at the image of God as Father as portrayed in the parable of the Prodigal Son. Understanding God as a communion of love, manifest in one way in the human face of the father of the prodigal son, we get a glimpse into the mystery of God and of ourselves. We stumble toward a grasp of the God whose image and likeness we are and, consequently, of who we are called to be.

No image will ever accurately capture who God is. Jesus refers to God as father, yet God is not father in the same way as many readers of this text are father. Saint Thérèse of Lisieux compared God to a mother saying that "I have long believed that the Lord is more tender than a mother" and continues to compare God's love to a parent's love. The prophet Isaiah speaks of God attending to us even more than a mother: "Can a woman forget her nursing child, / or show no compassion for the child of her womb? / Even these may forget, / yet I will not forget you" (Isa 49:15). So, the new *Catechism of the Catholic Church* wisely notes:

21

The language of faith thus draws on the human experience of parents....But this experience also tells us that human parents are fallible and can disfigure the face of fatherhood and motherhood. We ought therefore to recall that God transcends the human distinction between the sexes. He is neither man nor woman: he is God. He also transcends human fatherhood and motherhood, although he is their origin and standard: no one is father as God is Father (CCC §239).

Just as human parents are fallible and can disfigure the face of parenthood, so too false images of God can disfigure and distort who God really is and lead us to disfigured and distorted images of humanity and the moral life. Our reflections in this chapter call us to a more authentic image of God as communion of love in the Trinity, a communion not closed in upon itself but pouring itself out in love in Creation. Conformed to this Trinitarian love in the person of Christ, humanity would be marked by a life of giving and receiving love, responding to the initiatives first taken by God on our behalf.

CHAPTER TWO

Responding to Love in Love

The moral life is a response to God's initiatives of love. In many ways, the whole of life is about responses. The weather warms to the sunrise and chills at sunset. A plant moves in the direction of, and in response to, sunlight. A mother bear protects her cubs from danger. A watchdog responds to a suspicious person by barking or attacking. People smile or cry at the sound of joyful or sad news.

While all of these examples may be characterized as responses, a significant difference exists, we believe, between the last, a human response, and all the others. The first examples, while called responses, *must be* as they are. If the sun rises, the weather must warm; if the sun shines and a plant is in its path, the plant necessarily inclines toward the sun. A mother bear instinctively, as far as we know, protects her cubs from danger. Even an attack dog, as far as we know, responds, as Pavlov's dogs did, to a stimulus that it has been trained to "interpret" as threatening. One time, the trainer of our security dog explained what "goes on" in the dog's mind, as if we can even say that. He said, "It's not as if Bud has a nice personality and a mean one. He's always playing; but he responds in play that is violent and frightening when trained to do so. It's really all play to Bud." Intruders would have another opinion, undoubtedly. So, while all of these actions may be characterized as "responses," they are not like those human responses which ordinarily include some kind of awareness. As far as we know, the responses of these creatures are "automatic." They entail no feeling, thinking, or willing. Theirs are not conscious responses.

23

Human responses are different; they are conscious. Our level of awareness of them, however, may vary. We jump back "instinctively" from a hot stove or scream when frightened. We smile at the birth of a child and cry at the death of a friend. Tragedy and injustice anger us. We debate issues of public policy and argue in response to opinions that differ from ours. Science advances by reflection upon, and reaction to, competing theories. In these cases, our awareness of, and reflection on, how and why we are responding in a particular way will vary, but our moral responses entail some consciousness and freedom; otherwise, they are not moral.

In this chapter, we will examine the human response that is the moral life. We begin with the traditional requirements for a human moral action itself: knowledge and freedom. Then we move to an examination of other dynamics of the response, especially how our emotions and intellect are at work when we exercise our freedom. Next, we look at how patterned human responses, both emotionally and intellectually, shape our moral character; they are the emotional and intellectual dispositions that are the substance of virtue and vice. Finally, we discuss briefly the components of the moral act and under what conditions it may be termed good and virtuous.

1. The Human Act

Traditionally, Roman Catholic moral theology has made a distinction between a human act and the act of a human person. This distinction may sound like semantics, but it is important. If a driver of a car suddenly hits a patch of icy highway, slides and hits an oncoming vehicle, there is no question that a human being was behind the wheel of the car, but we would not call what happened a human act for which the driver is to be held responsible. Rather, we have observed an accident, something completely unintended by the person driving the car. Traditional moral theology would call this accident an act of a human person, but not a human act.

The distinctiveness of the human moral response lies principally in the capacity of human beings to know what they are doing and to freely will to do it. If we took the previous example, but in this instance the driver intentionally crosses the highway lines and crashes into an oncoming car, we have a human act for which the driver may be held morally responsible. The driver knew what she was doing and freely chose to do it. So the human moral response will entail freedom and knowledge on the part of the moral agent.

HUMAN KNOWLEDGE

What does it mean to say that knowledge is a requirement for a human act? It means that the person is aware of the rightness or wrongness of what he is about to do and brings this knowledge to his action. For example, I might think, "I know that lying to my boss about why I will miss work on Friday is wrong, but I am going to do it anyway. If I wait until Friday to leave for my vacation, I'll hit that weekend traffic." If this person approaches his boss and gives a false reason for his action, he does so knowing that his action is wrong.

Suppose a woman meets a man at a work-related party and they hit it off. They begin dating, and the man conceals from her that he is married. She continues to date him, without the knowledge that he is married and only much later finds out about it. The man was clearly more at fault for his double deception, to his wife and to his new friend, but the woman was doing something wrong but without possessing the knowledge to judge that it was wrong.

So, we might see human knowledge as that which is present or absent to the moral agent in moral action. We presume that when knowledge is present that moral consciousness of right and wrong is present as well. In the examples above, it seemed rather clearcut: either the person knew that the action was wrong or the person did not have the information to make that judgment. In this example, the rightness or wrongness of an action seems to hinge on a question of knowledge or ignorance. This clarity about moral matters, however, is not always present.

In our pastoral ministry, we have heard parents say something like, "I don't know why my son, John, doesn't go to Mass on Sundays. He knows it is wrong." How do we account for this kind of knowledge? John knows that he should go to Mass on Sundays but does not do so.

Sometimes we know things intellectually but we do not prize them in our hearts. We begin with the same example. John knows that he is supposed to go to Mass, but that knowledge does not compel him to act on it. So, even though he knows the third commandment about keeping holy the Lord's day, he does not attend Mass. John also knows that the fourth commandment is "honor your father and your mother." For the sake of this example, let us say that John is faithful to calling his parents, helping them in any way possible, remembering them on their birthdays, anniversary, Mother's Day, and Father's Day. In this case, John's knowledge of the fourth commandment compels him to act. What is the difference between the two examples?

The difference in these kinds of knowing, it seems, centers on the way in which the values that are proposed are personally esteemed by the moral agent. We do not suggest that we are in a world of moral relativism where rightness or wrongness depends on the whim of the individual. We only are attempting to understand how different ways of knowing may affect our moral action.

We suggest that these different types of knowing could be called "head knowledge" and "heart knowledge," but we do not want to infer, by doing so, that the head and the heart are disconnected. The emphasis in "head knowledge," however, is on information that a person possesses, whereas "heart knowledge" focuses on what is valued.

Shortly, we will use the issue of capital punishment as a way to illumine our moral reasoning in feeling, thinking, and willing. Current Church teaching says that capital punishment is an acceptable means of punishment only in very rare circumstances. Because this issue has received considerable attention in the United States in recent years, we believe that Catholics in the United States are aware of Church teaching on this matter; we presume that Catholics have "head knowledge" of Church teaching on capital punishment. Opinion polls, however, often report that more than 70 percent of American Catholics support the death penalty. "Heart knowledge" does not appear to be present in this instance. It is conceivable that John opposes capital punishment, although he does not attend Mass; and his parents attend Mass weekly but favor capital punishment. John could ask, "How can my parents support capital punishment? They know it is wrong." Perhaps this distinction in types of knowledge helps to explain what is going on in these instances.

A human act presumes some degree of "head knowledge" and "heart knowledge," even though we are aware that the former often precedes the latter. Moral responsibility and/or culpability is in proportion to the presence of "heart knowledge" because it indicates the moral agent's personal investment in the good or evil brought about by moral action.

HUMAN FREEDOM (CCC §§1731–1748)

The other distinctive mark of the human moral response is human freedom. As far as we know, there is no exercise of freedom in the examples from other nonhuman creatures listed on page 26. The weather, plants, bears, or dogs simply respond as they must; as far as we know, there is no deliberation or freedom in their response. This lack of deliberation or freedom is not so with human beings.

Human freedom is perhaps the most intriguing gift that God has given to us. Whereas all other creatures develop according to their genetic structure, subject to the circumstances of environment, human beings develop in large part due to the responsible exercise of their freedom. We, too, are certainly affected by our genetic makeup and environment, but our moral lives are marked chiefly by human freedom, our ability to shape our lives and to choose a course of action, for good or for ill.

Freedom from or freedom for? A tension exists between the understanding of freedom in popular Western culture and the notion of freedom that is at work in Roman Catholic moral theology. Keeping the distinction in mind will help us to understand how we might use our freedom responsibly in the moral life.

Popular western culture suggests that the essence of freedom is the ability to do what one pleases within the confines of civil law. "I am free to do whatever I want as long as I don't violate your rights." So, freedom is marked by being untethered; it is freedom from constraints. Some might argue that the law itself encroaches on freedom in the situation when the law is viewed as unjust or unreasonable. Examples of this view may range from the trivial, such as parking restrictions or "No turn on red" signs, to the more serious prohibition of gambling, prostitution, and the like. In the opinion of some, law cramps freedom.

Another central view of freedom in western thought is the ability to choose one thing over another. If I am buying a car and the only option offered to me at a particular dealership is a white Chevrolet Geo Metro, I might suggest that I do not have any freedom in the matter; there is no choice. I *must* buy a white Chevrolet Geo Metro if I am to have a car from this dealership. Similarly, elections of political representatives would be a farce if there were not at least two candidates running for office. We would say that our freedom is not really being exercised because there is no choice.

When we translate freedom as essentially a choice in the moral

life, the presumption is that one is free when one can choose between good and evil. I may choose to lie or not, to steal or not, to sin
or not. Following the logic of this popular understanding of freedom, we are free as long as we are not constrained from acting and
have a choice once we do.

According to the Roman Catholic Tradition, this notion of freedom is inadequate. As critical as human freedom is to humanity, it is
not an absolute value but is given to us for something more. The
Pastoral Constitution on the Church in the Modern World from the Second Vatican Council says that genuine "freedom is an exceptional
sign of the image of God in humanity. For God willed that men and
women should 'be left free to make their own decisions' (cf., Sir 15:14),
so that they might of their own accord seek their Creator and freely
attain their full and blessed perfection by cleaving to God" (§17).
Freedom, then, is not an end in itself, but rather a gift to direct our
lives in accord with our meaning and purpose, that is, giving and
receiving love and reaching fullness in union with God.

So, the focus of freedom is not "What am I free from?" where we
concentrate on laws and other constraints on freedom, where authority and others are viewed as threats to freedom; rather the question is: What am I free for? Why was I given this freedom? The Council
document suggests that it is precisely to shape myself into the image
and likeness of God. The *Catechism* puts it this way: "Human freedom is a force for growth and maturity in truth and goodness; it
attains its perfection when directed toward God, our beatitude" (CCC
§1731).

Pope John Paul II places the responsible use of freedom in the
context of what is truly good for the person, what we call authentic
human good. He writes: "Acting is morally good when the choices
of freedom are *in conformity with man's true good* and thus express the
voluntary ordering of the person towards his ultimate end: God himself, the supreme good in whom man finds his full and perfect hap-

piness" (*The Splendor of Truth*, §72). Put in a different way, freedom is used rightly when people choose those things that will contribute to their authentic human good, understanding this choice most fully as promoting right relationships with God, others, themselves, and all of Creation.

In this light, any exercise of freedom that would hinder our maturity in truth and goodness would be done *not* in freedom, but in slavery. To put this more concretely, while a contemporary view of freedom might say that I am free to harm another or not, true freedom would say that to harm another is *not* an exercise of freedom but of slavery. I have used my freedom not for truth and goodness but to harm another person, to break human relationships. If we harm ourselves or others, we contradict the very meaning of our existence as people made in the image and likeness of God. Freedom, rather, is for love, a gift to shape us to love well. How does this happen?

Freedom of self-determination through moral choices: Human freedom, manifest in moral choices, affects us on two different levels, one somewhat superficial (but very significant) and the other more profound. Consider, for example, the choice to pursue medicine as a career. That choice has an immediate and long-term effect on the person who makes it. The immediate effect is that a person has chosen a particular course of studies that will make tremendous demands on her as she prepares for a career in medicine. On a more profound level, however, this woman is making a choice about what type of person she will be, one involved in medicine and the care for others. While the short-term effect of the choice for the study of medicine is the more obvious one, this act is also indicative of freedom working at a deeper level in this person. Presuming that she commits herself to medicine for the best of motives, she will become one who cares for others.

Consider another example. A family decides that they will dedicate one Saturday a month to distributing food at a local soup kitchen. On one level, their decision and action involves perhaps four hours on a Saturday afternoon, once a month. On a deeper level, however, the family is shaping itself as people who care about the poor and the homeless, who care enough to invest time and energy to assist them.

We could go on and on with still other examples where abuses of freedom also shape a person. If someone finds it easier and easier to lie to protect himself from embarrassment, each lie is a choice in (or, really, abuse of) freedom, yet, at a deeper level, the man is shaping himself as a dishonest person, one who cannot be relied upon to tell the truth.

These examples simply point to the way that human freedom works in our lives. It has a twofold effect in that it brings about the particular choice of the moment (studying medicine, assisting at a soup kitchen, telling a lie) but also shapes our moral character for good or ill (fostering compassion for the suffering sick and for the poor, becoming untrustworthy, and so on). It is because freedom has such a determining influence on the type of people we will become that we must attend very carefully to its use. Unlike all other creatures, we were made in the image and likeness of God. The extent to which we actually mirror God to others is due in no small part to the way that we exercise our freedom in concert with God's grace, where our exercise of freedom should mirror God's freedom in loving as a community of persons within the Trinity and as a generous creative God. Freedom is not primarily about freedom from constraints, but the pursuit of excellence. It is not simply even about doing right and avoiding wrong, but becoming virtuous persons intent upon the good, being conformed to the person of Christ by the power of the Spirit.

2. The Virtuous Life: Gift From God and the Fruit of Freedom for Excellence (CCC §§1803–1845)

Freedom, then, has as its goal the shaping of a moral character to be like Christ's. The *Catechism* describes the virtuous person as one who "tends toward the good with all his sensory and spiritual powers; he pursues the good and chooses it in concrete action" (CCC §1803). A virtue itself is described as "an habitual and firm disposition to do the good" (CCC §1803). We might think of the virtuous person as one who longs for the good in all aspects of his or her life and acts so as to achieve it.

A common human experience of longing, a very physical phenomenon, is hunger. Although most of us have not experienced the devastation of life-threatening hunger, we know what it is to feel our stomach growl for food when it has not been satisfied for some time. We know the physical symptoms and the process that ensues once we experience hunger. We search for a way to satisfy it.

The whole of human existence is not unlike the dynamic of hunger and satisfaction of need. Sometimes we get it right; sometimes, however, we get it wrong. Sometimes we hunger for that which is not really good for us; other times we take steps to satisfy legitimate hungers in ways which are not appropriate. We hunger for affection and are satisfied with the touch of a loved one. We hunger for affirmation and are heartened by public recognition for a job well done. We hunger for justice and petition our political representatives to take steps to right wrongs. We might also hunger for vengeance against someone who has wronged us. We sometimes hunger for a sense of superiority over others by fostering unwarranted biases and untruths about people. We could hunger for power over others and manipulate situations to achieve it.

There is a constant movement back and forth from experiencing our human need and responding to that need in ways to meet it.

The hungers are of the heart and of the head, they are emotional and intellectual. The virtuous person's hungers are on target, longing for those things which will be truly beneficial to the person in relationship. So, too, are the actions which the virtuous person chooses to satisfy the hunger. In other words, the virtuous person is the one whose feeling and thinking "tend toward the good" and move one toward right willing and choosing in concrete actions. At the same time, right actions (or wrong actions) reinforce good (or bad) dispositions in the person.

We will say a few words about how concrete moral actions tend toward the good and then highlight seven virtues which the Roman Catholic Tradition has emphasized as particularly critical for the virtuous person. Within that Tradition, the Scriptures themselves, as we shall see in Chapter Six (p. 119), instruct us on the virtues. Virtuous actions flow from virtuous persons, and virtuous persons are formed by virtuous actions. There is an ongoing process of reciprocal reinforcement between our character and our actions. Virtues make living the moral life "easier."

CONTEXT FOR THE EXERCISE OF FREEDOM:
RIGHTLY ORDERED FEELING, THINKING, AND WILLING/CHOOSING

A free response in the moral life is not a simple process. It involves the interplay of feeling, thinking, and willing or choosing. Some might suggest that the only important thing is that persons do the right thing; that they choose to do what is right. This is important, of course, but right feeling and right thinking behind a moral choice render it more completely good, reflecting and reinforcing the goodness of the person. Perhaps an example can help us to understand the process at work in the exercise of freedom, particularly this interplay among feeling, thinking, and choosing.

Let us suppose that your state has a referendum to employ the death penalty as a legitimate means of punishing criminals convicted of grave acts. The proponents of the death penalty have spent considerable time and money researching the most horrific murder cases in the state in recent years to arouse the sympathy of the voters and to move them to favor the death penalty. One case involves the cold-blooded murder of a police officer by a drug dealer in the midst of a police sting operation. The murdered officer left behind a wife and two children under the age of five. Proponents of the death penalty believe that justice demands that the condemned murderer should lose his life. Opponents have argued that there is no reason to justify taking someone's life, no matter how terrible his deeds have been. How one responds to this situation on election day is clearly a moral choice and will involve right feeling, right thinking, and, finally, right choosing.

When feeling, thinking, and choosing are rightly ordered, freedom is exercised well. What do we mean by well-ordered feeling, thinking, and choosing? Expanding on Pope John Paul II's statement quoted earlier, we can say that these actions are well ordered and freedom is rightly used when they contribute to a person's authentic human good. That is, one's exercise of freedom indicates that one's feeling, thinking, and choosing are in conformity with one's true good "and thus express the voluntary ordering of the person toward" the ultimate end who is God. This freedom is freedom for excellence, for virtue. Let us take a moment to examine each of these: right feeling, right thinking, and right choosing or willing, in light of the example of the murder case outlined above and the death penalty as a response.

Right feeling: Conventional wisdom tells us that feelings, emotions, or passion are neither right nor wrong; they simply are. The *Catechism of the Catholic Church* notes that the passions are neither good nor bad, pleasurable nor hurtful, in themselves. They become so to the extent that they affect a person's reason and will and move that person toward action (CCC §1767). More commonly stated, emotions are not good or evil; it depends on what we do with them. Accepting the legitimacy of this statement, we might wonder whether or not what we feel is significant at all? Does this question mean that our emotions do not merit attention? Certainly not. Emotions play a critical role in moral choice, even if they have not always received the proper attention in moral theological reflection.

Love, desire, joy: How are the emotions at work in the moral life? Saint Thomas Aquinas said that three principal emotions, and their opposites, are evident in the exercise of freedom: love, desire, and joy. Love, he said, is the emotion which recognizes something as good, as lovable, potentially satisfying a human hunger. Desire is the emotion which moves us toward the good. Finally, we feel joy once the love is ours. For example, we may be attracted to someone (love), pursue them in friendship (desire), and delight in being with them (joy). We experience the opposites, hatred, aversion, and sadness, as well. Upon hearing the story of the murder of the police officer, we rightly would hate or abhor the act of murder, and avoid doing it, but experience sadness if and when it does occur. These emotions, we could say, are rightly ordered, loving what is truly lovable and hating what destroys love.

Disordered emotions or feelings: However, as our common human experience tells us, the emotions are not always properly ordered. At times, we love what is not right and good, and we hate that which should be loved. In the example that we have used, the criminal appears to have "loved" and pursued drugs, a disordered love. He also "loved," in a sense, taking the life of the officer because it is something that he, apparently, freely chose to do and saw as good, given his circumstances. Following the criterion that emotions are rightly ordered when they contribute to a person's authentic human good, we can reasonably say that the murderer's emotions were not ordered properly and moved him to an action that was fatal for a police officer and devastating for his family, to say nothing of the harm done to the criminal himself.

It is perhaps easier to understand and to evaluate the emotions of the convicted killer than our own. It seems perfectly clear that his loves, desires, and joys were disordered. What of ours, however? How do we account for the two positions on the death penalty? (Realize that we do not intend a thorough treatment of the death-penalty issue here but only use it as an example.)

Feelings and capital punishment: If we examine our own responses to the terrible murder outlined in the example, we can presume that both proponents and opponents of the death penalty experienced anger at the murder of the police officer. So, their emotional response to the killing was one of hatred, a rightly ordered response, hating that which is harmful to the authentic human good of another. What other emotions might be at work, however? What other hungers might be named in light of what we are feeling? Might there be anger and hatred not only for the act of murder but toward the murderer as well? Do our emotions of anger and hatred move from the act to the one who committed it, leading us to desire harm to the murderer himself, just as he inflicted harm on the police officer? Might there be fear that the murderer will get out of prison and kill someone else? In some cases where convicted murderers have been executed, it has not been uncommon to hear people express joy at the death of the criminal. "He got what he deserved," they might say. They appear happy to see the murderer dead.

As difficult as it may be to accept, according to the Roman Catholic Tradition, some of these emotions and hungers are properly ordered and some are not. The response of anger and hatred toward the act of murder is most appropriate precisely because the life of someone has been taken. However, the feeling of hatred toward the one who perpetrated the crime and a desire for his demise are disordered emotional responses—as understandable as they may be, humanly speaking. Accompanying them is a desire to harm another person. Thus, to act on those emotions either through violent personal acts on the murderer or through state-sponsored taking of life is a misuse of freedom. The only time that the Church in its teaching sees capital punishment justified is in cases where the state can no longer protect itself from a violent criminal (CCC §2267). Pope John Paul II spoke to this subject when he visited the United States in 1999. He said:

> The new evangelization calls for followers of Christ who are unconditionally pro-life: who will proclaim, celebrate and serve the Gospel of life in every situation. A sign of hope is the increasing recognition that the dignity of human life must never be taken away, even in the case of someone who has done great evil. Modern society has the means of protecting itself, without definitely denying criminals the chance to reform (see also, *Evangelium Vitae*, §27). I renew the appeal I made most recently at Christmas for a consensus to end the death penalty, which is both cruel and unnecessary (John Paul II, "Homily in the Trans World Dome," *Origins* 28/34 [February 11, 1999]: 600–601).

The same pope who summarized the purpose of life as giving and receiving love also reminds us of that vocation at the more difficult and heart-wrenching moments of our lives as well. As understandable as some emotions may be, they must always be examined in light of our call to give and receive love.

If our emotions were always and unquestionably directed toward giving and receiving love, we would have no need for further reflection on our moral action. There would be a simple movement from love to desire to joy, and from feeling to thinking to choosing. However, as the issue of capital punishment points out, as well as many other more ordinary examples from our daily lives, our emotions are not always properly ordered, and they must be evaluated in light of our understanding of who we are called to be as people made in the image of a Triune God revealed to us in Jesus, who is the Truth. It is through the use of our intellect that we attempt to grasp truth and to evaluate the rightness or wrongness of our emotional response to a particular situation.

Right thinking: The function of the intellect is to make certain that freedom is used to promote authentic human good. Remembering that authentic human good requires fostering right relationships between the moral agent and God, others, self, and Creation, right thinking ensures that these relationships are built up and not torn down. However, just as the emotions may be rightly or wrongly ordered, so too may one's thinking misfire in critical areas of moral reflection. Once again, when thinking is properly ordered, human life flourishes; when it is not, authentic human good is endangered.

In the example we have given of support for capital punishment, many ways exist to evaluate this action as a punitive measure for criminals. Many arguments may seem convincing. Some propose simply that justice demands a life for a life; there are no other ways to reason on the matter. In this case, thinking moves one to a particular concept of justice in which one life may be taken as a punishment for taking another's life. There are biblical foundations for this position in the Old Testament, yet the Church's developing moral teaching has moved away from this scriptural basis for capital punishment. Sometimes people argue that capital punishment serves as a deterrent for future crimes. Criminals will not pursue evil deeds, they claim, because they do not wish to die. In this case, the death of one person becomes a means to achieve the end of warning others of their fate should they commit the same crime. Others acknowledge that although capital punishment has not, in fact, proven to be a deterrent to future crime, it certainly prevents the executed criminal from future violence. Here, the death of the convicted murderer is used to protect the common good against future attacks, should the convict ever be released from prison.

Although each of these arguments may seem reasonable to some, they are flawed in their thinking process precisely because they take for granted some premises which Catholic Church teaching opposes precisely because of its impact on the human person. We are stewards of human life, not its masters. Even though the Church itself has had a mixed teaching on capital punishment and still allows for it in theory, current Church teaching, expounded most clearly by Pope John Paul II, argues that there are practically no situations in contemporary society to justify capital punishment. We have neither the right to take life out of a certain sense of justice nor to kill one person to serve as a word of caution to others. We cannot make the life of one person a means to achieve a perceived greater end. These opposing arguments to the reasons justifying capital punishment must inform all other thinking and feeling.

In light of this example, there is also a conclusion about the function of right thinking in regard to the emotions. Emotions must be evaluated by right thinking. Feelings are spontaneous and not morally good or evil in themselves (CCC §1767). However, because of the impact that they have on people's lives, a judgment must be made as to their legitimacy. Should I feel hatred for this criminal? Should I want his death? The intellect must intervene, suggesting that while anger is a most appropriate emotional response to the murder of someone, hatred for the murderer, while humanly speaking understandable, is not right feeling and could move persons away from rather than toward the good.

We could give many other examples, such as racism, where disordered thinking and feeling can lead to actions that attack authentic human good. Wrong thinking strengthens wrong feeling and vice versa.

On the other hand, right feeling and thinking tend toward the good and promote actions which guarantee or at least dispose one toward fuller humanity, toward the virtuous life. Disordered feeling and thinking move one to reason toward courses of action that present obstacles to human flourishing, either in part or completely.

Right willing/choosing: Following closely on what we have said of right feeling and right thinking, right willing or choosing is summed up precisely in Pope John Paul II's statement that "acting is morally good when the choices of freedom are *in conformity with man's true good*" (*The Splendor of Truth*, §72). The evaluation of moral action, just as was the evaluation of the hungers expressed in our feeling and thinking, is to be made in light of this criterion stated by Pope John Paul II.

We mentioned earlier that there are times when we hunger for the wrong things and make choices to satisfy that disordered longing. The moral choices of the convicted murderer in the case above are examples of disordered longings. At other times, however, we may long for something that is appropriate, such as justice, but might choose the wrong means to achieve it. The Church teaches that capital punishment is such a choice. Right willing and choosing humanize us and all our relationships. Wrong willing and choosing hamper our growth in maturity and goodness.

PARTICULAR VIRTUES TENDING TOWARD THE GOOD: HUMAN (MORAL) AND THEOLOGICAL VIRTUES

What we have outlined above is right-ordered feeling, thinking, and choosing as demonstrated in a particular act of voting for or against capital punishment. The ideally good moral act will embody all three aspects. What distinguishes virtue in the moral life, however, as the definition of virtue proposed earlier suggests, is an ongoing disposition toward the good. That disposition which is evident in a single act becomes habitual in a person's life. Right feeling, right thinking, and right choosing are not sporadic but persistent and even predictable.

We are all too familiar with "bad habits" of overdrinking, overeating, or smoking. We call them habits precisely because they are patterns of behavior in a person's life. We would not be inclined to call them virtuous, however, because as such they do not "tend toward the good." In fact, they are harmful to individuals, so we name them vices. The traditional seven deadly sins of pride, avarice, envy, wrath, lust, gluttony, and sloth are seen more as vices than as individual sinful acts (CCC §1866).

Virtues, on the other hand, nurtured as skills for living a life of love in union with God, who is love, are dimensions of one's moral character that make the perception of what is good easier. They are not merit badges which we wear to prove our goodness to others. Rather, they are the dispositions, demonstrated in action, which shape us as the people whom God has created us to be. Saint Thomas said, in fact, that virtues dispose one toward the good readily, easily, and delightfully. So virtuous persons, through ongoing right feeling, thinking, and choosing, form themselves as virtuous in cooperation with the grace of God.

In the Roman Catholic Tradition, a distinction has been made between the human or moral virtues and the theological virtues—the first set of virtues acquired, the second set infused. The human or moral virtues, also called the cardinal virtues of prudence, justice, fortitude, and temperance, are the fruit of human effort, always in cooperation with God's grace; in this sense, they are acquired. They are fostered by repeated actions which manifest virtue. Theological virtues, that is, faith, hope, and charity, are a gift from God; they are divine in origin, hence infused. Both types of virtue are operative in the moral life. We will say a word about each.

The human (moral) virtues (CCC §§1804–1811): The *Catechism* begins its section on the virtues with the following quote from Sacred Scripture: "Whatever is true, whatever is honorable, whatever is just, whatever is pure, whatever is pleasing, whatever is commendable, if there is any excellence and if there is anything worthy of praise, think about these things" (Phil 4:8). This list of virtues is only partial. We might also think of Saint Paul's letter to the Corinthians, which we will examine in greater detail in Chapter Six, where Paul describes qualities of love: patient, kind, forgiving, and the like. These, too, capture human virtues. The Roman Catholic moral tradition, however, has highlighted four cardinal or hinge virtues, which ought to be evident in every virtuous act and around which all other virtues are grouped (CCC §1805).

Prudence (CCC §1806): Saint Thomas describes prudence as a right judgment about what must be done. The prudent person is one who examines closely the situation presented to him or her, a situation requiring some kind of response. The prudent person will examine all the options to discern which one "tends toward the good" to the greatest degree. We might call the prudent person "wise" because he seems to know both what needs to be done and the best way to achieve the goal.

Sometimes people mistake the virtue of prudence for excessive caution or restraint. They associate it with fear in making decisions. In fact, sometimes people who are delaying a decision might suggest that they are being prudent by examining all possible options and going around and around reviewing them. These people are not prudent but indecisive. The prudent person is cautious and exercises restraint so as to make the right judgment when the right time arrives.

In some of the examples that we used earlier, the virtue of prudence would be required for the woman choosing a career in medicine and for a family choosing some kind of outreach service. The lack of prudence is evident in the man who repeatedly lies to disentangle himself from uncomfortable situations. Remembering that virtue tends toward the good, the judgments made by the young woman, the family, and the dishonest man are genuinely prudent only insofar as they tend toward the good. If the woman choosing medicine as her career has consistently done poorly in her academic performance, one could reasonably question whether her decision to study medicine is prudent and, consequently, whether she herself is prudent. If the parents who have chosen the soup kitchen as the way for their family to serve others are neglecting the care of a grandparent, one could reasonably wonder about the prudence of the decision and the real virtue of the parents. A judgment is prudent not simply when the action which flows from it produces some good but when that choice, in its whole context, is the best judgment tending toward the good.

Prudence is sometimes called the charioteer of the virtues because it guides and steers the other virtues by setting boundaries and standards (CCC §1806). It guides the moral agent to a right judgment about what must be done.

Justice (CCC §1807): If the virtue of prudence is described as right reason, justice marks right action. Justice is the key moral virtue that directs human beings to give what is due to God and neighbor consistently and firmly (CCC §1807).

A variety of ways exist to describe justice, for example, from the standpoint of philosophy or from the context of our Roman Catholic Tradition. Each point of view captures in some way what is required to give God and neighbor their "due." We begin with a general notion of justice, however, based on Sacred Scripture. The scriptural understanding of justice, or righteousness, is simply "right relationships." That is why the *Catechism* summarizes the virtue of justice as the disposition to give to God and neighbor their due. "Their due" is precisely what the nature of the relationship requires. As with all the virtues, one cannot say that one has ever become fully just because there will always be relationships to be harmonized. The just person is the one who performs the right action to meet the needs of a particular relationship, whether that be on the personal or social level.

Roman Catholic Tradition has accepted different descriptions of justice which can guide us in determining what is due in each situation. Some thinkers hold, for example, that to be just is to give the same thing to everyone, to divide things equally. Often when parents make out their wills, they divide their money evenly among their children so that no one will think that the parents have been unfair. Each child gets the same amount. This notion of justice is fine in some regard but is insufficient if there is a genuine need that one child may experience over another. If the money is distributed equally, some may argue that justice has been done, but this notion may miss the heart of justice.

Others hold that justice consists in giving people what they have earned; it is a notion of justice based on merit. This is appropriate, of course, as any student knows who has received an "A" for a well-crafted paper in college. Yet, you may remember the gospel parable of the master who goes out at three different times of the day to hire workers to harvest his field. At the end of the day, when the workers were to be paid their wages, the master first paid the workers who were hired toward the end of the workday, giving them a full-day's salary. When the workers who had put in a longer day came forward, they expected a wage greater than the others. Yet the master paid them the same full-day's wage. The workers who put in longer hours were outraged that they did not receive more. Their sense of justice was clearly that each one should receive according to merit, to what they earned; the master's sense of what his relationship with these other workers required of him was lost on the disgruntled workers. As we have said, then, these diverse expressions of justice help in some way to understand what is due to God and neighbor, but they ought always to be viewed in relation to the core understanding of justice as right relationships.

The examples of the young medical student and the family that volunteers in the soup kitchen point out how the virtue of justice is nurtured in the lives of these particular moral agents. The young woman, equipping herself with the skills of the medical field, will use her talent to build relationships, particularly among those who are ill and their families. Likewise, the family that dedicates several hours monthly on a Saturday afternoon to be with the poor and to serve them a meal fosters a sense of compassion for, and action on behalf of, the poor. The man who consistently lied not only broke trust with each untruth told but formed himself as untrustworthy and not dependable in his speech. On the other hand, the repeated actions of the young woman and the family cultivate the virtue of justice, moving them to right action, building up their relationships with God, others, themselves, and all of Creation.

Fortitude (CCC §1808): Fans of the movie *The Wizard of Oz* will remember the Cowardly Lion who was afraid of his own tail. His mission on the way to Oz was to ask for courage. What he found on the way to the Emerald City was a series of very difficult and challenging situations where he had to forge ahead in the face of adversity. When he finally made it to Oz, he realized that no one could give him courage but that he had indeed become a courageous lion through his constancy in adversity. This kind of perseverance is the essence of courage.

Fortitude is a key moral virtue that enables its possessor to endure the difficulties met in pursuing the good courageously and with purpose (CCC §1808). While prudence and justice are virtues qualifying the reasoning process and choice of action, fortitude and temperance are the virtues required to follow through on choices for the good. People strong in the virtue of fortitude are gutsy; they are brave. They see the good which they pursue and are willing to endure the difficulties that come with seeking it.

The difficulties which face persons of fortitude may come from inside and outside themselves. For example, fear is a powerful force to tempt one to abandon action for the good. Self-doubt about one's ability may work against one as well. On the other hand, external factors may raise obstacles. One's family might oppose a person's commitment to action for social justice. Peer pressure can sway people, young and old, from choosing what is right. In all instances, however, the person of fortitude will persist in the pursuit of the good even if and when sacrifice is required.

The young woman who has chosen a career in medicine would be foolish to think that a single choice for her career would be sufficient. That commitment to assist others through the medical profession will be challenged again and again by the unyielding grind of academic and "field" work, often tempting her to give up. She may encounter financial difficulties. In another example, the family may find the monthly trek to the soup kitchen trying at times. Other opportunities might arise which are more appealing, like a football game or a movie. How will they respond? The man who has chosen deceit has buckled in the face of adversity, exhibiting not courage but cowardice. The person of fortitude, on the other hand, grows in the virtue by pursuing the good with firmness and constancy.

Temperance (CCC §1809): "Virtue stands in the middle" is an adage used to describe the evenness of, or moderation in, the human or moral virtues. This statement applies to no virtue more than to temperance. A key word for this virtue is *balance*. Temperance is a key moral viture that deflects the excessive attraction of human pleasures and provides moderation in exercising one's passion. Not only does temperance provide balance in the use of created goods, but it also "ensures the will's mastery over instincts and keeps desires within the limits of what is honorable" (CCC §1809).

The nineteenth century saw temperance movements springing up in England, Ireland, and elsewhere as well. These societies, comprised of people who had sworn off alcohol, seem to capture for many people what the virtue of temperance is all about. Yet this understanding of temperance is faulty. The key term again for temperance is *balance*, not abstinence, except in the case of addiction.

Unlike temperance movements that avoided the created good of alcohol, the virtue of temperance asks the moral agent to measure carefully the use of created goods, not to avoid them entirely. While there are certainly examples of saints and people in our own day who have renounced ownership of all material possessions, the Gospel calls us to the reasonable use of material goods, money in particular, so that their use "tends toward the good." A lack of balance, leading to consumerism and materialism, can throw one's life off track and leave one devoting time and energy to amassing "things" while missing the purpose of human life.

Understanding temperance as moderation or balance is especially important when we are dealing with the emotions in the moral life. For too long, the emotions have been seen as mere distractions in the moral life, undesirable passions which raise obstacles to clear thinking. As our analysis of the moral response indicates, however, the emotions are critical in the moral life. They spark the initial movement toward the good. Yet, they must be measured and channeled so that they too "tend toward the good." Saint Thomas says that virtue does not banish emotions but orders them. Similarly, temperance does not refrain from the use of created goods, but uses them in moderation. Moderation and balance are the essence of temperance.

The young medical student displays temperance when she keeps in healthy tension all the aspects of her life as she begins her studies in medicine. An all-too-common error of people in high-pressure courses of study is to become so absorbed in studies out of initial zeal for one's project that other important dimensions of one's life are neglected. So, too, with the family that dedicates time each month in the service of the poor. Perhaps the most reasonable (prudent) judgment on the family's part was a monthly commitment. They might have said that they would volunteer every Saturday afternoon but might have ended up frustrated with their decision and incapable of attending to all their other responsibilities. Temperate persons will pace themselves so as to devote themselves adequately and well to the particular task at hand while attending to other responsibilities, such as family, friends, faith, and the like. The dishonest man failed to balance whatever short-term good he sought to achieve by lying with the long-term good of maintaining integrity of character and trustworthiness. His short-term solution, deficient in fortitude as well, indicates a lack of moderation and an inability to manage competing goods in his life.

The human or moral virtues, once again, are nurtured through repeated actions that are characterized by the virtues studied here. These cardinal or hinge virtues are ideally present in some way in every virtuous moral act. We turn now to the theological virtues, so named because they originate in God, are effective under his direction, and have him as their destiny (CCC §1812).

Theological virtues (CCC §§1812–1829): In this chapter, we have referred several times to the criterion for right moral action, that is, choices fostering authentic human good and, consequently, directing this human good toward God. In the Roman Catholic Tradition, authentic human good and union with God go together. In Chapter One we quoted Pope John Paul II's statement that "to ask about the good, in fact, ultimately means to turn towards God, the fullness of goodness" (*The Splendor of Truth*, §9). One can experience a certain degree of human contentment but genuine happiness, we believe, comes through union with the Triune God who made us. Genuine happiness will find us flourishing as human beings, conformed more and more to the image of God our Creator. Although one can speak of human virtue, acknowledging that people may arrive at a certain level of happiness as human beings without knowing God, the theological virtues focus on our journey toward union with God. This journey cannot be made on human effort alone. It is a gift. The theological virtues of faith, hope, and charity are given to humanity to find its way home to the Father more easily. These virtues are divine precisely because they originate in God and move us toward God. Human faith, hope, and charity will always find limits due to our human frailty and sin. Faith, hope, and charity given from a God who is boundless enable our formation in his image more than we could ever achieve on our own; although primarily about moving the moral agent out of himself or herself, the theological virtues further our excellence in the human virtues which are rooted in the theological virtues.

Faith (CCC §§1814–1816): The first theological virtue, faith, enables us to believe in God and to hold as true all that he has communicated and revealed to us, as well as what the Church holds out for our belief. The gift of faith draws one out of oneself not only acknowledging the existence of God but, more importantly, falling in love with the God who first loved us. All the virtues, human and theological, draw us out of ourselves in pursuit of the good and God, the fullness of goodness.

Although faith is a gift, it must be received and nurtured in order to flourish. Just as the cardinal virtues cannot possibly take hold of a person through a single act, neither does a person become faith-filled upon the acknowledgment of God's existence or the recitation of a creed. Rather, since faith is primarily about a relationship with

God, or even better, friendship with God, the virtue of faith is sustained and strengthened in proportion to the opportunities afforded to the person to come to know the God who reveals himself to us. We cannot pretend to be genuine friends with other human beings if we never have any contact with them; much less could we claim to know them. This observation holds true, too, as it applies to our relationship with God. The virtue of faith cannot be ours to any great degree if we do not allow God to reveal himself to us through frequent moments of encounter with him. Faith comes to us in and through a community of believers; for Roman Catholics, this community of believers makes up the Church.

The *Catechism* notes two consequences of faith: a good moral life and a spirit of evangelization. As we mentioned in Chapter One, our image of God is false if we think that we can believe in God, the God who created all that is, and yet not have any concern for the good of Creation, ourselves included. There is a necessary link between believing in God and right moral action precisely because the God we believe in cares for the well-being of his Creation. So, genuine faith demands right moral action. A second consequence of faith is a spirit of evangelization. Consider how difficult it is to keep good news to yourself. Instinctively, we want to tell the whole world. Again, think of how excitedly we tell others about the people we love: our children, nieces and nephews, our parents. We want to spread good news precisely so that others may share our joy. The same dynamic ought to be at work for those who are faith-filled. They should share the news with others.

Before we move to a discussion of the virtue of hope, we might reflect briefly on the impact of the virtue of faith on our moral lives. Accepting a God who created and loved us and who wills our happiness and union with him prompts not only a spirit of gratitude but also of determination to become the people God has created us to be. At the same time, the virtue of faith reminds us that there is a

God who is greater than we are who is always at work, even capable of bringing good out of evil, as in the redemption of the world through Jesus' own crucifixion and death. This realization that God trusts us to exercise our freedom to bring about goodness in the world should prompt a spirit and virtue of humility; at the same time, there is recognition that one greater than ourselves is at work. The virtue of faith prompts the believer to accept her place in Creation, as one entrusted with care for others, but under the overarching care of a God who loves us.

Hope (CC 1817–1821): The virtue of hope instills in the believer a joyful longing for the coming of the fullness of God's kingdom, both as the moment of salvation for the believer and as God's own crowning glory when all the forces counter to the God of love will be banished.

The virtue of hope has several effects on the believer; it is born of a confidence in God's presence and activity in the world. "It keeps man from discouragement; it sustains him during times of abandonment; it opens up his heart in expectation of eternal beatitude. Buoyed up by hope, he is preserved from selfishness and led to the happiness that flows from charity" (CCC §1818). The beatitudes, which we will examine in Chapter Six, raise our sights toward heaven as the fulfillment of the kingdom of God; they lay out the moral message of Jesus and gives his disciples a preview of the difficulties that await them (CCC §1820).

Although one may focus on the effects of the virtue of hope on the believer, one may also note the object of hope as a longing for God's glory. As people in relationship with God, a God offended by evil in the world, frustrated perhaps that his designs for Creation are often thwarted by abuses of human freedom, we long for the fullness of God's kingdom for God's own sake. This longing, too, is an element of the virtue of hope in the Roman Catholic Tradition.

One sees the virtue of hope at work in the moral life particularly in the expression of courage. Pursuing the good in the face of adversity is difficult on all counts. Courage is grounded in faith and hope that one who is all good is at work and will bring to completion good work begun in us.

Charity (CCC §§1822–1829): "Faith, hope, and love abide, these three; and the greatest of these is love" (1 Cor 13:13). Charity is the greatest of the theological virtues and ranked the highest (CCC §1826). The virtue of charity entails first receiving the love of God into our own hearts and loving God and neighbor in response to God's love. God loves us first, and out of the well of his love we are capable of loving others. Saint Thomas has said that to love someone is to make their loves, their concerns, our own (*Summa contra gentiles*, III, 117.3). To love God is to make God himself and all the things that God loves and cares for our own. Growth in the virtue of charity is manifest by a person being caught up in love for God and neighbor.

Just as we must avoid any image of God which presents him as unconcerned with the world and all its creatures, so too must we reject any suggestion that a truly charitable person could be unconcerned with the loves of God, especially his Creation. Rather, we are called to love as God loves, particularly the God revealed in Jesus. For this reason, Jesus says, "Love one another as I have loved you." With so many notions of love in contemporary times, the witness and love of Jesus provides *the* reference point for the way we are to love. The Lord asks us to love as he does, "even our *enemies*, to make ourselves the neighbor of those farthest away, and to love children and the poor as Christ himself" (CCC §1825).

Charity is the source and the goal of Christian practice (CCC §1828). As we have said, God loves us and in response we love others. Created from the source of Love itself, we are made for love. As we have mentioned several times, "the meaning of life is found in giving and receiving love." So charity is the source and goal of the moral life. It orders all the other virtues because it is the goal toward which they all strive.

After examining all these virtues in detail, we might lose sight of the bigger picture. Whatever virtues are proposed as contributing to authentic human good must be seen in light of the goal of human life. As people created in the image and likeness of God, we are gifted with freedom to shape our lives in conformity with that image. The Roman Catholic Tradition has held out these human and theological virtues as particularly characteristic of the disciples of Christ and most helpful in forming us in God's image.

TENDING TOWARD THE GOOD IN EVERY MORAL ACT

The virtues, as we have said, are the internal dispositions toward the good. They are expressed in concrete actions which either prove to be virtuous or not. We examine briefly the components of the moral act before closing this chapter so as to understand how "tending toward the good" is evident in individual actions as well as in ongoing dispositions.

The Roman Catholic Tradition has identified three elements to human moral action: the object, the intention, and the circumstances. When evaluating the morality of an action, we want to make sure that all three of these "tend toward the good."

An example can help us to understand these three components. Suppose that you are walking along the street and a person in need asks you for a dollar to help him get a bite to eat. You choose to respond and offer the man a dollar bill. What are the components of this moral act?

The object refers to the action that we are contemplating; the circumstances are all those factors that contribute to the moral dilemma that one is facing; the intention identifies what a person hopes to gain from performing the action.

The object of an act: The object of an action is the transfer of money from your hand to the other person's hand. For the object of a moral act to be good, it must foster in some way the authentic human good of the other. One could argue about the need for systemic change to help the homeless, but for the sake of our example we can say that the object of the action, giving money to a hungry person, is a good act.

The Church has traditionally held that some actions are always and everywhere wrong because they "radically contradict the good of the person made in [God's] image" (*The Splendor of Truth*, §80). Some examples cited in *The Splendor of Truth* are "homicide, genocide, abortion, euthanasia...slavery, prostitution and trafficking in women and children" (*The Splendor of Truth*, §80).

The circumstances: The circumstances refer to all the factors which make up the moral dilemma that we are facing. In our example, we come face to face with someone in need. What circumstances influence our moral response? We might ask ourselves whether it is best to give cash to someone on the street and whether we have the cash to give. We might wonder if we are the second or tenth person to be approached by the man. We might ponder the value of a short-term solution to a larger social problem. Many other factors could be at work, but none seem to indicate that giving money to the man would be harmful to him, or to us.

The intention: Intention focuses on why we act and what we hope to accomplish. The intention, or often intentions, must be evaluated in light of authentic human good. We presume that money is given to the man because we care for his well-being. In this case, our action tends toward the good. The whole virtuous character of our action changes, however, if we give money to the man simply to draw attention to ourselves as a charitable person. We might see friends walking along the street and want to impress them with our charity. In such a case, even though the man benefits from our action, the goodness of the act itself is missing because of our faulty intention. The intention most clearly reveals what is in the heart of the moral agent.

Throughout our discussions, we will be reminded again and again of these components of the moral act: object, intention, and circumstances. According to the Roman Catholic Tradition, the virtue of the moral agent and the goodness of a moral act will be evident in all three elements.

3. Conclusion

We have examined the human response to the God who first loved us. We noted that the uniqueness of the human response lies in the gift of freedom and awareness, the freedom to respond to God, to shape our own lives in community in the image of God. The human response is on target when marked by feeling, thinking, and choosing which moves one to action and fosters authentic human good.

Of particular importance in our development as moral persons are the virtues. The human or moral virtues make our tending toward the good easier and shape us as moral persons whose good behavior is both predictable and dependable. The theological virtues facilitate our relationship with God through lives of faith, hope, and charity. They encourage the proper use of freedom. Human freedom, says the *Catechism of the Catholic Church*, enables us to direct our lives toward truth and goodness and so mature as God's children. It is used responsibly when it directs us toward God who is our true happiness (CCC §1731). The virtuous person uses freedom for virtuous acts. We examined the components of the moral act, noting that the goodness of the act must be present in all three elements. The responsible use of freedom is manifest particularly by a life of virtue where one tends toward the good readily, easily, and delightfully. In doing so, one responds to Love in love.

CHAPTER THREE

Conscience:
Our Most Secret Core and Sanctuary

(CCC §§1776–1802)

Portrayals of conscience in both religious and popular language are many and varied and range from the seemingly ridiculous to the sublime. Perhaps your first association with conscience, as mine, was a cartoon figure of an angel whispering into the ear of a person who was about to do something wrong. The angel said, "Don't do it." Connecting conscience exclusively with "Don't do it," the comic-strip character, Broom Hilda, refers to conscience as "the fun stopper." Often people link conscience with intuition or with what feels right. Some Old Testament texts seem to identify the heart with conscience. Job, for example, says to his friends, "my heart does not reproach me" (Job 27:6). Wisdom is also an Old Testament expression of conscience. Others still refer to conscience as God's voice speaking to us. It is not surprising that something as complex as conscience should find expression in such a variety of images. As is often the case, no single description is complete but each one contains an element of truth.

The Second Vatican Council speaks of conscience as a "secret core" and "sanctuary" where persons are alone with God who speaks to them in their hearts (*Pastoral Constitution on the Church in the Modern World*, §16). The *Catechism* states that conscience is "a judgment of reason whereby the human person recognizes the moral quality of a concrete act that he is going to perform, is in the process of perform-ing, or has already completed" (CCC §1778). It says further that "con-science includes the perception of the principles of morality (synderesis); their application in the given circumstances by practi-cal discernment of reasons and goods; and finally judgment about concrete acts yet to be performed or already performed" (CCC §1780).

This chapter will draw out in further detail these very tightly packed descriptions of conscience in Church documents. We will begin with a general description of conscience and break it down into different moments in the formation and exercise of conscience.

1. Conscience: What Is It?

Perhaps the best way to describe conscience is the human person making a judgment about a specific action. This definition may sound acceptable to us, especially as our attention may move immediately to the words, "a judgment about a specific action." We might think, "Yes, conscience is activated when I must make a difficult decision and when I must make a judgment about the rightness or wrongness of a particular choice." Conscience certainly includes this, but we must not neglect the first part of the description, "a human person" who is making the judgment. Conscience is less adequately described as a voice, particularly a voice from outside ourselves, or some par-ticular "part" of who we are. Rather, as we will understand more fully as we go along, conscience encompasses that ability we have as human beings to desire and to know what is good and true as well as to make a judgment about which actions will attain them. Conscience includes both the disposition or inclination to do good and the prac-tical judgment for this or that action. Although formed in part by our family, our faith community, and many other cultural influences, conscience arises from within the person; it is not imposed from outside of us.

In the previous chapter, we spoke of right feeling, thinking, and choosing as characterizing actions which tend toward the good performed by virtuous persons who characteristically tend toward the good. Conscience is the "tool" to guide us to right action. It is not, however, a tool like a hammer which we pick up on occasion and put down when it is not needed. Conscience is always at work in that we are always either maturing in truth and goodness (CCC §1731) or closing in upon ourselves. For this reason, the Second Vatican Council says that conscience is "always calling [us] to love and to do what is good and to avoid evil," while moving us to make a judgment regarding a particular action, "do this, shun that" (*Pastoral Constitution on the Church in the Modern World*, §16). We examine next moments of conscience where we attempt to describe how conscience works.

2. Four "Moments" of Conscience

The *Catechism* and contemporary moral theologians identify three moments in the exercise of conscience. These are the perception of principles of morality (the Greek word, *synderesis*, is used to describe this dimension of conscience), discernment about a particular matter, and finally a judgment (CCC §1780). The *Catechism* also mentions a function of conscience as judging actions which we have already done. For this reason, we will add a fourth moment which is certainly included in the Tradition's understanding of conscience but which we name explicitly, that is, conscience as self-evaluating. The four moments then progress from an almost intuitive grasp of what is good to a discernment in a particular case of what should be done. Thus, we have a process by which we are led to make a judgment about the right action to follow; and the process concludes, at some point, with an evaluation of one's judgment.

Often the movement from moment to moment, from perception to discernment to judgment to evaluation, is very quick, perhaps even unnoticed. If we see someone trip and fall to the ground, we might move "instinctively" to help her to get back up, to ask her if she is all right, and to see if there is anything helpful that we can do. In hindsight, we might review what happened in a few seconds' time. Someone fell, we went to help her because we believe that we should treat others as we wish to be treated, and we actually did help. We can note that we perceived the good of helping our neighbor (perception of a principle of morality), discerned what to do (take some action to help *this* person), and made a judgment to do it (helped the person to get up and inquired about her well-being). Although we might consider this response almost "automatic," it required the exercise of conscience to assess the situation quickly and to act appropriately. Little reflection preceded the action.

We can imagine a different response if we saw someone seemingly trip and fall to the ground and steal a wallet or a purse from someone who attempted to help him to get up. If we observed this behavior repeated by the same person, our response to their "falling" would be different, and our deliberation prior to action more conscious. In this second instance, the exercise of conscience might be more evident to us.

For the most part, we draw on our moral character to guide us in our daily exercise of freedom. We are not often confronted with situations where we simply do not know what to do. We draw on a sense and knowledge of the good which guide us.

Occasionally, however, we confront a moment of crisis when we do not know what to do. Understand "crisis" here as a critical moment in our lives; it is not always a negative situation. It could be the choice of vocation, a career change, moving our family to a new location, or some other significant moment in our lives. Often at these critical times, we are uncertain as to what to do. As good and strong as our moral character is, it gives us no clear direction at this critical time. At points such as these, we will be particularly needful of our conscience and of a process to form and exercise it rightly. More specifically, the four moments of conscience will be more evident and require careful attention before we reach clarity about our choice.

We will use a fairly common and ethically uncomplicated example from contemporary healthcare to highlight these different moments. "Ethically uncomplicated" does not mean that the situation is not complex from a number of other viewpoints, that is, emotional, intellectual, economic, and the like. Let us suppose that you have been asked to make decisions about healthcare for a loved one if she should become incapacitated. Let us suppose further that indeed this person has suffered a terrible stroke and is being kept alive on a respirator. The medical personnel have told you that your loved one has suffered permanent brain damage and her heart and lungs will not function on their own. Further, as far as medical treatment is concerned, there is nothing more that the medical team can do. Although they are sympathetic to you and your two siblings, they would like you to make a decision as soon as possible; their recommendation is to withdraw the artificial means of respiration and to let your loved one die in peace. What are the four moments in the formation and exercise of conscience and how are they at work in the resolution of this dilemma?

FIRST MOMENT:
CONSCIENCE AS DESIRING AND KNOWING THE GOOD

The first moment of conscience we call "conscience as desiring and knowing the good," meaning that we have been made by God with a desire for what is good and true and given the capacity to know what the good and true are. When the *Catechism* says that conscience includes the perception of principles of morality, it is referring to this first moment of conscience. More than simply the perception of principles, such as "pursue the good and avoid evil," this moment of conscience refers to those human goods that we have come to love and prize. When we approach a moment of crisis in our lives, we come to it not with a blank slate but with a history of growth in maturity and goodness; we come already with some sensitivity to what is good and evil. The Roman Catholic Tradition referred to this state as habitual conscience because it was akin to moral character, an abiding sensitivity to good and evil which is brought to particularly critical moments in one's moral life. We might think, in light of the previous example about making a healthcare decision for a loved one, that you approach this burdensome decision already prizing the good of human life, the good of health, the good of a loving relationship with the person in peril and with your siblings, as well as many other human goods. The challenge will be to see how those human goods are to be guarded in the particular judgment about continuing or removing life support.

"Conscience as desiring and knowing the good" underscores the fact that human beings were created to love God and the good. Further, God has equipped us with a way to fulfill this basic human desire. Although our Tradition has often and legitimately emphasized the place of the intellect and reason in judgments of conscience, we should not lose sight of the importance of emotions as well. The desire for the good and the ability to know it are characteristic of the whole person. As we mentioned in the previous chapter, right feeling enhances and helps to order right thinking, just as right thinking can enrich and order right feeling.

The Roman Catholic Tradition sees this first moment of conscience as manifesting a very positive and optimistic view of the human person. While acknowledging that we have been tainted by original sin, social sin, and personal sin, the Tradition has maintained that human beings still desire the good and can know what it is.

A common question posed regarding this first moment of conscience is this: "If everyone has a desire for the good and the ability to know what it is, how can so many people, ourselves included, do evil things?" There are at least two related responses to this query.

61

The first answer is easier, though disheartening. Some people, knowing what is good, still choose to do evil. They choose to sin. There are, of course, many other factors involved, but in this first instance we simply point to the capacity of human beings to choose to knowingly and willingly do something that is wrong. Sometimes this choice may be an isolated instance, or it may be a pattern of behavior in the person's life. Quite simply, however, people sometimes choose to do evil.

The second response to the question of why everyone does not consistently choose the good is more complicated. As we have said, this first moment of conscience refers to a capacity that we possess to desire and to know the good. In order for us to have right desires and thoughts regarding the good, we must learn what they are specifically. We will address how we acquire this learning more completely in the chapter on natural law. However, something must be said here as well. God created us with an ability to desire and to know the good, but that ability must be nurtured by those entrusted with our care while we are young and by ourselves when we are old enough to make our own decisions. If the fundamental moral principle that we grasp almost intuitively is to pursue the good and avoid evil, the task of moral education and our moral formation is to learn what good and evil are in concrete matters (CCC §1784).

In some cases, people grow up in an environment which distorts their vision regarding what is good and true. We can imagine that many white children who were raised in South Africa during the time when a rigid system of apartheid was in place learned that their race was superior to that of the blacks and colored people (a class of mixed-race South Africans officially designated as such by law). Although it is clear that these white children should have learned that all people merit dignity and respect and that no race can claim superiority over another, most probably many growing up in South Africa during the 1980s never learned this way of thinking; on the contrary, they learned that it was socially and politically acceptable to deny rights to the blacks and colored of South African society.

Although God created these children with a desire for the good and a capacity to know it, their ability to grasp the good in the concrete matter of racial equality was severely hampered by their own sociocultural environment. So, in some cases, our environment is the principal factor affecting our capacity to desire and know rightly.

In other instances, people choose evil and, consequently, shape themselves as people of vice rather than virtue. Although made by God with the capacity to know the good, they repeatedly make choices contrary to what is good. Thus, they become insensitive to evil, making its choice easier. In the previous chapter, we used the example of a man who repeatedly lied when he found himself in an awkward or embarrassing situation. His habitual practice of lying affected his fundamental ability to know what is good. In the long run, it became not only easier to lie but he may well have believed that lying was a good thing.

In contrast to these two examples, there are others who grow up in an atmosphere where right feeling, thinking, and choosing mark the day. These people will be more apt to have their fundamental ability to desire and to know the good sharpened.

Even in the case where one's feeling and thinking are fairly on target regarding the good and the true, however, times occur when the precise response is not self-evident. The case of making a decision for a loved one regarding healthcare can help us here.

Application to example: Faced with the challenging responsibility of making a healthcare decision for a loved one, what do you bring to this crisis by way of habitual conscience or your own loves? What values do you hold that specify your intuitive grasp that good must be pursued and evil avoided? You might come with a love for human life and be concerned about the moral significance of removing this person from the respirator because you know that death will follow shortly thereafter. You would also bring a desire for the good of health for your loved one, wondering perhaps if any other measures can be taken. You would bring the good of a loving relationship with this person and with your siblings as well, concerned about what your responsibility is regarding all these relationships. Many other values may be at work as well. What is important for understanding conscience is that you do not approach the critical judgment of conscience (the third moment) in a disinterested way. Rather, you come with passions, in this case, passion for life, for health, and for a relationship with a loved one and siblings; you also come realizing that you must think clearly so as to make the right judgment. The loves that you bring, concrete loves of life, health, and relationship, color your thought process as well and will impact the discernment and judgment that you make in this instance.

This first moment of conscience, then, is significant because it indicates what lies in the head and the heart of the person who approaches a critical moment in life when a judgment about a particular action is not self-evident. People do not come to these crises with a blank slate in their hearts and their heads. Rather, they come already formed to some degree. The challenge of this first moment of conscience is to ensure that the God-given capacity to desire and to know the good is nurtured toward what is truly good and true. Regarding the case at hand, one must consider carefully prior to judgment what goods are at stake and how we are to act responsibly to ensure right action for authentic human good.

This first moment of conscience, however, is insufficient to guide us in the concrete decision facing us. Rather, it requires careful discernment prior to the judgment of conscience. Discernment is the heart of the second moment of conscience.

SECOND MOMENT:
CONSCIENCE AS DISCERNING THE PARTICULAR GOOD

The second moment of conscience we call "discerning the particular good." There are several tasks here: analysis of the situation, gathering information, and seeking counsel, followed by reflection which should move one toward a judgment of conscience. This whole process may be called discernment. In this moment of conscience, however, we move from a general grasp of principles of morality to a serious consideration of the concrete good in a particular situation, for example, whether to remove a loved one from a respirator. The *Catechism of the Catholic Church* notes that sometimes we are "confronted by situations that make moral judgments less assured and decision difficult." Still, we must "always seriously seek what is right and good and discern the will of God expressed in divine law" (CCC §1787). Precisely those situations in which we are less sure as to how to proceed bring this moment of conscience to the foreground.

This second moment of conscience highlights the need for the formation of conscience in a specific situation but also is concerned with the role of the broader human community in the process of the formation and exercise of conscience. The communal character of the formation of conscience is captured in the phrase from the Second Vatican Council, "Christians are joined to others in the search for truth" (*Pastoral Constitution on the Church in the Modern World*, §16). This communal search for the truth is even more explicit in the *Declaration on Religious Freedom* from the Second Vatican Council which states:

> The search for truth, however, must be carried out in a manner that is appropriate to the dignity and social nature of the human person: that is, by free enquiry with the help of teaching or instruction, communication and dialogue. It is by these

means that people share with each other the truth they have discovered, or think they have discovered, in such a way that they help one another in the search for truth (*Declaration on Religious Freedom*,§3).

This dimension of conscience focuses on our need for others, the Church in particular, to assist us in the formation and exercise of conscience. At times, people suspect that "follow your conscience" is another way of saying, "You're on your own; make up your own mind." While ultimately each one of us is responsible for our judgments of conscience, we would be foolish to believe that we have all the resources necessary to make these judgments unaided by others. At this second moment of the formation and exercise of conscience, we are saying, "I am not sure what to do, who can help?"

Tasks in the process of discernment: Three tasks mark this second moment of conscience: analysis of the situation, gathering of information and seeking counsel, and, finally, reflection. The process itself is not strictly a movement from one to the next; often the steps in the process are intertwined. However, for the sake of clarity we will separate these tasks, using the example of making a healthcare decision for a loved one to see the purpose of each one in the formation of conscience.

Task one: analysis of the situation: The Catholic moral tradition has offered questions to analyze a moral dilemma and to propose a course of action to resolve this dilemma. It offers several questions that we can use to uncover the complexity of the dilemma. We will consider questions such as: What is going on? Who is involved in this dilemma and its resolution? By what means will we resolve it? Are there other alternatives that we could choose? Why do we want to act? What will be the consequences of our action? When might we act to resolve this dilemma? Where will this occur? These questions can serve as helpful tools as we examine this case and others which arise in our moral lives.

WHAT IS GOING ON? We ask what is going on so that we might understand as fully as possible the crisis which we face. In the example we have been considering, we would want to know what is going on for the patient who has asked us to make a healthcare decision for her if she should become incapacitated. This question clearly requires input from experts; it cannot be answered by us alone. We would need to know, among other things, the medical condition of our loved one, what her chances of survival are, what benefit continued medical care would bring, and, finally, what the consequences would be of continuing or withdrawing life support. From the example given, we know that the medical staff has recommended that life support be withdrawn.

All of these questions, while associated with some of the other key questions, help us to get a clearer sense of what is going on. They should assist us in making as thorough an analysis of moral features as possible and in moving toward a clear judgment.

WHO IS INVOLVED IN THIS DILEMMA AND ITS RESOLUTION? The obvious answer to "who is involved in this dilemma" is the patient who is on life support. Certainly the judgment that is made must consider her well-being above all else. Yet it may seem surprising to some that the Roman Catholic Tradition, recognizing that we are people in relationship with God, others, self, and all of Creation, would want to know what is happening in terms of these other relationships as well. How does the moral dilemma affect them? For example, if there is hope that the loved one might become conscious again and have time to harmonize her relationships with family and/or with God, might there not be a benefit to maintaining medical treatment for a while? Another significant question is what impact the illness and care of the loved one is having on the whole family, both psychologically and financially. These deliberations may appear surprising to some. Yet the Congregation for the Doctrine of the Faith wrote in its *Declaration on Euthanasia*:

> It is also permissible to make do with the normal means that medicine can offer. Therefore one cannot impose on anyone the obligation to have recourse to a technique which is already in use but which carries a risk or is burdensome. Such a refusal is not the equivalent of suicide; on the contrary, it should be considered as an acceptance of the human condition, or a wish to avoid the application of a medical procedure disproportionate to the results that can be expected, or a desire not to impose excessive expense on the family or the community (Congregation for the Doctrine of the Faith, *Declaration on Euthanasia*, Section IV, "Due Proportion in the Use of Remedies," *Origins* 10/10 [August 14, 1980]: 156).

Those who have been attending to our loved one medically and pastorally must also be considered in terms of their professional expertise and personal commitment to the patient. When we ask who is involved, we will want to consider all those people who are affected by the crisis that we face. In the example that we have been using, little information is available regarding all of these questions, but let us suppose that these relationships are not strained and that our loved one is at peace.

BY WHAT MEANS WILL WE RESOLVE IT? When we consider the way in which we will act to resolve a moral dilemma, we must bear in mind the criterion for right and wrong action which we have raised repeatedly in this book: does this action contribute to authentic human good and is it, consequently, directed toward God? In other words, we want to ensure that the way we intend to resolve the dilemma is consistent with right feeling, thinking, and choosing. A helpful axiom underscores the importance of paying attention to how we will act: "The end does not justify the means." We cannot use any means to resolve a moral dilemma and suggest that it is morally licit (permissible) because we hope to bring about some good. The good must be present in the means as well.

Making decisions in healthcare requires careful attention to the means used to reach desired ends. In the case at hand, two options seem to be presented to us: continue or discontinue life support, in particular, the use of a respirator. Continuing life support, the medical personnel have said, will bring no benefit to the patient, but simply prolong the process of dying. Discontinuing life support would, according to all evidence, allow the pathology from which the patient suffers to run its course; she will die. Since the latter choice has the more drastic consequences, it merits more attention. What precisely are we doing when we remove a respirator? If we were directly taking the life of the patient, we would have to conclude that removing a person from a respirator is an evil action because it harms the good of the life of the person. In fact, however, the patient has already suffered a stroke which has left her unable to breathe on her own. Although the machine has assisted her for a while, no moral obligation exists to prolong the dying process. Removal of life support is not a direct attack on the life of that patient as much as it is a sad recognition that her earthly life has ended and that nothing more medically can be done nor anything ethically which must be done. Consequently, one could legitimately discontinue the use of the respirator and allow the patient to die.

Notice the careful analysis that must be considered regarding the means to be used. How we choose to resolve a moral dilemma is critical.

ARE THERE OTHER ALTERNATIVES THAT WE COULD CHOOSE? The question regarding alternatives may be superfluous if one takes the process of conscience formation seriously. One could hardly be acting with integrity if one settles on only one way to resolve a dilemma to the exclusion of others and then proceeds to justify why it is the right way. On the contrary, examining alternatives is both wise and necessary. One's imagination is critical here as one attempts to broaden one's grasp of the issue by examining various ways of resolving the dilemma.

Our experience and human psychology remind us, however, that crises in our moral lives affect the whole person. At times, the jarring effect of the crisis is that people lose a clarity of thought as to what to do. They may be overcome with fear, with sadness, with guilt. Many emotions may emerge as a response to the moral dilemma. The example that we have been considering is helpful precisely because the continuation or withdrawal of life support is emotionally charged. The decision is not simply a matter of getting information and making a judgment.

Two points arise in particular: the formation of conscience is more effective when one engages others in the process. When we are upset, we often fail to think and even feel rightly. Our imaginations, too, may shut down. Sharing our experience with others can bring clarity to our own thinking as well as expand the possibilities before us. The second point, then, is that allowing another into our moral dilemma invites other proposed solutions, other alternatives. Left to ourselves, we may not see all the options that are available. Letting someone else think and feel with us opens up possibilities of resolution.

In the case we have been considering, it is not difficult to imagine that a person would be hesitant to withdraw life support from a loved one precisely because it is a final judgment. There is no turning back once the decision has been made. Often when loved ones die, those who are left behind wish that they had resolved difficulties with the person who has died; they wish that they had apologized for wrongs, and the like. In the face of a situation like this one, the decision-maker may believe that the only option is to continue life support, hoping that someday they will be able to harmonize the relationship. As laudable as this motive is, it is unrealistic given the medical condition of the patient. Other options, such as withdrawing life support, must be considered in order to make the best judgment possible. There may well be other possibilities that the attending physicians might suggest.

An important question, then, when considering a course of action is what alternatives exist? How else might this situation be resolved? As important as what we choose to do, however, is why we choose to act as we do.

WHY DO WE WANT TO ACT? T. S. Eliot's words from *Murder in the Cathedral* ring true for us as we analyze and attempt to resolve a moral dilemma: "The last temptation is the greatest treason: To do the right deed for the wrong reason." Although some actions are morally wrong because the object of the act itself is contrary to authentic human good and needs no further examination, often the morality of an action will be determined by the intention of the moral agent in conjunction with the object and circumstances. Certainly, the moral culpability of the person acting is linked closely to intention. So, why we act is of critical importance as we stand before God accountable for our use of freedom. Brutal honesty with ourselves is required in the formation and exercise of conscience. Asking ourselves why we wish to proceed in a certain fashion is critical.

In the example that we are considering, one would hope that our reason for making any kind of healthcare decision for our loved one would be to make the best judgment for her. But what is the particular expression of that general desire for the good? Why continue or terminate life support? We might prefer to keep someone alive on life support because we are not prepared for their death. We might hope against hope that a medical breakthrough will occur or even wish for a miracle. On the other hand, we could argue to discontinue life support because the medical professionals have indicated that no further medical assistance will offer any promise of recovery. Further, we may reason that we should discontinue life support because our loved one has suffered for a long time, has no hope of recovery, and has experienced failure of her own bodily organs. Acting with integrity, we might judge that we are leaning toward removing our loved one from the respirator because it seems to be the best action given her medical condition, her own wishes, the recommendation of her attending physicians, as well as the morally neutral character of the means used. No matter what we choose, our intention, the "why" of our action, indicates how closely we personally tend toward the good. Of all the questions asked, "why" we act is most revealing of our own moral character.

WHAT WILL BE THE CONSEQUENCES OF OUR ACTION? In attempting to discern the best response to a moral dilemma, we should examine the desired results and how this particular resolution to the situation is the best one. One way of judging the adequacy of a response to a moral dilemma is to examine the consequences, both short-term and long-term, that we believe will follow from a particular action. The consequences of an action must be measured carefully. We must remember the axiom mentioned earlier, that the end does not justify the means. Simply because the results gained from an action will bring some good, we are not justified to use any means to achieve them.

For example, if the situation were different in the case that we are considering and the respirator was only a temporary medical treatment, if the patient would most probably breathe on her own again, we would not be justified in removing life support. Although a short-term consequence of removing life support at this time might be the immediate relief from suffering, the long-term consequences, given the circumstances, would be tragic. We would have deprived someone of her life by focusing too narrowly on the short-term benefit of ending her suffering while failing to see this temporary suffering in light of her long-term recovery. This example underscores the significance of the timing of a judgment of conscience.

WHEN MIGHT WE ACT TO RESOLVE THIS DILEMMA? The question about the timing of a judgment of conscience is not always significant. For example, if I am contemplating harming someone, it will be morally unacceptable whenever I choose to do it. The same is not true for all circumstances, however. In the case that we are considering, for example, the timing of the decision is crucial.

We mentioned earlier that premature removal of someone from life support would be immoral. The same would not be true in the case that we have been considering. Other factors may enter into the decision as to when life support is withdrawn. All family members may wish to be present. It would be prudent to wait until they all arrive so as not to exclude them from an important moment in the life of a loved one and in their own lives.

Many factors may enter into determining the right moment for judgment and action. Consideration must be given to them in order to exercise one's conscience responsibly.

WHERE WILL THIS OCCUR? The final question, like the former, is not always morally significant. If we are considering doing something which is morally wrong, where it occurs is of little or no import. A lie told to protect oneself while harming another is wrong whether told in a courtroom or a living room. Although one could argue that the courtroom is a more serious location for falsehood, it is not appreciably more grave. Whether we speed on a highway or in a school zone when children are present is morally significant because of increased danger to others in the school zone.

In the case of the healthcare decision, *where* a judgment about healthcare is made is not terribly weighty. It could be important for family members and for the patient that the person die in her own home. Whether this wish were honored would not impact the morality of the act to any degree, but it would show a sensitivity to all concerned and make a heart-wrenching experience perhaps a bit more bearable for all concerned. In the end, however, where an action occurs is not always significant. It must be considered, however, in order to analyze appropriately the moral dilemma facing us.

These questions, handed on from the traditional books of moral theology, may be helpful in uncovering the particularity of a crisis in our moral lives and in leading us to a sound resolution of the difficulty. Our example has helped us to see how these questions might function in determining what is at stake and how best to pursue authentic human good for ourselves and others.

Task two: gathering information/data and seeking counsel: A second task in the formation and exercise of conscience entails gathering information so as to understand the moral dilemma more clearly and seeking counsel as to how to resolve it. As mentioned previously, all of these tasks are intertwined; they are not carried out in a linear fashion. Implicit in many of the questions raised in the last section is the need to ask others for information and help. According to the *Catechism* we must strive to interpret the information from our own experience and the changing events of human history with the help of the Holy Spirit and his gifts, with the assistance of the moral virture of prudence, and aided by the guidance of competent advisors (CCC §1788).

Whom we approach for information and wisdom will vary according to the nature of the moral dilemma. In order for us to exercise our freedom and conscience responsibly, however, we must seek the truth wherever it may be revealed. The virtue of humility prompts us to admit truthfully what we do not know and seek counsel from those who might assist us. It would be disingenuous to seek information or counsel only from people who tell us what we want to hear. The dignity of conscience requires a willingness to be challenged in the process of forming one's conscience.

The case that we have studied reminds us that sometimes we merely seek information. What is the medical condition of our loved one? What are the effects of various medical treatments? What are their benefits or burdens?

We expect experts to recommend something precisely because they have more experience from the professional standpoint than we do. Their counsel, however, is based more often than not on the facts, an objective reading of the situation. As the analysis of the situation earlier suggests, many other factors are at work as well.

As a community of faith, we have several resources at our disposal for the formation of conscience. We have Sacred Scripture which is the normative text (the one that establishes standards) for our community. We also have the Tradition of the Church, the way the faith has been passed on from generation to generation over the centuries. In particular, we have the magisterium (from the Latin word for "teacher"), that is, the bishops of the Church who, in union with the pope, offer the moral wisdom of our faith community for the formation of conscience. The magisterium is not one voice among all others within our Roman Catholic Tradition, but an authoritative voice of the community. Its teaching in the area of morality is to be received by the faithful and acted on in their daily lives. We will discuss the relationship between personal conscience and Church teaching in greater depth in Chapter Eight.

In addition to Scripture, Tradition, and the magisterium, we also have other members of the faith community who have experienced moral dilemmas similar to ours. They can assist us by offering the wisdom that they gained from their own experience.

Simply put, we should pursue all avenues to moral truth in our effort to understand a particular moral dilemma. Having gathered information and wisdom from those competent to advise us, we must move to the task of reflection, a time in particular where we are alone with God in the "secret core" and "sanctuary" of ourselves (*Pastoral Constitution on the Church in the Modern World*, §16).

Task three: reflection: The *Catechism* states that "it is important for every person to be sufficiently present to himself in order to hear and follow the voice of his conscience. This requirement of *interiority* is all the more necessary as life often distracts us from any reflection, self-examination or introspection" (CCC §1779). The task of reflection, although characterizing this whole process of the formation and exercise of conscience, is brought forward at this point. Although many might suggest that there is an ease in the movement from gathering information/seeking counsel to making a judgment, an easy transition from one step to the other is not the experience of most people. Wise people, including the magisterium, advise us but they do not make the final judgment of conscience for us nor do they live with the consequences. We must do that. Therefore, we must take time to be alone with God and to be present to ourselves with all the information and wisdom that we have gathered. Although the whole process of conscience formation may be marked by prayer, this task requires it more than any other. Just as we do not make serious judgments of conscience without the assistance of others in our faith community and family and friends, nor should we do so without a conscious presence to the God who calls us to the fullness of life.

Reflection involves a review of all that we have heard by asking questions to clarify the moral dilemma; it includes the further information that we have gained, as well as the wisdom that we have heard from others. At this moment, we attempt to sift through all that we have heard in order to hear God's voice which is indeed present in a limited way in the other voices. We personalize all that we have heard because this judgment of conscience will be an exercise of freedom, affecting others, especially our loved one, and shaping us for good or ill. Integrity in this process of reflection is essential.

THIRD MOMENT:
CONSCIENCE AS A JUDGMENT FOR RIGHT ACTION

The third moment in the formation and exercise of conscience is a "judgment for right action." Having moved through the first moment which reminds us of our desire for and capacity to know the good, and the second moment of discernment, we come to the time of judgment, "do this, shun that," as the *Pastoral Constitution on the Church in the Modern World* puts it (§16). Here we will judge the rightness or wrongness of a particular action under consideration in order to resolve the moral dilemma that we face. The task of evaluating judgments already made will be left to the fourth moment of conscience. Significantly, the Roman Catholic Tradition has the highest respect for the judgment of conscience precisely because, as the Second Vatican Council says, God speaks to us through our conscience, through the process of discernment that we have followed.

Obligation to follow conscience: Given that one has acted with integrity in the formation and exercise of conscience, one is obliged to follow the judgment which conscience determines as right. Again, the *Declaration on Religious Freedom* states: "All are bound to follow their conscience faithfully in every sphere of activity so that they may come to God, who is their last end. Therefore, the individual must not be forced to act against conscience nor be prevented from acting according to conscience, especially in religious matters" (*Declaration on Religious Freedom*, §3).

The obligation to form and to follow one's conscience arises from the Church's long tradition of respect for the freedom and the highly personal character of both the search for what is true and good and the moral choice made to attain it. Once again, the *Declaration on Religious Freedom* states that "it is by personal assent that they must adhere to the truth they have discovered" (*Declaration on Religious*

Freedom, §3). Personal assent is made through the judgment of conscience.

So great is the Tradition's respect for the judgment of conscience that it is the opinion of some theologians in the tradition, Saint Thomas Aquinas among them, that one must follow one's conscience even if it is objectively wrong. He gave the example of those who honestly believed that they should *not* believe in Christ and accept Christianity. If that is what their conscience told them, even though objectively wrong, they would stand justified because they followed their consciences. We will say more about this later, but this example underscores the weightiness of a judgment of conscience both in terms of the obligation to form it properly and the responsibility that accompanies a judgment of conscience.

When one makes a judgment of conscience, one stands before God saying, "This is what I believe I must do." The *Catechism of the Catholic Church* says that if one were to act against this judgment of conscience, a person would pronounce himself guilty (CCC §1790). Although we will often have to account for our actions to others, the personal assent to truth that we make in our conscience is ultimately before God.

Types of conscience: Despite the sincerity with which a person may follow the process of forming his or her conscience and the profound respect that is given to a judgment of conscience, it is possible to err in making such a judgment. "Conscience is not an infallible judge" (*The Splendor of Truth*, §62). The moral tradition has named several "types" of conscience. We will focus on two critically important types.

Correct conscience (CCC §1794): A correct conscience judges as good that which is truly good and judges as evil that which is truly evil. If we have described virtuous persons and virtuous acts as those which tend toward the good, the correct conscience embodies both: the moral agent as well as the judgment made tend toward the good. No evidence can be found in a correct conscience of a person moving away from the good, either in terms of the grasp of the principles of morality (first moment of conscience) or the pertinence and manifestation of these principles in a particular moral dilemma (second moment of conscience).

Erroneous conscience (CCC §§1790–1793): When people make a judgment of conscience which is mistaken, the tradition has termed this type of judgment erroneous. An important distinction has been made regarding the concept of an erroneous conscience. Sometimes the error in judgment is in no way the fault of the person who made it; at other times, the person is at fault. Some examples may help to clarify these points.

Invincibly erroneous conscience: We recall that a fully human act requires knowledge and freedom on the part of the moral agent. In this first instance of an erroneous conscience, the tradition recognized that knowledge was lacking regarding the moral significance of an action. Saint Thomas Aquinas, underscoring the obligation to follow one's conscience, gave the example cited earlier of someone who believed that the Christian faith is evil. If a person, upon serious reflection similar to the process that we have outlined above, comes to a judgment of conscience that Christianity is evil and that it would be sinful to become a Christian, that person must follow his conscience and avoid Christianity, even though his judgment of conscience is objectively wrong. Why? Because we presume that a judgment of conscience is made with integrity and that the "truth" that a person arrives at after this process of the formation of conscience is what they must act on. As we mentioned earlier, once a person comes to a conviction about what they must do, they have an obligation to follow through on that judgment of conscience.

In this example of an erroneous conscience, one can appreciate the wisdom of the tradition which recognizes the good will of the person forming his or her conscience and respects their judgment of conscience accordingly. Saint Teresa of Ávila once said to her sisters, "God doesn't look so much at the greatness of our works as at the love with which they were done." This statement does not diminish the attention which should be given to right action, but it recognizes that the intention of the moral agent is of particular significance when assessing where a person stands before God.

Vincibly erroneous conscience: The examples which we have offered previously attest to judgments of conscience where the moral agent has come to a judgment which is in error through no fault of the agent's own. As far as we know, the person has not chosen to remain ignorant of the moral relevance of refusing Christianity.

The same cannot be said of the vincibly erroneous conscience or a judgment of conscience made by a person who has not tried to understand fully the moral significance of his or her action. The Second Vatican Council, while acknowledging the possibility of the invincibly erroneous conscience, has something quite different to say of those who are culpable for their judgments of conscience: "Yet it often happens that conscience goes astray through ignorance which it is unable to avoid, without thereby losing its dignity. This cannot be said of the person who takes little trouble to find out what is true and good, or when conscience is gradually almost blinded through the habit of committing sin" (*Pastoral Constitution on the Church in the Modern World*, §16).

One can imagine several instances as examples. A surgeon is about to perform surgery but does not take the time to inform himself about the risks to a particular patient. During the course of the surgery, the person experiences cardiac arrest. A person gets into a serious relationship with another without ever inquiring whether the person is single or married. After several dates and a sense that they might be right for each other, one partner finds out that the other is married. An employer, anxious to get drivers for his taxi service, fails to inquire about the health of applicants, knowing that this may compromise the safety of the company's passengers. The board of a multinational company is making a decision to set up offices and work forces in a developing country; there have been complaints in other counties about insufficient wages and the poor conditions under which employees are working. The executives fail to inform themselves of these complaints and proceed with their plans because of the economic promise this decision holds out for them.

In each of these instances, people are making judgments and seemingly choosing to remain ignorant about important information that has significant moral implications, caring "but little for truth." Their ignorance can be overcome in some cases with a simple question so that they might make a more informed judgment of conscience.

For others, their conscience becomes darkened and insensitive to evil through habitual activity. We mentioned in a previous chapter the example of the man who found lying easier than telling the truth at times. Although initially he may have felt guilty about being untruthful, one can imagine that it became easier through repeated lies. This numbing of conscience to good and evil is often at work in the vincibly erroneous conscience. The moral agent has an obligation to become properly informed so as to make a good moral judgment.

Application to example: Returning briefly to the example that we have used to illustrate the four moments of conscience: making a judgment about the healthcare of our loved one. Either choice, continuing or discontinuing life support, is morally acceptable; however, it would seem that the best judgment of conscience, given the medical condition of the patient and all the factors that we discussed earlier, would be withdrawing life support and allowing the patient to die in peace. If we were to choose this latter course of action, we would be acting with a correct conscience, seeing as good for the patient that which is truly good; our feeling, thinking, and choosing would be properly ordered.

Summing up, the judgment of conscience is made after reflection on the principles of morality and after a serious process of gathering information and wisdom. The judgment which one arrives at must be followed. Our own experience tells us that we often have greater clarity after we have made a judgment of conscience and lived with its consequences. The fourth moment of conscience acknowledges this reality and sees it as crucial for our ongoing moral development.

FOURTH MOMENT:
CONSCIENCE AS SELF-EVALUATING

In the days when American football was played almost always on Sundays, a term was used to describe the fans who, after the game was over, saw with great clarity all the errors and the ways that they could have been prevented. These fans were referred to as "Monday-morning quarterbacks." They knew exactly how the game should have been played, but it was too late. The same reality is captured in the phrase "hindsight is 20–20."

This fourth moment of conscience is akin to the Monday-morning quarterback and requires hindsight. The tradition has spoken of conscience as that which guides moral action that we are considering, in the process of doing, or have done. Most of this chapter has dealt with a judgment of conscience in process. We have reserved this fourth moment to focus on the task of conscience which praises or blames one for what one has done.

At this point in the formation and exercise of conscience, we look back at our judgment of conscience. We do so out of integrity, out of a desire to evaluate and to learn from our moral experience. If, upon reflection, we praise our judgment of conscience, we confirm the sensitivity to good and evil present in that judgment of conscience and strengthens our moral character. On the other hand, a negative evaluation of our judgment of conscience invites us to correct that judgment when possible and also to learn from the mistaken judgment.

There is a circularity to the formation and exercise of conscience. We begin with a general perception of the good and principles of morality and move through a process to discern the particular good in a given situation. After a judgment has been made, the decision becomes part of our moral history and should guide us in the future, should we come upon a similar moral dilemma. If at the fourth moment of conscience we affirm the judgment of conscience that was made, we steep ourselves more fully in the good; if we challenge the judgment, however, we are fine tuning our sensitivity to good and evil and should not make the same error in judgment if we confront a similar situation in the future. It is only through our lived experience that we come to understand better how the good and the true are to be grasped concretely. In evaluating our judgments of conscience, we realize that we are not always sound in our decisions: sometimes we get them right and sometimes we err. This fourth moment of conscience is designed to assist us in a process of conversion so that we do not repeat the same errors and so that we use our freedom more responsibly the next time.

The evaluating function of conscience occurs in its own time. We may be in a position to evaluate a judgment of conscience within a day of the judgment or it may take years. In the case of our loved one on life support, we may make the judgment to withdraw life support and be troubled for some time as to whether or not it was the correct judgment. Although we may know intellectually that it was a wise decision, we may still wonder whether we had done enough for our loved one, whether we acted with complete integrity. These questions which we raise are important both for a thorough analysis of our action as well as to caution ourselves in the future. We believe that conscience-as-evaluator would affirm the judgment to withdraw life support from our loved one, while acknowledging the judgment as terribly burdensome with no entirely happy result.

3. Conclusion: Conscience As Heart

We began this chapter by calling to mind images of conscience which impact our moral imagination. We conclude by focusing on one in particular: the heart. Although the brain is the most important bodily organ, the heart bears a symbolic import that the brain cannot rival.

Several years ago, we heard a homily which left us pondering one line in particular: "Be careful about what you allow to dwell in your heart." The preacher was a bishop addressing a young man about to be ordained to the priesthood, but his advice is good for everyone. "Be careful about what you allow to dwell in your heart."

We are advised to "be careful" precisely because whatever lies there, as we mentioned before, will characterize us as persons and make its way into our actions. It will either build us up along with the whole People of God or tear us down. If hatred and revenge are our loves, they will give way to hurtful actions. If kindness, compassion, and love fill our hearts, they will break forth in kind, compassionate, and loving acts. In light of our discussions in the preceding chapter, if our hearts are virtuous they will produce virtuous actions; the opposite is true regarding vices.

The Roman Catholic Tradition recognizes conscience as a special moment of contact between God and our hearts. For this reason, it has always taught the faithful of their obligation to follow their consciences, always respected the inviolability of moral conscience, while recognizing its fallibility. Equally aware of this awesome gift of human freedom and conscience, moral agents must attend very carefully to its formation and exercise.

The responsible use of conscience will move one toward or away from God, toward or away from the fullness of life. In the end, good advice is "Be careful about what you allow to dwell in your heart."

CHAPTER FOUR

Sin: The Betrayal of Freedom

It is not unusual to hear religious people say such things as "no-body seems to talk about sin anymore," "whatever happened to sin," or "the understanding of sin has changed." There is certainly an element of truth in these observations. In recent years, we have witnessed people doing grossly harmful or unjust things without any apparent understanding that they have done something evil or that they are somehow accountable for their actions. Acts of geno-cide, abuse of innocent people in times of war, and acts of interna-tional terrorism are some stark examples. The reason for occurrences like these could be that people see themselves more as victims of circumstance or evil forces than the actual doers of evil who make others victims. Even if there is some recognition of responsibil-ity on the part of the person, any reference to God in describing the attitude, act, or omission that caused harm is usually absent. Thus, we are more likely to hear such explanations as: "I made the wrong choice," "I wasn't true to myself," or "I know it was wrong but I could not help myself. He, she, or they made me do it."

Such an approach was illustrated in *The Washington Post* newspa-per some years ago. In his article "Getting Away With Murder," Charles Krauthammer, referring to comments made by figure skater Tanya Harding and singer Michael Jackson after their public offenses, concluded that "the themes are self-betrayal and self-forgiveness. They reflect perfectly a culture in which one no longer sins against God, natural law, moral order, society or even one's fellow man...but against oneself" (February 4, 1994, p. A–19).

These observations tell us something about our era and culture. First, we underestimate our freedom and our ability to choose. Perhaps a tendency exists to blame our destructive attitudes, actions, and omissions on forces out there, be they an unhelpful ethical climate, people who influence us, or pressures of everyday life and work that cause tension, and these in turn cause us to "slip up." It is the "out there" that is responsible rather than the "in me." This approach allows us to avoid acknowledging the negative side of ourselves. It suggests that it is unhealthy, too depressing, or destructive to admit that we are actually sinners.

Perhaps you have even observed how recent changes in the texts of popular hymns help us to avoid seeing ourselves as sinners. Where once we sang, "Amazing grace! How sweet the sound that saved a wretch like me," we may now be singing "Amazing grace! How sweet the sound that saved and strengthened me."

Second, sin is essentially a religious term; it is not just a personal transgression, the breaking of a law, or the failing in some ethical principle. It may well be all these things, but for the transgression to be really acknowledged as sin, a link needs to be made between my action or attitude and my God. How we make this link is important for a proper understanding of sin. We could argue that God has created laws to be followed, and sin is the breaking of these laws. This approach to sin was very common in the past as is evidenced in the moral theology books that were used to train priests before the Second Vatican Council. There was a certain consistency in the approach. If God was primarily seen as Lawgiver and Judge, who not only issued laws but punished criminals who broke the law, then sin was essentially a crime or the breaking of God's law. The problem with this approach is not that it is false, but rather, that it is too limited or narrow.

God is more than a lawgiver and a judge, and our relationship is more than abiding with or going against God's law. Consequently, sin is much more than merely breaking the law. When we speed and we are caught by the authority, we get a ticket, we have to pay the fine, and then we move on. But sin has a greater impact on our lives because it is linked to loving, to relationships, and to fidelity. When we sin, we do in a sense sin against ourselves or betray our true selves. We do harm to who we are called to be by sin because the human heart is made for right relationships with God and our brothers and sisters. But we need to turn to the Scriptures with its images and stories to paint a more complete picture of the sin and the sinner.

1. A Word on Sin

Even the English word "sin" can give us some insight. It derives from the German word "*sunder*," which means to sunder or break from another. When we come to the Hebrew words, the reality of human sin becomes even more apparent. The Hebrew word "*hatta*" expresses the idea of missing the mark or the target, the target being a relationship (Prov 19:2). Another Hebrew word "*awon*" signifies bending or twisting, deviating or going off the track (Jer 30:15). Finally, the word "*pesha*" means the breaking of a covenant, a revolt or a rebellion (Jer 33:8). It can be a revolt against the law (Hos 8:1) but also a revolt of the people of Israel against their God (1 Kgs 12:19).

All these words are linked to a common theme, namely, that sin has something to do with a personal, binding relationship with God. This relationship or covenant with God that is broken or transgressed is not so much a legal one but rather one modeled more after a family relationship that has been ruptured. When we hit the target, stay on the right road, remain in right relationships, we flourish as human beings and become the type of people we are meant to be. When we miss the target, go off the road, and break the familial relationship with our God, we are actually doing violence to our true selves who are made in God's image and made for a relationship with God. We are made for the giving and receiving of love. Sin is the choice for evil, a choice made with freedom and knowledge. As we shall see, the consequences of sin do not stop with us, but rather, like a stone thrown into a pond, send out ripples disturbing those around us.

IN THE BEGINNING (GENESIS 1–4)

In the Old Testament, the epic story of the Creation of man and woman stresses that sin is about breaking a covenant or relationship with God because of pride. This human pride is expressed through a desire to be totally free from God, in fact, to be like God. Adam and Eve, made in God's image with the gift of freedom, live in paradise. With God they share a relationship of trust, friendship, and familiarity. The command given to our first parents, namely, not to eat the fruit of a particular tree, is not an instrument of oppression, rather it highlights the fact that Adam and Eve have the freedom to choose. God has made them this way. The command not to eat the fruit of the tree of good and evil does, however, set limits and delineation. The creature is not the same as the Creator; there is an inequality, for Adam and Eve are not God. This command is much more than a legal precept, for it is set in a context of love, trust, and friendship.

The sin of Adam and Eve: Sin enters the garden when, in their freedom, our first parents choose to break the relationship by disobeying the command which is a summary and symbol of the covenant between God and them. In fact, they want to be like God, for they believe what the tempter tells them, namely, if they eat the fruit, they will have the knowledge and wisdom of God. Their inordinate pride leads them to betray the very gift of freedom that God gave them. What are the consequences? Adam and Eve see themselves as naked for the first time (Gen 3:7). This nudity is not limited to the sexual, rather, it signifies a loss of dignity, a dignity that was based on their relation with the Creator. Sin is recognized for what it is, an empty promise, an illusion, a misuse or betrayal of freedom in the vain attempt to be free of God, to be like God.

In our very nature we are made for God, yet here we are using our freedom to attempt the opposite. Rather than choosing the true good, the lasting good, that is, God's plan for our happiness and fulfillment, we choose to make our own plans which exclude God and result in harm to ourselves and others. John Paul II sums it up in a phrase, "sin is an exclusion of God, rupture with God, disobedience to God" (*Apostolic Exhortation on Reconciliation and Penance*, §14).

When the relationship with God is ruptured, the strain begins to surface and deepen between Adam and Eve and their children. Before the Fall, Adam accepts his partner, Eve, as a gift from God, an intimate partner, "flesh of my flesh and bone of my bone." After eating the forbidden fruit, he refers to Eve as "that woman whom you gave me." Cain eventually kills his brother Abel (Gen 4), and as a result of his sin becomes a vagabond, a wanderer in the land of Nod (Gen 4:16), isolated from the relationships that once sustained him.

THE PRODIGAL SON (LUKE 15:11–32)

We have already referred to the story of the Prodigal Son in the first chapter of this book to emphasize the image of God as Father. This story, recorded in Luke's Gospel, also gives us a deeper understanding of the intimacy that the Creator wills to share with us creatures. It underlines the fact that sin is really a separation of children from their Father and from one another.

The point of departure of the story is set out in the second part of the parable, when the Father says to the older son, "Son, you are always with me, and all that is mine is yours." No doubt the Father had the same attitude to the younger son. There exists a relationship of love between the younger son and his Father, a sense of belonging, receiving all as gift from the Father. It all changes when the younger son asks for his share of the inheritance so that he can go off to a distant country.

What is happening here, why would he want to go away, what must he be thinking and desiring? The younger son wants to plot his own life, be his own boss, to become what he thinks of as free. He wants to take his life and his future into his own hands, free of the restrictions and duties that come with being a son. Now this situation may sound commonplace to many of today's parents, but remember here we are dealing with a gospel story from an eastern culture, a family structure of two thousand years ago. The story illustrates that we are never the uncontested director of our own lives, especially when we believe that we are made in the image of God and belong to God's family. As in the Creation story, we are the creature, dependent on the Creator; it is a part of who we are. No matter how we shut our eyes or block our ears to this fact, we are never God's equal and can never really escape the reality that all we have is gift. Freedom seen as absolute autonomy, total independence, not having to rely on anyone, is a myth that will in time only disappoint because it is not how we will find our happiness and flourish.

The reaction of the Father to the son's request is a profound respect for the boy's decision and what he may falsely think will bring him true liberty and happiness. The dynamic has changed from "all is gift" to "this is my right," from "I am your son" to "I want to go it alone," from closeness to the Father to distance from the Father, from a healthy relationship of love and belonging, to an attitude of pride where the son thinks he no longer needs a Father. It is all freedom *from*.

The consequences of sin: The consequences of the young son's choice and actions should not surprise us. Just as Adam and Eve, grabbing for God's knowledge of good and evil, find themselves naked, so this son grasping the Father's goods in order to be free of him, finds himself unclean with the pigs. Saint Augustine touched upon a wonderful insight into love when he contrasted grasping from the hand of God to clinging to the hand of God. Grasping implies taking and going, while clinging suggests a certain dependence, a continuous receiving, and a staying.

Further repercussions arise out of the prodigal son's past actions, despite the fact that he returns home and is accepted by his Father. The story continues with a telling description of the older brother's anger and resentment when he learns that the prodigal has returned. Jealously and bitterness surface between the two brothers, just as there was trouble between the sons of Adam and Eve. The sin of the younger brother may be forgiven, but further work must be done in order to heal the damage it has caused.

ORIGINAL SIN (CCC §1440, §§1871–1872)

The reader may be sensing a missing element or character in our reflection on the Creation story and sin. Something or someone is missing. The serpent has not been accounted for, that most clever of animals, shrewder indeed than Adam or Eve (Gen 3:1). A snake has the ability to sustain in most of us all sorts of reactions. It is poisonous, insidiously strong, capable of moving swiftly, inextricably on its belly without legs; it has a forked tongue and can even leave its own skin. So far in our reflection on the Creation story, we have focused our attention on the choices and sinful actions of Adam and Eve. Yet, even before the symbolic eating of the fruit of the tree, the presence and influence of the serpent is a given fact. Our first parents are created and placed in the garden, but the serpent is already there. Evil is lurking in their surroundings even before they sin.

The origin of evil: In the scriptural account of the beginning times, there are references to a fallen angel who was created naturally good by the Creator but who rejected and opposed God (1 Chr 21:1; Job 1:6; Zech 3:1). The Church's Tradition and Scripture refer to this fallen angel as "Satan" or the devil (CCC §391). While sin, strictly speaking, needs the knowledge and consent of a person, the Church does refer to "original sin." Here "sin" is being used in what is referred to as an analogous way, that is, it is like sin, but it is not exactly the same as sin. Adam and Eve committed a personal sin; however, their sin of disobedience has affected our human nature. Their sin has, in fact, wounded our human nature so that we are subject to suffering, ignorance, and death, and we as well have to do battle with the inclination to evil. This original sin is not committed by us, rather it is passed on to us. It is a state which we inherit rather than an act that we do.

This concept of original sin may raise many questions for the thinking lay person and the theologian. Just how evil entered Creation at the beginning, even before Adam's and Eve's sin, remains something of a mystery. "I sought where evil comes from and there was no solution," concluded Saint Augustine. Just how the sin of Adam and Eve is transmitted to all human beings is also a mystery that we cannot completely comprehend (CCC §404). What we do know however is this; "where sin increased, grace abounded all the more" (Rom 5:20), and the Gospel is the revelation in Jesus Christ of God's mercy to sinners (Lk 15). The very name "Jesus" tells us that God will save his people from their sins (Mt 1:21). Our human nature may be wounded, our minds blurred, and our wills weakened, but our hope is firm in Jesus Christ our Savior.

2. The Catholic Tradition and Sin (CCC §§1846–1942)

The different kinds of sin may be distinguished in many different ways. We could make a division based on whether the sin is primarily against God, against our neighbor, or against ourselves. We say "primarily" because all sin is against all three of the above. Take, for example, a serious lack of prayer in a Christian's life, to the extent that he or she does not even bother to keep the Lord's Day holy. While God is certainly not given praise or thanksgiving, those who have abandoned prayer are causing themselves spiritual damage which in turn will affect their relationships and attitudes towards others. So, in a sense, an offense against one is an offense against another.

MORTAL SIN AND VENIAL SIN

The Scriptures do not directly use both words "mortal sin" and "venial sin," although they *do* frequently make the distinction between the gravity and consequences of sins (Mt 25:41–46; Gal 5:19–21; Mk 3:28–29; 1 Cor 3:10–17). The reality of the mortal/venial distinction is also attested to in 1 John 5:16–17. The distinction between mortal and venial sin that is familiar to many Catholics, perhaps being more clear to a certain generation or generations, was specifically taught by the Church at the Synod of Carthage in 228 A.D., reaffirmed by the Council of Trent (1545–1563), and restated by Pope John Paul II in his *Apostolic Exhortation on Reconciliation and Penance*, published in 1984. These distinctions in sin developed over the centuries in the Church. Saint Augustine taught, especially in his work on lying, that the gravity of sin is able to vary, and Saint Thomas Aquinas supplied theology with a systematic explanation of the mortal/venial distinction. Their thought took hold in the Catholic Tradition and remains with us today.

Saint Thomas Aquinas basically explains sin as a disorder. We human beings should be moving towards an end or a goal for which we have been made. The ultimate goal is to be totally united with the God who made us, and an important way to this goal is by loving our brothers and sisters who are also made in God's image. To somehow cut ourselves off from God and from others is a radical distortion of who we are and where we are going. Normally, it is not just a matter of turning away, or cutting ourselves off, from God. We find a substitute, some finite created thing or pleasure, thinking or hoping that it will fulfill us and make us happy. This explanation is why Saint Thomas calls sin a disorder. The disorder consists, if you like, in disordering our loves, for we would love something else rather than our God. The only way to happiness is to strive for the goal God has given us, namely, to love him and our brothers and sisters.

Mortal sin destroys love in our hearts, referred to in the *Catechism* as sanctifying grace (CCC §1861). It turns us away from God who is our ultimate end, and consequently turns us away from eternal happiness (CCC §1855). For such a radical disorder to occur, three conditions must be met; the object or the concern of our action must be grave; we must choose with full knowledge what we are doing; and we must give deliberate consent (CCC §1857). Some examples of grave matter are listed in the Decalogue and would include all kinds of direct killing of the innocent, adultery, stealing, false witness, defrauding, and not keeping the Sabbath holy. Pope John Paul in his encyclical, *The Splendor of the Truth*, lists many more grave matters which, if chosen with knowledge and will, would certainly fall under the category of mortal sin—for example, euthanasia, slavery, abortion, degrading working conditions, and torture (§80).

Venial sin, on the other hand, wounds or weakens charity in our hearts. It also weakens the virtues, but it does not turn us away from our God. Of course, one sin can lead to another sin and over time what began as small can slowly grow into something serious. Taking small amounts of money, spreading uncharitable tales about others, those little bursts of anger and uncontrolled thoughts may lead to grave matters. Perhaps the American bishops have provided a common-sense description of sin in their pastoral letter, *To Live in Christ Jesus: A Pastoral Reflection on the Moral Life* (1977). They conclude that personal sin is different from unavoidable failure or limitation because it is a spirit of selfishness in our hearts and wills that wages war against God's plan for our fulfillment. It is rejection, either partial or total, of one's role as a child of God and a member of God's people, a rejection of the spirit of sonship and daughtership, love and life (*To Live in Christ Jesus*, §5).

FORMAL AND MATERIAL SINS

Another distinction among types of sin exists which we might not know by its theoretical terminology, but hopefully we are aware of its practical consequences. We are talking about what has been traditionally referred to as material and formal sins. Material sins are those which violate a moral order. For example, prostitution is a violation of the natural order because genital sexual expression is reserved for marriage and not for the marketplace. We can make a judgment on the act itself and say that the act is materially sinful. It violates a moral order and brings about wrong. Formal sin, however, is a subjective judgment about the guilt of the person who performs a particular action. Returning to our example, anyone who has visited cities of appalling poverty and has seen women with hungry, sick children would think twice about a quick assessment of the guilt or culpability of the person who has turned to prostitution to survive. Such a reservation of judgment is not to deny the material sin of prostitution, but rather to pay heed to the Lord's words about not judging and condemning another (Jn 8:1–11).

It is always crucial to remember that it is much easier to call an action evil (material sin) than to make the judgment that someone has committed a formal sin, implying their culpability. As with original sin, the use of the term "material sin" is only an analogous use of the word "sin," since formal sin which involves the person's knowledge and freedom, is, strictly speaking, the only real sin. In other words, you have to know and freely choose what you are doing; otherwise you are not sinning. The *Catechism of the Catholic Church* wisely observes that, although we can judge, after careful consideration, that an action is in itself a grave evil, we must leave the judgment of personal culpability to God alone (CCC §1861). Pope John

Paul II recalls that "both in moral theology and pastoral practice one is familiar with cases in which an act which is grave by reason of its matter does not constitute a mortal sin because of lack of full awareness or deliberate consent on the part of the person performing it" (*The Splendor of Truth*, §70).

If we find it difficult to separate our judgment of the acts of another from the judgment of the person themselves, we need only look at the planks in our own eyes which will help us be less judgmental about the splinters in the eyes of others (Mt 7:1–5). It is a common blind spot for many Catholics not to recognize the seriousness of spreading gossip and ruining another person's name. Even if the facts and faults of the other person which make up our gossip are true, we have the material sin of detraction; and if the facts and faults are false, we call the material sin "calumny." How many of us sin materially in this matter without the awareness that it is a grave matter that demands restitution according to the order of justice? Once we are aware of its gravity and once we become aware of what we are doing, the revealing of the faults and failings of others to those who do not need to know may well move from being one of our material sins to becoming a formal sin.

SINS OF COMMISSION AND OMISSION

Sins are not only the actions we do, they can be actions we fail to do. Thus, a distinction is always made between sins of commission and those of omission. In general, one may say that sins of commission are more serious because there is a willful attempt to bring about moral evil. However, the same intention could exist in someone who refuses to do something. Sins of commission refer, then, to acts which a person performs which correspond to the elements necessary for a fully human act, namely, sufficient knowledge and full consent of the will. These actions would rightly be called sins, sins of commission.

On the other hand, the Scriptures dramatically speak to us of sins of omission, with the famous last judgment scene in Matthew 25:31–46, where the sheep and the goats are separated. The goats are condemned for actions which they failed to do. What didn't they do? They did not feed the hungry, give drink to the thirsty, clothe the naked, visit those who were sick or in prison. Our *confiteor*, the first option for the penitential rite at Mass states "in what I have done and in what I have failed to do." We should readily acknowledge that there are good things which we ought to do but avoid, and such a decision or lack of decision can be sinful. Just as the priest and the Levite sinned because they did nothing for the man robbed and beaten on his way from Jerusalem to Jericho (Lk 10:25–37). We can sin by failing to act.

SINFUL THOUGHTS AND ATTITUDES (CCC §1869)

It is tempting to limit our consideration of sin to external actions performed by the knowing and free moral agent. However, sinful actions flow out of a person and often the thoughts, attitudes, and vision of the moral agent will help explain the sinful actions committed. Suppose you notice a series of changes in a close friend of yours. The changes are first detected in her actions, the things she does, the words she says, and the actions and words she omits. Unfortunately, it is a turn for the worse, because your friend becomes highly critical of everyone. She cannot stop putting mutual friends down by revealing many of their secret faults. Where once she was generous, she has now become mean. We may say to ourselves: "What has happened to her?" We might even judge some of her behavior as materially sinful.

Now, while we cannot look into a person's heart, it is possible that something deforming has happened inside of her which flows out in external action. Perhaps she has given her thoughts over to envy, jealousy, and revenge. Wanting what others have, being sad at the good fortune of others, thinking all the time about striking back and getting even, can completely cloud a person's vision of others and of themselves. Thoughts are powerful, and thoughts can be sinful. As with action, thought can lack the required freedom and knowledge to render it sinful, but we do have the ability to deliberately choose to stay with destructive thoughts and attitudes. These sinful thoughts and attitudes will eventually become concrete in external action. To remedy such a situation, a person must at times not only attend to individual sinful acts but also confront a sinful direction or attitude he or she has decided upon or gradually slipped into over time. It will take perhaps a harder gaze into the mirror to see the destructive thoughts as well as the sinful external actions.

SOCIAL SIN (CCC §1869)

In the late 1960s, Christian theology developed a renewed appreciation of the fact that sin has social repercussions. The question was raised; can sin be a social phenomenon? Theologians started to coin the terms "social sin" and "sinful structures." How is sin social? As we have already mentioned, each individual's sin in some manner affects other people, and in this way sin is social. However, some sins may be said to be more directly social when they are attacks against our neighbor. For example, our own personal laziness or sloth does have an effect on those with whom we live, but stealing or damaging public property is a sin with more direct social consequences. The social nature of sin becomes even more obvious when we consider sins committed against the basic rights of communities, for example, acts against the freedom of religion or the right to education and healthcare.

So far we have been really speaking about the social consequences of personal sin. The term "sinful structures" raises our awareness of the social nature of sin to an even higher level. Let us paint a picture of some sinful structures and their role in social sin. Sinful structures could be identified as political institutions that oppress persons and violate their human dignity; they stifle freedom and foster inequality. They are usually the product of some person's or group's greed, egoism, ambition, or even cruelty. Structures and institutions in a country may uphold discrimination according to race or religion, may encourage corruption and the taking of bribes, may eradicate all political opposition and keep a certain proportion of the population in dire poverty and virtual slavery. The politicians, the police force, the judiciary, and the armed forces may all be involved on some level. We can refer to such institutions or structures as sinful. They are all the more insidious because often seemingly good people cooperate with them, numbing their consciences and social sensibilities either because the structures themselves or the attitudes they promote have become commonplace over time, or because people are afraid to oppose what is in place. When such structures are in place, they are often very difficult to change. We need only think of racism and the political, religious, and economic structures that can support this sin to realize that false visions and attitudes built into structures are hard to shake.

Church teaching on social sin: As with the terms "original sin" and "material sin," the expression "sinful structures" employs the word "sin" in an analogous way. By this we mean, strictly speaking, an institution or a political structure may not have an individual will and knowledge. In fact, the sinful structure or institution is indeed the product of many individual wills and decisions that have opted for sin. In other words, the accumulation of many personal sins can create this unjust and oppressive monster. Pope John Paul II has emphasized this point often in his writings on sin.

> Whenever the Church speaks of situations of sin, or when she condemns as social sins certain situations or the collective behavior of certain social groups, big or small, or even of whole

nations and blocs of nations, she knows and she proclaims that such cases of social sin are the result of the accumulation and concentration of many personal sins....The real responsibility then lies with individuals (*Apostolic Exhortation on Reconciliation and Penance*, §16).

We can talk of structures of sin in that they are rooted in personal sin and linked in the end to concrete acts of individuals who introduce the structures, consolidate them, make them hard to remove and influence others to sin (*On Social Concern*, §35).

So we have to determine whether we are blindly cooperating with structures and institutions that are causing grave injustices, and we must ask ourselves if there is any way that we can help to dismantle the product of so many accumulated sinful acts and attitudes. Pope John Paul II reminds us: "All sin is personal and social under one aspect, all sin is social in that it also has social implications" (*Apostolic Exhortation on Reconciliation and Penance*, §15).

3. In Him There Is Plentiful Redemption

This chapter may seem to be burdensome to the reader with its heavy emphasis on sin. Like Saint Paul, however, we need to be able to confront the dark side of life so that we can truly appreciate what Christ has done for us. Saint Paul, in his first chapter to the Romans, vividly portrays human sinfulness. "They were filled with every kind of wickedness, evil, covetousness, malice. Full of envy, murder, strife, deceit, craftiness, they are gossips, slanderers, God-haters, insolent, haughty, boastful, inventors of evil, rebellious toward parents, foolish, faithless, heartless, ruthless" (Rom 1:29–31). Luckily, his reflection does not end with sin. Like a soothing cool breeze entering the stifling heat, verse 24 of the third chapter of the Letter to the Romans announces: "They are being justified as a gift by his grace, through the redemption which has come about in Christ Jesus." The righteousness of God enters the grim picture of human sin. The God of love and saving faithfulness is loyal to us despite sin, and Christ is the enfleshed expression of this loving faithfulness. We are drawn back into right relationship with our God and with others through redemption.

What is redemption? Saint Paul explains redemption in Romans 3:24–25: "They are now justified by his grace as a gift, through the redemption that is in Christ Jesus, whom God put forward as a sacrifice of atonement by his blood, effective through faith." Jesus Christ dies on behalf of the Father so that we can be changed. This God of saving faithfulness and love, like the father to the prodigal son, through the costly death of Jesus Christ, changes us and welcomes us back while we are still sinners. This wonderful work happens through the grace of the Holy Spirit who cleanses us from sin. We are saved from sin and the consequences of sin. "Much more surely then, now that we have been justified by his blood, will we be saved through him from the wrath of God" (Rom 5:9).

4. Conversion: Turning From Sin to God Through the Grace of the Holy Spirit

In the gospels of Matthew (3:2), Mark (1:4), and Luke (3:7), John the Baptist calls people to repentance or conversion. The actual Greek word used is *"metanoia."* Jesus himself proclaims, "I have come to call not the righteous but sinners to *metanoia*" (see Lk 5:32). From the stories in the gospel to the present day, there are numerous accounts of conversion. Conversion stories, though different in details and unique to each character, have something in common; namely, they are all tales about turning from something and turning towards God. Perhaps we remember the life of the woman caught in adultery, turning from a life of sin to following the Lord, or the dramatic conversion story of Saint Paul as related by Luke in the Acts of the

Apostles: the voice from heaven, the blinding light, the falling to the ground, the subsequent blindness, the journey to the prophet, the changing of Saul to Paul, the turning from being a persecutor of the Christians to an extraordinary apostle called to preach the gospel message of Jesus Christ. Saint Anthony of Egypt, the founder of monasticism, was moved by the Holy Spirit when he heard the gospel about the rich young man being read in church; and many of us are familiar with the story of Saint Augustine as he relates his conversion in his *Confessions* and recounts the role of his mother's prayers in this struggle to change.

While personal and mysterious in its nature, conversion is basically the experience of being in love with God without restrictions. Once this love is accepted, we see life in a different light, we have a new vision or outlook and we act differently. This experience of conversion is not the product of human effort; rather, it is the work of divine grace, that love of God that has been poured into our hearts by the Holy Spirit. Strangely, we can often resist this love with our wills and our minds for a variety of reasons, mostly because of an attachment to other goods that oppose God's love or because of a disobedient heart that insists on what it calls "my freedom." While conversion is a pure gift from God, it needs humans to cooperate as intelligent and free beings so that the transformation can take place. It is gift and response, an overcoming of the fear of letting go and letting God work in us and change us.

Many of us do not have dramatic conversion stories like that of Saint Paul, but this lack should not lead us to mistakenly conclude that we are not converted or experiencing an ongoing turning to the Lord and a turning away from sin. It may be in the daily ups and downs, the going forward and the slipping back, that we experience conversion. The continuous movement towards God and away from sin can be as gradual as silently growing crops, without any dramatic events occurring. For some, the reading of the Scriptures during a quiet moment of the day enlightens their minds to the goodness of God while, for others, the example of the saints touches the heart.

The sacraments of the Church are special moments of this conversion when we encounter the healing power of Christ as a community of faith. The grace of the Holy Spirit through baptism has the power not only to cleanse us from original sin but also to sanctify or to make holy our whole being so that we become new creations for God and for one another. In the sacrament of reconciliation we can become aware of our own brokenness and sinfulness as a community and, as a community, seek conversion and reconciliation with one another and with God. We admit that we are sinners at the beginning of each Eucharist in the penitential rite so that we can truly celebrate the presence of the Lord and be nourished by his body and blood. Conversion is not just between myself and God; other people in my life often call me to change and help me to change. Often the hardships and suffering of others can be a powerful instrument used by the Lord for conversion. It was the witness of such suffering on her doorstep that turned around the life of Mother Teresa of Calcutta. Conversion is the constant struggle to be "dead to sin and alive to God in Christ Jesus" (Rom 6:11).

5. Conclusion

Each Ash Wednesday at the commencement of the Lenten season, when the ashes are placed on our foreheads, the following words are proclaimed: "Turn away from sin and believe the Good News!" All sin is a betrayal of the gift of freedom given to us by our Creator. It is a choice, made with knowledge and free will, that destroys or at least damages our relationship with God, others, and our true selves. Like Saint Paul, we can admit that often we do not do the good but rather the evil that we should not do. However, like the great apostle, we can answer the question "Who will save me from this struggle?" with the words: "Thanks be to God through Jesus Christ our Lord" (Rom 7:25).

SECTION TWO

Avenues to Moral Truth

Introduction

S ome people suggest that the three most difficult words to utter are "I don't know." Perhaps you were expecting "I love you" or "I was wrong." "I don't know" acknowledges one's inadequacy and limitations, hard things to admit. Yet, these words can be most important when we are in need of assistance from others.

When we studied conscience in Chapter Three, we noted that the second moment in the formation and exercise of conscience consists in gathering information from whatever sources are available to assist a person in making a responsible judgment of conscience. To fail to seek information and advice from others is irresponsible and a disservice to the gift of conscience that we have.

Resources for moral theology, or avenues to moral truth, are many and varied. If we are to analyze issues of justice from a moral standpoint, we will need the expertise of economists, sociologists, political scientists, and many other specialists to grasp the impact of particular issues on the lives of people. Psychology and other human sciences offer insights into sexuality which are indispensable for moral reflection precisely because these sciences assist us in understanding authentic human good. As advances in science and technology raise hopes for breakthroughs in medicine, we need solid information from these sciences to understand their impact on the human person and, consequently, to make a sound moral judgment. Finally, as the earth's population continues to increase and as we become more conscious of our responsibility to be good stewards of the many gifts of Creation, we must attend to the effects of our efforts on the whole environment. Input from sciences, demographics, and the like will be necessary to assess what means of development respect the good of Creation and what ones do not, attending in particular to the human good.

The Church recognizes its competence and limitations in the field of science but has an important word for those sciences as well. The Congregation for the Doctrine of the Faith writes in its *Instruction on Respect for Human Life in Its Origins*: "The Church's magisterium does not intervene on the basis of a particular competence in the area of the experimental sciences; but having taken account of the data of research and technology, it intends to put forward...the moral teaching corresponding to the dignity of the person and to his or her integral vocation" (*Instruction on Respect for Human Life in Its Origins*, "Introduction"). Thus, the Church does not claim a particular competency in science but reminds all the sciences that they must be at the service of the human person, that the sciences are most valuable when they promote "integral development for the benefit of all; but they cannot of themselves show the meaning of existence and of human progress" (*Instruction on Respect for Human Life in Its Origins*; see also *Pastoral Constitution on the Church in the Modern World*, §35).

We make these remarks at the beginning of this second section of the book which deals with avenues to moral truth. We do not and could not offer a thorough treatment of all resources available and necessary for analysis of moral issues. We focus, instead, on four areas: The Living Roman Catholic Moral Tradition, Sacred Scripture, Natural Law, and the magisterium, the teaching office of the Church.

All reflection in moral theology takes place within the context of the living Roman Catholic Tradition. Chapter Five describes Tradition as a river flowing from the source, Jesus Christ, receiving the Truth and transmitting it through the centuries. Truths are eternal but their expression is always in a particular time and space so that they may be understood.

How are these truths handed on, however? What are the resources available from one generation to the next? *The* reference point for moral theology, of course, is Jesus Christ, the fullest revelation of God. In our liturgical and prayer lives, we come face to face with the God revealed to us in Jesus Christ.

Principal among places of revelation for the Christian community is Sacred Scripture. There we grasp more fully who God has called us to be and what behavior is consistent with our vocation. Chapter Six speaks of Scripture as the authoritative source of moral formation. It is interpreted by the teaching office of the church in each historical context and continues the ongoing development of the Tradition. The inspired Word of God, written within a particular historical context, must be reinterpreted constantly so as to be heard afresh in the contemporary world.

Roman Catholic thinking in moral theology has also been characterized by a confidence in reason, expressed most fully in the natural law tradition. Simply put, natural law is characterized by correct reasoning consistent with our human vocation, people called to give and receive love. Chapter Seven offers a summary of the natural law tradition, linking it with Sacred Scripture.

Finally, Chapter Eight describes the responsibility of the teaching office of the Church which interprets Sacred Scripture authoritatively for the church community. It also draws on the natural law tradition, and analyzes moral issues, offering an authoritative teaching to the Catholic community.

This second section on avenues to moral truth should assist us in understanding the ongoing grasp of revelation through the living moral tradition. This revelation is grasped through reflection on the normative documents of Sacred Scripture and church teaching in dialogue with the contributions of the sciences so that the living Roman Catholic moral tradition may continue to develop faithful to Jesus Christ and for the good of humanity.

CHAPTER FIVE

The Roman Catholic Tradition

A story is told that during the First Vatican Council's debates about Scripture and Tradition in the Church, Pope Pius IX turned to one of the cardinals and said, "Tradition! I am it." Frequent appeals are made to "tradition" and the "living tradition" in Roman Catholic theology and in Roman Catholic moral theology. Indeed, the importance given to Tradition, as well as Scripture, is said to be a distinguishing mark of the Catholic Church. Since Tradition is an important source of our moral knowledge, let us turn our consideration to it in this chapter.

1. What Is Tradition?

Many communities appeal to their traditions as a source of meaning, moral direction, and guidance. Tradition can be understood as a fundamental structure of human and social life. It can be seen as a basis of various cultures throughout the world during their long history. Often, the core of the tradition can come from what is conceived as a divine source, or at least an authoritative source. It is to be found in the myths of peoples, the way people act, speak, and worship with the help of sacred texts, rituals, and liturgy. It also is expressed in the way people think and believe, aided by precepts and doctrines. In fact, tradition is all about the transmission, or the handing on, of the meaning of life; it usually concerns life's essential questions, such as how to be happy, who is God, what causes suffering and punishment, how to be saved, and how to be lost. Traditions are, therefore, a guide to living, a map for the difficult terrain of living, surviving, and even flourishing with meaning and purpose. The map, the guide, is normative, that is, it can tell us what we should do and what we should not do. It has an authority; and so institutions usually develop to preserve the core of the tradition, to safeguard its authority, and to monitor what goes in and out of the tradition.

Tradition is all about truths received and transmitted in order to be in turn received and transmitted further along the line of humanity. Like a river flowing through the centuries, a tradition has the same source, even though it may have to transport the water along some new terrain. We are speaking here of a living tradition, as distinct from a dead tradition, for, in order to be considered living, a tradition needs to be communicated to new generations who have new questions and different experiences. Sometimes a living tradition must even cope with unnerving crises. Naturally, the kernel of truth and wisdom of tradition must be preserved, otherwise a particular tradition would cease to be.

2. Christian Tradition According to Catholic Teaching

God's Word of revelation, that is, the manifestation of God and his plan of salvation for humankind, is revealed through Our Lord Jesus Christ. Tradition, according to Catholic teaching, is one of the sources of this divine revelation, together with the Sacred Scriptures. "Tradition and scripture make up a single sacred deposit of the word of God, which is entrusted to the church" (*Dogmatic Constitution on Divine Revelation*, §10; see also CCC 80–83). So God's Word of revelation is handed on from generation to generation through the Scriptures and through Tradition. This sacred Tradition includes all of what the apostles "received—whether from the lips of Christ, from his way of life and his works, or by coming to know it through the prompting of the Holy Spirit" (*Dogmatic Constitution on Divine Rev-*

elation, §7). The apostles handed the Tradition on through their preaching, their example, their instructions; and, in turn, the Church through her teaching, worship, and life continues to pass on the Tradition (CCC §173).

3. "Big" Tradition and "Little" Traditions

Theologians often make a distinction between big Tradition (beginning with a capital "T") and small traditions. The Catholic Church has a rich and venerable Tradition (with a capital "T")—from the great creedal statements of faith, the Apostles' Creed and the Nicene-Constantinopolitan Creed, to dogmas of the faith such as the Immaculate Conception and the Assumption of Mary into heaven, to the teachings of the ecumenical councils. This Tradition is not separate from the Scriptures; it is implicitly part of the Gospel message even though it may have taken centuries for this part of the Gospel message to move from implicit teaching and belief to explicit teaching and belief. "Flowing from the same divine wellspring, both of them merge, in a sense, and move towards the same goal" (*Dogmatic Constitution on Divine Revelation*, §9).

Along with what we might refer to as "Word of God" Traditions (beginning with a capital "T"), that is, Tradition as part of the Gospel message of Jesus, there also develop in the Church various traditions (with the small "t"). These particular beliefs or practices are maintained in certain regions or ethnic groups of the Church. The touching and kissing of statues of Jesus, Mary, and the saints may be an ancient practice in certain churches, an aid to prayer and devotion, yet such a practice is not to be put on the same level as the "Word of God" Tradition, which is part of the deposit of the faith. Sometimes such traditions spring up, change, and die out; sometimes they need to change, to be refined, or even to cease.

4. The Catholic Moral Tradition

When it comes to the particular concerns of who we are called to be in Christ and what we should do in response to Christ's invitation, we turn to our moral tradition. Nearest to the time of the moral teaching of the New Testament, we have the teaching of those people known as the Apostolic Fathers. Their writings contain a wealth of moral catechesis (or instruction in the faith), for example, the *Letter of Pseudo-Barnabas*, the *Letter of Clement of Rome*, letters of Ignatius of Antioch, *Letter to the Philippians* of Polycarp of Smyrna, the anonymous writer of the *Shepherd of Hermas*, and the *Didache*, an ancient book of basic instructions for Christians. We also have the great apologists who attacked superstition and false moral teaching. These include, Justin (d. 165), Irenaeus of Lyons (c. 130–c. 200), Tertullian (c. 150–c. 240), Origen (185–c. 254), and Clement of Alexandria (c. 150–c. 211). Moral teaching flourished, too, in the great monastic movements in both east and west. Here we think of Saint Basil of Caesarea (330–379), his brother Gregory of Nyssa (c. 336–c. 395), and Saint Anthony of Egypt, Father of western monasticism whose life was written by Saint Athanasius (c. 295–373). From these early writers and from countless other sources, the Church's moral tradition continues to flow even to the present generation of believers.

Let us take just one example from the Catholic moral tradition, namely, helping people to deal with the sinful dimension of their lives and the effect of healing the sin on the individual and community. The chapter on sin in this book is a witness to the centuries of reflection given to this dimension of the Christian life in our Tradition. Starting from the teaching of the Old Testament (the Fall of Adam and Eve, among other texts) and the New Testament (for example, the story of the Prodigal Son), the Church developed its teachings on sin further at the synod of Carthage (228 B.C.). Saint Cyprian, the bishop of Carthage, had to deal with a particular problem in the

Church. What should be done with Christians, who, because of the fear of persecution, had denied their faith? Could such a sin be forgiven, and could such a Christian experience God's forgiveness and be welcomed back to the community? These questions caused much dispute within the Church, and it was necessary to reflect anew on the mercy of God and the Gospel message. Eventually, practices were developed to welcome back into the Church apostates and others who had committed the serious sins of murder, adultery, and idolatry and to enable them to experience the forgiveness of God. The Celtic world with its large monastic communities also contributed to people's struggle to cope with sin and find mercy through the use of repeated confession.

Through the reflections of the master theologians such as Saint Augustine (345–430) and Saint Thomas Aquinas of the Middle Ages (1225–1274), who contrasted sin to the virtues, that are brought to their fullness by the gifts of the Holy Spirit, and to the Beatitudes, the Church continued to reflect on the experience and consequences of sin and the ways of healing its consequences. In more recent times, a greater stress has been laid on the social dimensions of sin, as exemplified in the words of Pope Paul VI which are quoted in the introduction to the *Rite of Penance*, "By the hidden and loving mystery of God's design men are joined together in the bonds of supernatural solidarity, so much so that the sin of one harms others just as the holiness of one benefits the others" (*The Rite of Penance*, "Introduction," §5).

Obviously, this example is but one instance of the Catholic moral tradition being handed on to future generations through the centuries. If we were to take the topics of the sanctity of human life, the gift of human sexuality, the call to care for the poor, and so many other aspects of our moral life, we would continue to be amazed at the wisdom to be found in the Tradition.

While this small book constantly draws on some of the giants of the Catholic moral tradition, from Saint Augustine, Saint Thomas, and Saint Alphonsus Liguori, as well as on the teaching of the great Councils of the Church, the teachings of popes and theologians, it also acknowledges that the Catholic Tradition is to be found and transmitted through many ways apart from formal theological thought, treatises, and dogmas. The way people pray and worship, their devotional life, their sentiments, their belief and hopes, are all channels through which the Catholic Tradition continues to flow. This sensitivity of the faithful to true belief and morality has a technical name in Catholic teaching, *sensus fidei*, or a sense of the faith. The Second Vatican Council taught that the "whole body of the faithful who have received an anointing which comes from the holy one...cannot be mistaken in belief. It shows this characteristic through the entire people's supernatural sense of the faith (*sensus fidei*) when...it manifests a universal consensus in matters of faith and morals" (*Dogmatic Constitution on the Church*, §12). Naturally, this sense of the faith is guided by the teaching Church. When it comes to individuals who have passed on the Tradition, some may have been recognized by the Church as canonized saints, others perhaps are only known by their family, friends, and local church community, but all can be carriers of our great Tradition. The process of passing on the Tradition is the work of the whole Church, as one theologian expresses it: "It occurs whenever a parent catechizes his or her child, whenever liturgy is celebrated and the gospel proclaimed, whenever the values of the gospel are testified to in work habits and attitudes of Christians in the marketplace" (*Teaching With Authority*, 78). Likewise, we can use the words of the Second Vatican Council regarding the transmission of the Tradition:

This comes about through the contemplation and study of believers who ponder these things in their hearts....It comes from the intimate sense of spiritual realities which they expe-

rience. And it comes from the preaching of those who, on suc-
ceeding to the office of bishop, have received the sure charism
of truth (*Dogmatic Constitution on Divine Revelation*, §8).

5. The Living Moral Tradition

The Catholic Tradition is not just a collection of some historical hap-
penings or insights of the past to be remembered; rather, it is a living
and informing reality for us now, even as it is progressing through
the centuries. The Second Vatican Council explicitly taught that our
Catholic Tradition develops. "The tradition that comes from the
apostles makes progress in the church, with the help of the Holy
Spirit. There is a growth in insight into the realities and words that are
being passed on" (*Dogmatic Constitution on Divine Revelation*, §8). Two
recent encyclicals of the Church also stress the importance and the
development of the moral tradition. The first, *The Splendor of Truth*,
speaks of a "constant" deepening of knowledge with regard to morality (§4, footnote 8) and how the Church's moral reflection has
developed in moral theology. "The role of moral theology is to seek
to bring the living tradition into contact with the modes of thought
and feeling of different cultures" (*The Splendor of Truth*, §29).

In the encyclical, *One Hundred Years of Catholic Social Teaching*,
Pope John Paul II also refers to that great treasure of the Church's
Tradition which contains what is old, received, and passed on from
the very beginning and which enables us to interpret the new things
in the midst of which the life of the Church and the world unfolds.
The pope refers to the activities of millions of people over time who
have taken the Church's teaching to heart, especially in the area of
social justice, and so have enriched the Tradition, the life of faith,
and the society in which they live (*One Hundred Years*, §3). It is note-
worthy that the fruitful and faithful activity of people can enrich
and pass on our Tradition. In fact, in the Second Vatican Council's
listing of the ways in which the Holy Spirit continues to make the

Church grow in the truth, the role of the faithful precedes that of the preaching of the bishops.

TRADITIONALISM AND ENTHUSIASM

Human beings do have a tendency to be attracted by the extremes in life and faith. Perhaps these extremes seem less complicated, or more clear-cut, but usually they are misleading. When a tradition is irrevocably bound to the past, in the sense that it cannot incorporate or deal with present realities and questions, or if, in fact, a tradition pretends that these realities simply do not exist, we get a state of affairs called "traditionalism." In these circumstances no room exists for the development and deepening of the tradition. Perhaps traditionalism is based on the assumption that we humans can master the truth and give full expression to it once and for all, that we humans have nothing else to learn. With such a mind-set, tradition becomes a dead thing rather than a living reality of the Church and her faithful. On the other hand, certain enthusiasts could claim that their tradition is in some kind of radical evolutionary process in which what is past must be continually left behind. With this mind-set, sometimes referred by the term "modernism," only contemporary insights are viewed as valuable, and the past experience and reflection and expressions of faith have to be let go, even if this means leaving behind the core of the tradition and changing its very identity. The Church takes a more balanced and nuanced understanding of tradition than these extreme approaches, realizing that communication and passing down of the Christian truths can both preserve the deposit of the faith and at the same time engage new questions and insights through the living Church as it is alert to the present age and cultures.

IMAGES OF TRADITION

Some writers have used the three images of the quarry, the sponge, and the prism to ensure that we appreciate all the dimensions of the concept of the living Tradition. The image of the quarry stresses the aspect of the faithful digging into what is already there, the treasure of the Tradition buried and safe, needing just to be continually brought to the surface. Using this image, we mine the riches of the long Catholic Tradition. Using the metaphor of the sponge which is a living organism, which takes in and keeps what is nutritious and expels what is of no use, we see the living Tradition as taking in present-day concerns, questions, knowledge, and culture. These stresses and realities over time become part of the life of the Church. The living Tradition absorbs and develops through the contribution of thousands of nutrients, while discarding all that is unnecessary.

A prism allows us to see the light from a different perspective, that is, the same light is seen reflected through a variety of angles. So the light of the living Tradition may be reflected through the theology and faith experience of our Eastern brethren in the Catholic Church, or through the great schools of moral theology linked to particular saints and their religious orders or congregations, for example, Saint Thomas Aquinas and the Dominicans, Saint Bonaventure (1221–1274) and the Franciscans, Saint Alphonsus Liguori (1696–1787) and the Redemptorists, and Juan Azor, the Jesuit professor of Rome (1536–1603), and the Jesuits.

All these images attempt to express the fact that the Catholic moral tradition shapes, enlightens, sustains, and gives meaning to moral living and is transmitted through the living Church. This task falls to the official teaching Church, the preaching of the successors of the apostles, the bishops (what we call the magisterium), as well as the believing communities of the centuries, faithful to the teaching of Christ and the apostles.

6. Conclusion:
Tradition—The Quest for Wisdom

One of the most influential moral theologians of the last century, Father Bernard Häring, once described the moral tradition as a stream of life and truth under the guidance of the Holy Spirit who introduces each generation in its own dynamic historical context into the one great truth of Jesus Christ. Sometimes we must grapple to find the truth as it is transmitted through the Catholic moral tradition; this has particularly been the case in recent times with the developments in medicine and genetics. Such grappling at times should not shake our confidence in the Tradition but urge us to meet the challenge of enabling our great moral tradition to continue to transmit wisdom. Listen to the encouraging words of the Second Vatican Council:

> The Church is guardian of the deposit of God's word and draws religious and moral principles from it, but it does not always have a ready answer to every question. Still it is eager to associate the light of revelation with the experience of humanity in trying to clarify the course upon which it has recently entered (*Pastoral Constitution on the Church in the Modern World*, §33).

This *Essential Moral Handbook* reflects the Catholic moral tradition, drawing on the light of revelation and the rich experience of the many people who have reflected on and lived the faith. It certainly does not exhaust the Catholic moral tradition, nor should it, nor can it, for it is the mystery of faith that possesses us and not we who restrict it.

CHAPTER SIX

Scripture:
The Soul of Moral Theology

S cripture has traditionally been seen as an authoritative source of moral formation, inspiration, and instruction, somehow express-ing God's will concerning who we should be and what we should do. "All scripture is inspired by God and is useful for teaching, for reproof, for correction, and for training in righteousness, so that eve-ryone who belongs to God may be proficient, equipped for every good work" (2 Tim 3:16). The Second Vatican Council, in fact, rec-ommended that Scripture should be the soul of all theology (*Decree on Priestly Formation,* §16). So, while morality, in general terms, is concerned with preservating and fostering the standards judged to be required for human well-being and flourishing, and while it at-tempts to give direction and meaning to an individual's life and the lives of others, Christian morality flowing from a religious faith in Jesus as the Son of God and as revealed in the Scriptures, has some-thing special to offer. How does belief in our Savior of the cross and the Resurrection, as revealed in the Scriptures, influence both our moral behavior and who we are called to be?

1. Scripture Calls Us to Greater Things

The first thing to be said is that the New Testament exhorts us to be holy. "Therefore be imitators of God, as beloved children, and live in love, as Christ loved us" (Eph 5:1–2). The primary concern is not merely discerning what is permitted and what is prohibited; rather, the primary concern of the Scriptures in terms of morality is to exhort people to be and do more than the minimum. Scriptures offer encouragement to walk towards Christian sanctity and to live as Christ did, to imitate his freedom of heart, his love for the poor, his chastity, his kindness, and compassion. In other words, the Scriptures call us to do more than just avoid certain behaviors or even to be satisfied with behavior that does not harm. Scripture should make us ask the question: "What will lead to Christian fullness and what will lead the Christian community to grow in love and hope?" The document on priestly formation from the Second Vatican Council called for a renewal in all theological disciplines. Speaking of moral theology, this document said that this discipline should draw more fully on the Scriptures and speak to people of their exalted vocation as followers of Christ and their obligation to bring forth charity for the life of the world (*Decree on Priestly Formation*, §16). Of course, we can only ask this more generous question and bring forth the fruit of charity if we have experienced the love of God.

2. Scripture: The Basis for Love Responding to Love

The Word of God reveals to us that we are loved by God. So much does God love us that he sent his only Son to take on our humanity and die for our sins. This reality is the basis of the Christian moral life. Once we believe its actuality, that is, this is how it is, God really loves me in Christ, then the same Word of God calls or exhorts us to respond. It gives an imperative: "Be this and do that." This idea seems so simple: listen to, meditate on, and pray with the many texts of Scripture that reveal that all people are precious to God. We may turn to the prophet Isaiah and read that we have been known by God in our mother's womb, that we are precious to him, that we are carved in the palm of his hand (Isa 49:15–16). We can look to the sayings of Jesus, for example, that every hair on our heads has been counted (Mt 10:30) or meditate on the supreme proof of love, the death of Jesus on the cross. Having heard this Good News, we then also look to the Scriptures to see how we should respond to the One who loves us. We respond by becoming a certain type of person and by acting in a certain way. Important commands in the Word of God concern what kind of character we should form and what sort of actions we should perform. However, these commands come as a response to God's love. "In this is love, not that we loved God but that he loved us" (1 Jn 4:10). Saint Augustine knew this ancient truth when he asked if love brings about the keeping of the commandments or whether the keeping of the commandments brings about love. In other words, which is more fundamental? He responds to his own question. He had no doubt that love comes first. For the one who does not love has no real reason for keeping the commandments. Made in the image of God, redeemed by Christ's love, we are called to lead lives "worthy of the gospel of Christ" (Phil 1:27). We become capable of responding because the love of Christ through the Holy Spirit has been poured into our hearts (Rom 8). Thus we can be "imitators of God, as beloved children, and live in love" (Eph 5:1–2).

3. Scripture: A Catechesis of the Twofold Commandment (CCC §§1822–1832)

Whether we ask "what must I do to inherit eternal life" (Lk 10:25) or "which commandment in the law is the greatest" (Mt 22:36, Mk 12:28), the gospels respond with the same answer, the double commandment of loving God and loving our neighbor as ourselves. This great command is the summary of the law and the prophets (Mt 22:34–40), the first and second of all the commandments (Mk 12:28–34), the means to eternal life (Lk 10:25–28). In fact, it is truly a new commandment when we are asked to love others as Jesus has loved us (Jn 13:34). Loving God and loving one another is the proper response of the Christian to God's all-embracing and all-merciful love

(Jn 13:34). Who is my neighbor? Any person in need: the hungry, the naked, the sick, and those in prison (Mt 25:34–46); naturally, also my family, my friends, my fellow workers, members of my faith community, and, yes, even my enemies and persecutors (Lk 6:35–36). How am I to know the type of love my neighbor wants? "In everything do to others as you would have them do to you; for this is the law and the prophets" (Mt 7:12). This love, characterized by mercy, is to come even before heroic and devotional sacrifice of time and energy to God: "I desire mercy and not sacrifice" (Mt 12:7), "leave your gift there before the altar and go; first be reconciled to your brother or sister" (Mt 5:24). Keeping our eyes on the double commandment prevents us from developing split personalities when it comes to loving God and yet not being concerned with our neighbor's needs. (Is it easier to love God whom we cannot see or our neighbor whom we can see?)

Saint Paul explains what love is, and what love is not, in his famous text in 1 Corinthians 13:4–8. "Love is patient; love is kind; love is not envious or boastful or arrogant or rude. It does not insist on its own way; it is not irritable or resentful; it does not rejoice in wrongdoing, but rejoices in the truth. It bears all things, believes all things, hopes all things, endures all things. Love never ends."

Reflecting on this text and making it the foundation of his prayers, the patron of moral theology, Saint Alphonsus Liguori, had the following insights into the practice of Christian love in his work, *The Practice of the Love of Jesus Christ.*

"Love is kind." As Christians, we should request rather than demand. If we need to correct others, we should do it with firmness and not harshness, for we should always leave another with gentleness and a word of kindness, especially after disagreements or heated exchanges. It is kindness and tenderness that convert another rather than accusations. We need to practice kindness towards ourselves as

well. To be overly annoyed with our own faults and shortcomings is a form of pride. How can we be kind to others when we are not kind to ourselves? Our kindness should be especially extended to the poor, the sick, and those whom we do not like.

"Love does not envy." A sinful envy resents the talents and the material possessions of others. A sure test for envy, according to the saint, is whether we can rejoice at the good others do, or have a sense of pleasure as if we ourselves had done the good. We should only envy those who love more than we do. This is holy envy.

"Love is never boastful." The person who is humble of heart realizes that all talents and accomplishments are due to the generous gifts of God. The proud of heart eventually fall because they rely on themselves. No matter how strong we may appear, we need to remind ourselves continually that we rely on the strength that comes from the Lord. If we take offense at every slight and are so sensitive to the comments of others, Saint Alphonsus suggests that we have become hollow reeds that are crushed so easily or like porcupines that react with their needles, all because our love has not been purified of pride.

"Love is not conceited." To praise yourself is faint praise, and rampant ambition tramples over Christian love. The saint recommends the advice of Saint Paul: "In humility regard others as better than yourselves" (Phil 2:3).

"Love is never selfish." Self-love can hinder us from loving the Lord our God with our whole heart. This is not to say that we should not have a healthy respect for ourselves and appreciation of our God-given gifts; rather, it means that we should have a certain detachment from wanting things to always go our way, in our time, and in the place and manner that we desire. If we lose respect, recognition, wealth, social position and even health, do we also lose our faith in God because life is not running according to our plans?

"Love does not take offense and is not resentful." Saint Alphonsus warns us of the dangers of being so sensitive to the words, thoughts,

and actions of others that we see offense and insult at every corner. "Some people," he says, "think that they deserve honor in proportion to their own conceit!" Can we accept reasonable correction, can we admit that we make mistakes, or do such experiences make us vindictive and angry? There are practical ways to remain at peace; divert your thoughts to something else of more importance, turn to God with a short prayer, remind yourself that all is passing and that the fire of vindictiveness will not relieve the sting of being offended.

"Love delights in the truth." Here the Doctor of Prayer, Saint Alphonsus, reminds us that all holiness consists in doing God's will. The will of God is the source of our truth and it brings a rejoicing and a sense of peace. One should keep in mind that God's general will for all of us is that we be saved, that we flourish as human beings. In our prayer, the one request that should be repeated is "Lord what would you have me do?"

"Love is always ready to excuse, to trust." Can we understand the limitations and mistakes of others or are we one-sided perfectionists in the sense that we expect perfection of others and not of ourselves. Trust in the Gospel message, the summation of which is the beatitudes, that happiness will be ours if we follow Christ's way.

"Love is always ready to hope." It is when we have confidence in the goodness and the providence of God that our own weakness ceases to weigh us down and we have a sense that we can do all things in him who strengthens us. Such a confidence gives a person a certain calmness.

"Love is ready to endure whatever comes." Trials come in many guises. Our commentator on the text to the Corinthians narrows his focus here to the trials of temptation. We should not allow temptations to cause us to revert to our old selves, to our unbelieving selves, our unloving selves and hopeless selves. Temptation does not have to unnerve us, for "God is faithful and he will not let you be tested beyond your strength" (1 Cor 10:13). Just as stagnant water becomes

useless, so the person who is without struggle and temptation can become stale because of an exaggerated conception of his own virtue. A certain smugness can settle in.

This insight into the call to love from one text of Saint Paul and the reflections of one saint prepares us for the summit of the moral teaching of the New Testament. We begin with a catechesis of the beatitudes.

4. Scripture: A Catechesis of the Beatitudes
(CCC §§1716–1724) ·

The beatitudes depict the countenance of Jesus Christ and portray his charity. They express the vocation of the faithful associated with the glory of his Passion and Resurrection; they shed light on the actions and the attitudes characteristic of the Christian life (CCC §1717). Saint Augustine, in the early life of the Church, reflected on the central role of the beatitudes for the Christian moral life in his sermons and in his commentary on the Sermon on the Mount as found in the Gospel of Saint Matthew. His insights are clear and applicable to every Christian.

"Blessed are the poor in spirit, for theirs is the kingdom of heaven." "What does it mean?" asks Augustine. Simply this, whoever is puffed up with pride does not have the humble heart of Christ and cannot enjoy the kingdom of heaven.

"Blessed are the meek, for they will inherit the earth." If you are not meek, then, rather than possessing the earth, the earth will possess you. Avarice will spread its cloak over all that the earth offers rather than you offering your cloak to those in need. Search the Scriptures for its treasures, Augustine advises, rather than searching the earth and others for their riches. This beatitude challenges us to rearrange our priorities in order to find true happiness.

"Blessed are those who mourn, for they will be comforted." Conversion to Jesus Christ entails a certain letting go. We leave behind and at times lose things that we used to embrace as precious. This letting go may cause us to grieve just as the departure of a person in death may rightly cause us to grieve. The promise is that there will be consolation and we will not be left desolate. The Holy Spirit, the Comforter, will come to us.

"Blessed are those who hunger and thirst for righteousness, for they will be filled." Right relationships bring true satisfaction to the human heart, a satisfaction that lasts. Our real food is to do the will of God, and the will of God is for us to be in right relationship with him, others, ourselves, and all of creation.

"Blessed are the merciful, for they shall receive mercy." Augustine reminds us that we are in need of mercy and that we are beggars. As we treat the beggar so will our God treat us. Do unto another with mercy so that God may do unto us with mercy.

"Blessed are the pure in heart, for they will see God." We may be on fire to see God, but unless we have the means our desire will be in vain. Augustine uses the image of a person who desires to see a sunrise but has bleary eyes. With such an eye condition you can desire your heart away but never see the beauty of this new day. So it is with seeing God, the means is a pure heart and to have a pure heart is to cleanse it by faith (Acts 15:9). What kind of faith is needed?—a faith which works by charity (Gal 5:6) and keeps the heart simple.

"Blessed are the peacemakers, for they will be called children of God." To control our passions, or to school our spirited emotions of anger and fear so that they can be used in a positive way, will engender peace in ourselves and build up the kingdom of God.

"Blessed are those who are persecuted for righteousness' sake, for theirs is the kingdom of heaven." For Saint Augustine, this beatitude returns us to the beginning, where Christ also promises us the kingdom of heaven when we are poor in spirit. The blessedness of those who live

the beatitudes cannot be overcome or attacked by any tribulation, for tribulation works out endurance, and endurance works out trial, and trial works out hope, and our hope will never let us down (Rom 3–5).

Of course, the beatitudes are only part of the Sermon on the Mount, justly called "the charter of the Christian life." The Sermon offers the believer the essential teaching of Jesus on justice. This particular section of the Sermon develops five of the precepts of the Decalogue by means of a vivid contrast, "You have heard it said...but I say to you." Here Jesus explains justice not on a minimal, exterior action level. He goes to the heart of the matter and includes a probe of our inner thoughts so that justice can reveal itself even in the love of enemies and the striving to be merciful and perfect as the heavenly Father is perfect (Mt 5:39, 44, 48).

5. Scripture: A Catechesis of the Human (Moral) Virtues (CCC §§1803–1809)

The *Catechism of the Catholic Church* refers to a catechesis of the human virtues which causes one to grasp the beauty and attraction of right dispositions towards goodness. A good character is based on acquiring virtues, that is, the dispositions to desire, feel, think, and act in a manner that leads to excellence, to human flourishing. "If there is any excellence and if there is anything worthy of praise, think about these things" (Phil 4:8).

Do the Scriptures instruct us on the nature and acquiring of such human virtues? Let us consider the virtue of fortitude, or courage, that is, the moral virtue that enables human beings to firmly and consistently pursue the good even though the path is strewn with difficulties (CCC §1808). Courage moves a person to desire, feel, think, and act in a way that is not too timid and not too foolhardy. "Anyone who seeks his life will lose it and anyone who loses his life will find it." This saying of Jesus, one could argue, gives us a moral insight about character and virtue, namely, that there is always a tension in any decision-making or acting between (1) the world of security and safety, the known territory and (2) the unknown, the world of insecurity, and the courage needed to take a risk. The Gospel instructs us to be courageous, yet it does add a particular twist. "Anyone who loses his life for my sake will find it." We are exhorted to take the risk, and to have courage for his sake and with his help. Perhaps we are reminded of Jesus calling out to the apostles on the stormy sea, "Courage, it is I."

In contrast to such Gospel courage, the writer George Eliot portrays a character in *Middlemarch* as follows: "His soul was sensitive without being enthusiastic, it was too languid to thrill out of self-consciousness into passionate delight, it went on fluttering in the swampy ground where it was hatched, thinking of its wings but never flying." Henry James in his *Portrait of a Lady* gives an account of one Gilbert Osmond who is very decisive, and definitely courageous. "A mind more ingenious, more pliant, more cultivated, more trained to admirable exercises, she had not encountered. Underneath all this culture however lay his egoism hidden like a serpent in the bank of the flowers." Courage it seems is not enough for an integrated moral life.

Other virtues also make for the morally mature person. Again we can turn to the Scriptures for guidance. "Clothe yourselves with compassion, kindness, humility, meekness, and patience" (Col 3:12–14). In fact, while we can talk about natural virtues as distinct from the theological virtues of faith, hope, and love, which are infused and originate with the grace of Christ, once we believe, the Word of God transforms or deepens our philosophical knowledge of the so-called human virtues and develops them beyond our unaided human thoughts and hopes.

6. Scripture: The Story to Which We Belong

The virtues, for example, the moral virtues of prudence, justice, fortitude, temperance, and the ability to have compassion, are often portrayed in stories, images, and parables in the Scriptures. Some theologians maintain that one can only know who one should be and what one should do if a person can answer the prior question: "To what story or stories do I belong?" The Creation story, the exodus story, the story of Christ's life, Passion, death, and Resurrection, and indeed the stories he told of the Good Samaritan, the Prodigal Son, the Unforgiving Servant, and the Sheep and the Goats are all grand narratives to which we belong. Moral education and formation is not only a knowledge of a collection of moral principles for use in moral decision-making, it is often an attempt to find one's way through the hazards, tragedies, and challenges of life by means of the virtues, which, in turn, come from a map of the living Christian tradition or story. How often Catholic people have taken courage from the life of the Mother of God as it is portrayed in the Scriptures—the invitation or call to be the Mother of God, the fear and the questioning that the invitation generated, the reassurance given by God through the angel Gabriel, the acceptance in faith of the call by Mary, the times of trial, immense suffering, and blessedness that come from firmly believing and experiencing that all the promises made to us by the Lord will be fulfilled. So when the Scriptures tell the story of Israel and the story of Jesus, we are drawn into the stories themselves. The saving deeds of the past become present to us in an efficacious way.

As well as the grand narratives, we also find short stories or parables that often have the uncanny ability to shake our everyday assumptions, assumptions that are often incorrect— the last worker who is given the same wage as the one who toiled all day in the sun (Mt 20:1–16), our sympathy for Martha who is doing all the work and

Mary who is said to have chosen the better part (Lk 10:38–42), the statements saying that to those who have, more will be given and to those who have little, what little they have will be taken from them, as well as the saying that the first shall be last and the last first (Mt 19:30).

All these grand narratives, short stories, and parables are set in the context of God's covenant with his people. We now treat the commandments, the articulation of the expectations of this covenantal relationship with God.

7. The Ten Commandments in Sacred Scripture
(CCC §§2052–2550)

The word "decalogue" means literally "ten words" (Ex 34:28; Deut 4:13; 10:4). This word is also used as a term for the Ten Commandments which are in a special way a gift from God and an expression of Divine providence, handed down to us in the Books of Exodus and Deuteronomy. In the New Testament, when the young man asked Jesus what he must do to inherit eternal life, Jesus cited the commandments that concern the love of neighbor (Mt 19:16–19): "You shall not murder; You shall not commit adultery; You shall not steal; You shall not bear false witness; Honor your father and mother." These are known as the social commandments on which Jesus placed so much emphasis. While the first three commandments concern our love for God and the other seven concern our love for neighbor, all ten are given and are to be understood within the framework of the Covenant. The papal encyclical on the moral life, *The Splendor of Truth*, states that the Decalogue requires from us more than mere legal obedience, it requires a response of faith and love to what is God's gift of wisdom, goodness, and holiness.

A word about goodness is called for here. We all have a natural inclination towards goodness; it is like some primitive inclination. We seek and do the good thing not primarily out of a sense of obligation, but out of an attraction to the good. What is good attracts us and causes a response of love. What a difference it makes if we approach the Decalogue primarily not as a list of commands or negative prohibitions to which we must respond because of obligation, but rather as an expression of God's goodness and care for us. As such, the commandments are attractive, offering us the way to embrace goodness, which in turn will give us joy in our living. When we say that the Ten Commandments are an essential part of God's law for us we are really understanding law in the biblical sense, namely, as the articulation of the expectations and demands of a right relationship with God and with others. The wisdom that the Ten Commandments offer in fact corresponds to our deepest yearnings for goodness and truth. It should not surprise us, then, that the Tradition of the Church has acknowledged and emphasized the importance of the Ten Commandments in the moral life of the faithful.

While the division and the numbering of the commandments have varied throughout history, this present chapter follows the division found in the *Catechism of the Catholic Church*, a division established by Saint Augustine.

THE FIRST COMMANDMENT

"I am the Lord your God, who brought you out of the land of Egypt, out of the house of slavery; you shall have no other gods before me. You shall not make for yourself an idol, whether in the form of anything that is in heaven above, or that is on the earth beneath, or that is in the water under the earth. You shall not bow down to them or worship them" (Ex 20:2–5; see also Deut 5:6–9).

We notice that the first commandment begins with calling our attention to the nature of God. Our God rescues, saves, and is full of mercy. So, from the very beginning of the Decalogue, we are to acknowledge that it is futile looking to other things for our rescue and salvation. Our God alone is almighty, all merciful, and infinitely beneficent. It follows that we should have complete faith in God alone, place our hope in him and respond in love to the God who made us and in whose image we are made. Such an acknowledgment of God expresses itself in adoration. "You shall worship the Lord your God, and him only shall you serve." These are the words Jesus cites from the Book of Deuteronomy. We adore through prayers of praise, thanksgiving, intercession, and petition. We truly acknowledge the mercy of God by being merciful and compassionate to others. God demands this sacrifice of mercy: "I desire mercy, not sacrifice" (Mt 9:13; 12:7; see also Hos 6:6).

THE SECOND COMMANDMENT

"You shall not make wrongful use of the name of the Lord *your God"* (Ex 20:7; Deut 5:11).

We only have to consider the many ways in which we can injure another through ridicule and bad mouthing of their name to realize how we refer to or use another's name often indicates the type of relationship we have with that person and in what regard we hold that person. Using another person, through their name, as the butt of jokes or as an expression of hatred is an act of destruction. So it is with the name of God. If our tongue uses God's name with disrespect, or with the intention of convincing another of something that is really a lie, that is, using a false oath, we are in fact saying to ourselves and to others that our relationship with God is not important and that God can be used simply to further our own ends. While offensive use of the name of God, Mary, and the saints may be unintentional and the result simply of a bad habit, we are to remember that such disrespect, rightly or wrongly, may well say to another that persons who are holy do not deserve respect.

THE THIRD COMMANDMENT

"Remember the Sabbath day, and keep it holy. Six days you shall labor and do all your work. But the seventh day is a Sabbath to the Lord your God; you shall not do any work" (Ex 20:8–10; see also Deut 5:12–15).

A contemporary moral theologian suggests that this commandment forms us and encourages us to rest, to celebrate and to gather (James Keenan, *Commandments of Compassion*, Sheed and Ward, 1999, 15). Interestingly, this commandment was used in the early Church (in the sixth century) to ban servile work so that serfs could have time to celebrate the Lord's Day through the Eucharist. The temptation today is to fail to recognize our own limitations, our need for rest so that we can gather and be together as a family and as a believing community in worship. To devote time and energy to the care of family and relatives can be so difficult during the other rushed days of the week. To keep up the tradition of good works for the sick and elderly on a Sunday demands a break in our daily routine. The *Catechism of the Catholic Church* even refers to the Sabbath as a day of protest against the servitude of work and the worship of money (CCC §2172). Naturally, for Christians, the celebration of the Resurrection Day, the Lord's Day, is Sunday, the first day after the Jewish Sabbath. The Sunday celebration of the Eucharist fulfills the moral command of the Old Covenant and continues the practice of the Christian assembly which dates from the beginnings of the apostolic age. It is the foremost holy day of obligation in the universal Church (CCC §§2177–2178).

THE FOURTH COMMANDMENT

"Honor your father and your mother" (Ex 20:12; Deut 5:16).

This fourth commandment is often referred to as opening the second table of the Decalogue, meaning that we now begin to consider our love for neighbor in the order of charity. Our first reaction is to relate this commandment to the honor and obedience that is due to parents from their children. After all, it was our parents who gave us life and usually handed on the faith to us. Of course there are other ways of showing honor apart from obedience. A parent may not feel particularly honored if all their children can offer them is obedience. Besides, parents deserve to be honored by their offspring well after they have grown out of childhood. To spend time with another, to show affection and concern, to express gratitude and to make the effort to know our parents and their history of struggles and joys, is to really show them honor and respect. This is what makes Christian family life, that primary community of faith, hope, and love. No one doubts that our experience of and attitude toward the family set the foundations for the life and well-being of society. So this commandment has far reaching consequences for public morality, cooperation, and security.

THE FIFTH COMMANDMENT

"You shall not murder" (Ex 20:13; see also Deut 5:17).

This commandment taps into our natural inclination to preserve life and into the divine source of this inclination. The *Catechism of the Catholic Church* begins its reflection on this commandment with a quotation from a document of the Church called *Instruction on Respect for Human Life in Its Origin and on the Dignity of Procreation.*

Human life is sacred because from its beginning it involves the creative action of God and it remains forever in a special relationship with the Creator, who is its sole end. God alone is the Lord of life from its beginning until its end: no one can under any circumstance claim for himself the right directly to destroy an innocent human being (*Instruction on Respect for Human Life in its Origin and on the Dignity of Procreation*, "Introduction," §5).

Obviously, a commandment on life itself touches a wide range of moral issues, including intentional homicide, abortion, euthanasia, war, self-defense, respect for health and health needs, respect for bodily integrity (including such things as kidnaping, hostage-taking, terrorism, torture, mutilations, and direct sterilizations), and respect for the spiritual integrity of the whole person which includes the avoidance of scandal. As we have stated from the outset, our lives are a reflection of God's life; we are made in his image and given life as a gift. In this context, these prohibitions make sense for the believing Catholic. We will return to many of these specific issues in more detail in the chapter on bioethics.

THE SIXTH COMMANDMENT

"You shall not commit adultery" (Ex 20:14; Deut 5:18).

We are bodily and we are sexual. It is through our human body and sexuality that we feel, communicate, have relationships, and express love and commitment. Thus, it should come as no surprise that we have a specific commandment dedicated to this fundamental component of ourselves. Attitudes towards our bodies and our sexuality affect so many aspects of our living, our maturity, and our faith. As Christians we strive to be virtuous in this area of our humanity. "Chastity means the successful integration of sexuality within the person and thus the inner unity of man in his bodily and spiritual being" (CCC §2337). Defined as such, all men and women, be they married, single, priests, or religious, are called to the virtue of chastity; and it is to this positive virtue that the sixth commandment points us.

While this commandment seems to focus on the married life, on people who have made a vow to each other, it really concerns us all. In married life, part of the vow to the other is the sharing of one's body, for the body can express so much about a relationship and commitment. Attitudes to, and actions with, our own body and the bodies of others touch the core of our identity, our relationships, our bonds of affection, our commitments, and our love of God. This commandment gives witness to the fact that human beings are to value, esteem, and respect the dignity of themselves and others as bodily, sexual beings. Offenses against chastity listed in the *Catechism* include lust, masturbation, fornication, pornography, prostitution, homosexual acts, conjugal infidelity, and contraception (CCC §§3251–2400).

THE SEVENTH COMMANDMENT

"You shall not steal" (Ex 20:15; Deut 5:19).

As well as respecting persons, we are to respect the goods of people. This command is so because these goods, the fruit of men's and women's work, bring a security to human life that is often threatened by poverty and violence (CCC §2402). While this basic provision is true, a Christian must not lose sight of the fact that God made the world and its riches not just for a few but for all human beings. This view raises the question of justice and fairness. We work to provide food, shelter, and many other goods for ourselves and our families, but we also have a responsibility for the promotion of the good of the whole human family. This aspect of the Christian life is one that is often forgotten or conveniently overlooked. It has been said that the Church's social teaching is one of its best-kept secrets, meaning that Catholic people are often very aware of the Church's teachings on sexuality and liturgy but ignorant of the richness of the Church's reflection on the issues of justice and fairness.

Disrespect for the goods of others and also for their natural right to have the basics of life expresses itself in many guises. There is simple stealing, business fraud, paying unjust wages, working poorly, tax evasion, forgery, waste, not paying debts, refusing the restitution of stolen goods to their owner, and unjust manipulation of the marketplace. People today are still being sold into slavery, chained to machines in sweatshops, and living in countries that are crippled by debt. The Scriptures tell us that it is in fact the poor ones, "the *anawim*," the widow, the orphan, the outcast, the stranger, who are God's favorites. The *Catechism of the Catholic Church* also places the welfare of animals and our environment under this commandment (CCC §§2415–2418). In many parts of the world consumerism and greed have been the cause of the breakdown of right relationships and have created a new god molded by grasping humanity. A special Chapter Eleven (page 257) is devoted to justice issues and Church social teaching.

THE EIGHTH COMMANDMENT

"You shall not bear false witness against your neighbor" (Ex 20:16; see also Deut 5:20).

The eighth commandment ensures that there is always a space so truth may be told and heard. Saint Thomas wisely concluded that one can sin in this area by not revealing enough of what is true and by revealing too much of what is true. The former sin would include deliberate lies, false witness in a court, perjury under oath, and calumny, which is making remarks contrary to the truth that harms another person's reputation or good name. The latter sin would include detraction, disclosing without a sufficient and valid reason another person's faults and failings to others who did not know them. Most of us struggle each day with the commonplace things, such as gossip and exaggeration, rather than the revealing of national secrets or acts of perjury. By "putting away falsehood," we are to put away "all malice, and all guile, insincerity, envy, and all slander" (Eph 4:25; 1 Peter 2:1; see also CCC §2475). Even if things are true, not everyone has a right to know them. People have a right to privacy in their ordinary dealings and all the more so when confidentiality is expected from professionals. Are we open to hear the truth or do we have selective hearing blocking out all that shakes our prejudices or rattles our preconceptions? Do we encourage others to speak their truth or by our judgmental attitudes and air of superiority do we stop many stories from being told and many truths being heard? On a larger scale, the media carry heavy responsibilities for revealing and withholding what is true just as governments can be held accountable for propaganda and falsifying the truth.

THE NINTH COMMANDMENT

"You shall not covet your neighbor's wife" (Ex 20:17).

Covetousness refers to our desires, the things for which we really long. What a difference our desires make to our lives, our mental state, and our spiritual lives. It is not difficult to recall deep desires making us feel happy, frustrated, impatient, or disappointed. It is good to desire some things, but it can be not only very unsettling of the moral life but even sinful to desire other things. Our desires are usually linked to the image of our hearts, because they flow from the deeper part of ourselves and our emotions. We can love with all our heart but also "out of the heart come evil intentions, murder, adultery, fornication" (Mt 15:19). In the Catholic catechetical tradition, this ninth commandment usually focuses on carnal concupiscence (CCC §2514). We might think of the husband or wife who begins to focus his or her desires on another's spouse, the attention, the energy and the deepest desires are no longer given to the one to whom they are committed. These actions will have consequences not only for the primary relationship of marriage, but it may also prove destructive to another couple's relationship as well. What we desire is important. How many have thrown away vital and life-giving relationships on account of fleeting passionate desires. This commandment reminds us that it is not just our external actions that are part of the moral life: the yearnings and desires of the heart reveal where our treasure lies (Mt 6:21). "But I say to you that everyone who looks at a woman with lust has already committed adultery with her in his heart" (Mt 5:28). Sometimes, it seems, desires can engage a person against the good as much as any exterior action.

THE TENTH COMMANDMENT

"You shall not covet your neighbor's house...or ox, or donkey, or anything that belongs to your neighbor" (Ex 20:17; Deut 5:21).

Have you ever encountered the type of person who is never happy with what he has? "If only I had this, if only I had that, then I would be happy." We can spend so much of our time wishing for things that we never really appreciate what we already have. The human heart, rather than expressing gratitude, can be eaten up with the vice of envy. Envy is a strange human trait; it is actually being sad at the sight and thought of another's goods and can lead to the desire to acquire them for oneself. Envy can even reach the stage where one desires the other harm so that his goods may become one's own.

We do not just envy people for the things they own. Power, position, praise, and giftedness can all be the objects of envy. A person can be so obsessed with things that greed, the desire to amass goods without limit, dominates every thought and action. This last commandment asks us to consider the source of our true satisfaction. It should also cause us to pause and to ask ourselves: What is the cause of my dissatisfaction, and will riches, earthly goods, power, and the praise of others really be the remedy? Perhaps we will come to the realization that our hearts need to be set on the Lord and on thanksgiving for what we already have.

8. Scriptures As a Lens and Source of Motivation

In our reflections on the Decalogue, we have been considering a great deal of ethical content, that is, things to be done and not to be done. As we have mentioned before, however, Scripture offers us more than simply directives for right and wrong action.

Scripture presents us with a way of viewing or interpreting the world that is distinctive. For example, we view one another as brothers and sisters in Christ. Nonbelievers and non-Christians may not take this stance. We view Creation and one another as sacred because all is gift from God entrusted to us as stewards, not masters. In light of Christ's Passion, death, and Resurrection, we view suffering as a place where new life may emerge. So, Scripture and its interpretation in the Tradition provide us with a lens through which we view reality. It also provides motivation for our moral lives.

What motivations do the Scriptures give us to lead the moral life? Certainly, as we have already stressed, the ultimate motivation is a response to love. This primary motivation can take other guises, for example, the desire to be like Christ. We could call this the "imitation model" of viewing Scriptures. How many of the saints spent their lives imitating the virtues and the actions of Christ because they desired to be like him? There is also what we might call the eschatological motivation of viewing Scriptures, namely, the promise of heaven or hell, happiness or pain, in the next life. The Scriptures can also motivate us by revealing that the way to peace and happiness in this life is a moral life based on the Gospel. This point of view arising out of Scriptures is certainly an important aspect of a Christian ethic, in contrast to a secular ethic. The Scriptures can provide motivation for the things we do, the actions and thoughts we shun, and the people we strive to become. The Scriptures force us to ask the fundamental question of why lead a moral life at all. They are a powerful source of motivation and inspiration.

9. Scripture: Source of Formal and Material Norms

The word "norm" is a term that we often use but rarely stop to define. The following attempt at a definition may lay some groundwork for a broader understanding of this term. A norm is an action guide that describes conduct to be avoided as morally wrong (proscribed) or to be done as morally right (prescribed). Formal norms, also called general norms, relate to our character, with its virtues and vices. Formal norms do not tell us what we ought to do in any great concrete detail, but rather bring into focus the sorts of persons we ought to become. Such norms exhort, challenge, and encourage us to become a certain type of someone. Be gentle, compassionate, humble, chaste. "Let love be genuine; hate what is evil, hold fast to what is good; love one another with mutual affection; outdo one another in showing honor. Do not lag in zeal, be ardent in spirit, serve the Lord (Rom 12:9–13).

Material norms, on the other hand, are particular, behavioral, specific, and concrete. Some examples would include: Do not steal, do not fornicate, do not murder, do not lie, do not divorce and re-marry. For example, we find such concrete directives on divorce and remarriage in the sayings of Jesus (Mk 10:2–12; Mt 5:32; 19:3–9; Lk 16:18, and in the writings on fornication of Paul (1 Cor 7:10–16). But some of these norms often need serious consideration when ap-plied to very specific situations. What if during the Second World War you were living in Europe and in the dead of night you heard Nazi troops herding Jewish people out of houses and into trucks to be taken to extermination camps. You have been sheltering a young Jewish family in your basement for weeks. There is the brusque knock at your door, some of the troops ask, "Are there any Jews in this house?" Does the scriptural command to tell the truth and not to tell a falsehood bind here? What do we do with this particular mate-rial norm? One could perhaps argue that people do not have a right to all information and so you need not answer the soldier's ques-tion. What if the demand is followed by the real threat: "Answer me or your family will be sent away?" Could I answer, "There are no Jews in this house?" This case shows why the application of material moral norms, even those found in the Scriptures themselves, has been the focus of centuries of reflection in the Catholic moral tradi-tion. Perhaps the real question I have been asked by the troops is,

"Are there any Jews in this house who deserve to be transported to a concentration camp and murdered?" Understood in this way, my answer may be very different. Thus, one needs to be appreciative of the complexity of material norms, even moral norms derived from the Scriptures.

If we consider the commandment "do not steal," we need to understand first what stealing really is. It is not just taking something that belongs to someone else. It is the taking of something that rightfully belongs to another. Doctor of the Church Saint Thomas Aquinas taught that no one has an absolute right to property. If my small children and I are starving to death, am I stealing if I take some food from a very wealthy person who has an overabundance of food rotting in the basement and is unwilling to give me so much as a crumb? "Thou shalt not kill" also raises many ethical considerations. Does it mean you should never kill another human being? Or does it really mean you should never kill another innocent human being? Then again, every war kills innocent human beings, so on what basis does our Tradition accept legitimate forms of warfare? What of capital punishment? This discussion is not to deny that we find concrete material norms in the Scripture, but it is to say that it takes more than a simple quoting of such a norm to discover its meaning and application. Once again, our Catholic Tradition gives us guidance in these areas and ongoing theological reflection can help develop this moral tradition.

10. Scripture and Fundamentalism

A pastor keen to build a new church and facing opposition from many of his parishioners chose a text from the Old Testament for one of his homilies, namely, the Second Book of Chronicles where God said to Solomon, "Build me a temple." The pastor thought this would settle the argument, for since the Bible says God wanted a temple built, therefore God must also want this new church to be built. Needless to say, the parishioners had a different interpretation and application of this particular text.

This simple story illustrates the temptation to settle any moral problems by recourse to one phrase, command, or story from Scripture. The problem with this approach is that biblical fundamentalism (a view that tends to take the words of Scripture literally) fails to take into account the whole of Scripture. Are we still bound by the prohibitions we find in the Old Testament concerning the eating of shellfish, the stoning to death of those found committing adultery, and the covering of their heads by all women in church? We have to see these prohibitions in their proper context. A humorous line often heard among young theology students is that "a text without a context is a pretext!"

Fundamentalists find apparently conflicting stories in the Scriptures very disconcerting. How do we reconcile the two Creation stories in Genesis, and who was actually first to get to the empty tomb and speak with Jesus? Why does Matthew's account of Jesus' teaching on divorce add the exception clause, "except in the case of adultery," and the other evangelists do not? Did they just forget or did they not hear of this exception clause? Besides what does it actually mean? Even the central question raised in the Gospels, who is Jesus Christ, and Peter's confession of faith are treated differently by the evangelists, Matthew, Mark, and Luke.

A danger always exists of an arbitrary use of Scripture to support our own arguments or even our own bias in moral matters. We need to look to the guidance of the teaching Church and the insights of scholars to ensure a responsible use of Scripture in the moral dimensions of our life. How disconcerting it is to witness people in the heat of a moral debate hurling various texts of Scripture at one another like misguided missiles, often taking the text out of context, and misinterpreting it in the vain hope of winning an argument. Christians do not win people for Christ this way.

11. For a Balanced Interpretation and Application of the Scriptures

While Catholics believe that the Bible is the Word of God written under the influence of divine inspiration, we also believe that biblical texts need to be interpreted correctly according to the living Christian Tradition and modern biblical scholarship. Scholars often refer to the world behind the text, meaning that a biblical text has an author, a language, a culture, an audience, a history, and local circumstances and expectations. For example, when Saint Paul recommends that those who are unmarried should stay single in his First Letter to the Corinthians, the expectation at the time was that the world as we know it was coming to an abrupt end. The Second Coming of the Lord was very near. Knowing this world behind the text, we do not give today exactly the same advice on this matter as Paul did. A differing admonishment to unmarried people is not to say that the text has no meaning for us. It certainly does. It exhorts us to put our concerns and preoccupations in the right perspective, for this world is passing, and we need to see to spiritual matters with minds and hearts that do not forget the life to come.

Every text also is part of a whole. For example, a couple of verses taken from the Gospel of Luke is part of a chapter of Luke, which in turn is part of the whole Gospel of Luke. The Gospel of Luke is one of the four gospels. Isolating a particular text from this broader context can lead to misinterpretation. This example introduces us to the world in front of the text, namely, our world, our concerns, and our questions. Just as the original audience had their world and their concerns, so we have ours. It is a valid world of concerns and questions, and the biblical text can engage it and inform it. But we must be mindful of the human temptation and weakness to force our ideology, mind-set, or preconceived ideas onto the text rather than letting the inspired text work on us. We also need to remember that we belong to a living Tradition that has interpreted the Word of God down through the centuries, that we have a teaching Church and modern scholarship both guiding us to a fuller understanding of the Bible and its inspiration in matters moral.

12. Conclusion: The New Law of the Grace of the Holy Spirit

As Christians, we have and enjoy a New Law. According to Saint Thomas Aquinas, this New Law is the love of Christ poured into our hearts through the grace of the Holy Spirit. The New Law is essentially an internal law, not an external law. Thus, it touches the heart and is written there (Jer 31:33). How does this grace of the Holy Spirit, however, come to us from our faith in Jesus Christ? It comes to us through tangible realities since we are not pure spirits but human beings. We have seen that the Scriptures are a rare and wonderful tangible reality that dispose us to the grace of the Holy Spirit, instruct us, and inspire us in the moral life. This New Law coming to us through the Sacred Scriptures gives a whole new meaning and experience to law as we usually understand and experience it. Not only is it an interior law, it is not a master-slave type of law. It is a law between friends (Jn 15:15) that creates in us a great freedom because we want to follow it rather than just feeling we have to obey it. This is what it means to be truly living in the Holy Spirit.

CHAPTER SEVEN

The Natural Law

(CCC §§474–476;
The Splendor of Truth, §50–53)

Modern-day proponents of a healthy diet often suggest foods which are "natural," those that have no artificial ingredients. They argue that by introducing artificial ingredients either into the foods themselves or into the animals or plants which provide them we might do harm to ourselves and impact the nutritional value of what we eat. In this instance, the "natural" is contrasted with what is artificial. Our chapter on environmental ethics will address more fully the issue of respect for the earth and the concern that many have about destroying the natural beauty of the earth through construction, scientific experimentation, and so forth. Many environmentalists argue that we are dealing with a living cosmic organism and that human beings should not interfere with and upset the balance. In this view, nature is pristine and is damaged by human intervention. A common expression that we use when referring to people's personality is "by nature." "She's just very easygoing by nature. He's very competitive by nature." These descriptions, while seeming to be accurate descriptions of a person's personality, suggest that the people are constitutionally "easygoing" or "competitive." Nature is descriptive of who people are.

When we use the term "natural law," the word "natural" refers to human nature, to what it means to be a human being. We refer to the term "law," not because the natural law is written down somewhere, but because it is like an inner directive that flows from human beings and directs them to the fullness of life.

We stated earlier that the meaning of life is giving and receiving love. Our Roman Catholic Tradition would say that our nature, then, as human beings, is to give and to receive love. The natural law tradition focuses on how we discern the best way to do that, not solely by recourse to Sacred Scripture, a very important avenue to moral truth, but through the use of reason. Natural law argues further that the conclusions reached in its deliberations are valid not simply for believers but for all people precisely because we are talking about human nature.

1. Definition of Natural Law

The most basic definition of natural law comes to us from Saint Thomas Aquinas who calls it "right reason." When one reasons rightly one will make judgments which are consistent with one's human nature and which will promote human flourishing. Natural law, our Tradition holds, is written within our hearts by our Creator and is our ability to grasp in some way the mind of the Creator for us. We have spoken earlier, when addressing the virtues, about humanity's "tending toward the good." Natural law theory begins with a focus on how we have been created to tend toward the good.

There are natural springs within us, which bring knowledge and truth to the human mind and heart. We now wish to consider the basic human inclinations which are planted in our depths. Through the centuries, thinkers and philosophers have referred to these universal inclinations of the human heart and mind as pertaining to the natural law. A proper reflection on these natural inclinations will see them, not as something purely biological, but always with regard to the rational human person who seeks what is good so as to reach fulfillment. In other words, the human person, who is rational by nature, uses this God-given gift of reason to reflect on his or her natural inclinations. Why? Because by doing so we hope to discover what is good, and by discovering what is good we can reach fulfillment. "Natural inclinations take on moral relevance only in so far as they refer to the human person and his authentic fulfillment, a fulfillment that can take place always and only in human nature" (*The Splendor of Truth*, §50).

From the outset, it is vital to stress that the natural law is not primarily external to us, "nature out there somewhere," restraining us. Rather, it is the inclinations and yearnings in us, within our human nature, that should really attract us, enlighten us, lead us, and help express our true selves as human beings in society.

What are these inclinations? From where do these inclinations come? Answering the second question first, we believe they come from the God who created us and that they reflect, although in a limited way, the eternal law or wisdom of God. In other words, God has created us with our own particular nature, our human nature, and this nature, who we are as human beings, has its own special purposes. How do we get in touch with this natural law, these natural inclinations, yearnings, or purposes which point us in the direction of what is good? We have been created with the power of reason, and this gift of intelligence, reflecting on Creation and human experience, can discern these purposes.

> The natural law is written and engraved in the soul of each and every man, because it is human reason ordaining him to do good and forbidding him to sin...But this command of human reason would not have the force of law if it were not the voice and interpreter of a higher reason to which our spirit and our freedom must be submitted (Pope Leo XIII, *Libertas proetant issimum*, 597).

We also have the Word of God to come to the aid of our struggling reason in its reflection. As we shall discover, the Word of God and our reason, striving to discern the natural law, are not two distinct and disconnected realities; rather, they both direct us to the same basic insights that come from the Wisdom of God and God's plan for us.

2. Primary Principle of Natural Law

Enough of abstract theory for the moment, for we have not answered the first question posed, namely, what are these natural inclinations in the human mind and heart? While we find reflections on the natural law in the ancient writings of Aristotle and Cicero and numerous philosophers and theologians, the outline of this chapter and treatment of natural law will be based primarily on the insights of Saint Thomas Aquinas and the scholastic theologians. This focus is not to say that the understanding of the natural law has not developed since the time of Aquinas. In fact, we will refer to more contemporary understandings of the natural law as we proceed. We are simply claiming that the Thomistic approach offers us a very useful framework from which to begin our reflection on this very Catholic source of moral knowledge.

"The natural law is nothing other than the light of understanding placed in us by God; through it we know what we must do and what we must avoid. God has given this light or law at the Creation" (Saint Thomas Aquinas, *De Trinitate*).

Saint Thomas says that the most basic or fundamental inclination we have is "to do good and to avoid evil." This primary natural insight makes sense, since we strive for happiness, and the way to be happy is to know what is good and to participate in it. All humans have this primary law within them. Do not let the word "law" confuse you. It is not some arbitrary external law we are speaking about here. We use the word "law" to identify our natural inclinations and purposes, an internal law that leads us to do good.

Returning to a discussion of our primary inclination, the reader may object: "If this is the case, then why is it that so many people do evil and avoid the good?" There are two possible reasons for this circumstance. First, a person may make a mistake in moving from the basic inclination to do good and translate this inclination into particular actions. In other words, a person may make the mistake of thinking something is an expression of good when in fact it is not. For example, a doctor gives the very elderly and dying a lethal injection to end their pain or poor quality of life. He may think he is expressing the search for what is good in a very practical way. In fact, what he is doing is gravely mistaken. He is not doing the good, and he is not avoiding what is evil in his practice. Something needs to be done on the part of the doctor to come to the realization of a proper transition from the basic inclination he has, that is, to do what is good, to the specific expressions of it. In other words, while he is attuned to his most basic inclination as a human person to do good, something goes wrong in his thinking when it comes to deciding what is the best way to express what is good in specific concrete actions. This particular example will be considered more fully towards the end of this chapter.

Second, humans can willingly go against the inclination to do the good and embrace it. In Christian theology, we call this sin. A decision to run against the grain of the basic inclination of the human heart and mind is very possible as we discussed in our treatment of sin. Despite sin and despite mistakes, the great theologians tell us that this natural spark of knowledge, to do the good and avoid the evil, cannot ever be fully extinguished, although it can be seriously dimmed. To use an image of Saint Bonaventure, it can be like a jockey who has fallen off his horse, but he is still attached by the reins. Of course, the natural law offers us more specific insights than just this primary but general insight of our human nature.

3. Four Inclinations of the Human Heart and Mind

TO PRESERVE YOUR LIFE

How many times have we experienced the natural inclination to preserve our life, from our almost automatic responses to danger to planned strategies to avoid life-threatening forces and circumstances. Springing from this inclination is the natural desire to be healthy and the right to preserve our bodily integrity. This natural desire to preserve our life expresses itself also in our quest for food, clothing, and shelter. Nor is it just our own lives that we know we ought to protect. In fact, the fifth commandment, "thou shalt not kill," is an expression of our duty to respect the natural inclination to preserve our own lives and the lives of others.

Our lives are not to be limited to the physical dimension however. To preserve our lives will also entail the protection of our moral and spiritual selves. At times, these aspects of ourselves can take priority over the physical, to such an extent that one may put his physical life in danger for the sake of others, for the sake of faith, and for the sake of country. A stark reminder of such a priority in recent times would be life of Saint Maximilian Kolbe, who offered his own life in a concentration camp in order to preserve the life of another person. This choice was not a wish to die and so against the natural law or his natural inclination to preserve his own life; rather, it was the heroic expression of the knowledge that preservation of physical life is not an absolute good at any cost, and, at times, risks have to be taken to preserve other goods.

Abortion, torture, terrorism, euthanasia, all direct attacks on innocent life, on the other hand, are attacks on one of our natural inclinations to protect the lives of others. The alarming rate of suicide in some developed countries should be a warning light that something is radically wrong in such societies. What is it that can dim the knowledge of one of the most basic natural truths, namely, that my life is of value and deserves to be preserved? Other self-destructive acts common across the globe indicate that a basic human inclination and yearning is being radically dimmed. Drug and alcohol abuse, dangerous driving, deadly sexual practices, all indicate that the inner law to protect our own lives and the lives of others has been overshadowed by disordered or unruly desires or unclear thinking.

TO MARRY AND TO GENERATE, PRESERVE, AND EDUCATE OFFSPRING

Humans also have a natural desire to find a spouse, to have children, and to care for their offspring. In fact, thinkers of the past have suggested that we share these inclinations with the animal world just as we share, too, the inclination for the preservation of our lives with the animal world and the whole of living Creation. While this statement may be true, what pertains to us as human beings from the natural law needs to be distinguished from what is natural to animals. The human person can bring to perfection what is observed as natural to the animal world. Have you ever seen some disturbing scenes on nature shows where the male tiger or lion in fact kills his offspring. As men and women made in the image of God, we would not want to imitate all the natural inclinations of animals, for we are endowed with reason and freedom. While many of us watch nature programs on television and are astounded at the beauty and complexity of animal life, it soon becomes obvious that their patterns of mating, partnership, and parenthood are different from our own. While animals live by instinct, doing what is natural for them, we live as reasoning and believing people, reflecting on what it really means to be made in God's image.

It is no accident that we can perhaps detect already a similarity between the dictates of the natural law for humans and the Ten Commandments. This relationship exists because the principles of the natural laws are manifest in the Ten Commandments, or Decalogue, of the Old Testament (CCC §1955). We need only think of the fourth commandment, to honor our mother and father, the ones who have generated us, cared for us, and educated us, to realize that the Word of God expresses what we may already know, perhaps vaguely, from our reason reflecting on our own human nature and experience.

The same can be said about the sixth commandment, that sexual intercourse and the commitment it should entail are reserved to marriage, or the ninth commandment that reminds us that our deepest yearnings for another in lust are destructive of the marriage relationship and the family.

TO SEARCH FOR THE TRUTH

Just as plants naturally strain for the sunlight, so we yearn for knowledge and for truth. Part of this search for truth is the natural desire to come to know God. Indeed, all our communication and relationships is based on this human inclination. To know another, to have them know me, and to know the God who created me and loves me forms a great part of the human endeavor. With Saint Augustine, we can spontaneously pray, "Would that I might know myself and know Thee." Knowledge is not divorced from love; this fact gives knowledge a particular attraction or drawing power, for the more we know a friend, a spouse, and God the more we love them. The eighth commandment, which deals with lying and false promises, supports this inclination to search for the truth. From this insight of the natural law, we also sense the obligation to educate ourselves and others. The ancient maxim, namely, that a life lived but not reflected upon is a life not worth living, is an attempt to touch this truth. Perhaps we have never thought of a life of reflection in this way, but to refuse to know the truth, nor to want to hear or learn, nor develop or be open, is to stunt a natural inclination of the human heart and mind, and, therefore, to place limitations on our ability to love. The reasons may be many: fear, laziness, not wanting to change, or prejudice, but the consequence is a severe limiting of our freedom since it is the truth that sets us free.

TO LIVE IN SOCIETY

Cynics would say that we human beings only cooperate with one another because it is necessary for survival. If you are going to survive, you need the support and the protection of others around you. It is a dog-eat-dog world, and the only reason we do not eat the other dog is because there is always another hound that might inspire to eat us! Despite such cynicism, could it be that this yearning to be with others and to cooperate with them stems from something deeper than mere survival? To be understood, heard, loved, forgiven, appreciated, to belong, to feel with, rely on, be useful, are all part of our everyday language that gives voice to a natural inclination to be social. When we frustrate this inclination in ourselves or others and block its path, we pay the consequences. If we have a vision of ourselves as primarily isolated individuals, exercising our freedom and demanding our personal rights in competition with other humans of a similar nature, what becomes of friendship, affection, a sense of solidarity? We cannot appeal to our individual rights to demand friendship, a sense of belonging, and encouragement. Contemporary theology is beginning to rediscover the importance once given to friendship in the spiritual and moral life by medieval theologians and mystics. Listening to the elderly talk about the good-old days, one can often detect a sense of loss—loss of the experience of a community, a common goal, a trustworthy neighbor, an innate respect for the common good. Forms of radical liberalism that choose to ignore the importance of community and solidarity are flying in the face of a human need or inclination, in other words, going against part of this natural law. We are social, rational animals, but much more than this. Our God is social, too, Father, Son, and Holy Spirit communicating and loving; and we are made in that Trinitarian image. No wonder it is natural for us to be social!

4. Reducing the Natural Law to the Physical

Unfortunately, it is not always easy to determine the natural law when we come down to specifics. An easy way out might be to say: "Do not go against what our *physical* nature tells us." Is this the meaning of the natural law? In fact, this is not the meaning of the natural law and, if we follow such an interpretation rigidly, we could end up with some very strange moral evaluations indeed. Consider the donating of a kidney or having a valve replaced in your ailing heart. What would you think of the following argument. God made me with my two kidneys and you with your two and thus God did not intend that my kidney should ever function in you. This exchange would be going against what is natural; and, therefore, it is against the natural law and is therefore morally wrong. In a similar fashion, if God created me with a faulty heart valve, then it is natural to me. To interfere with it would be going against what is natural. Most of us would be uneasy with such reasoning and such an interpretation of the natural law. Why? Because it attempts to reduce completely to the physical dimension what is natural to us, the natural law, those natural inclinations and yearnings discovered by our reason.

In the history of moral theology, this mistaken interpretation of the natural law has been called "physicalism." It is not as if our physical and biological laws have nothing to say to us; they do. "Listen to what your body is telling you" has become a popular expression, meaning physical signals can give you an insight into how your whole life is going. Being unable to sleep, lacking an appetite, being reduced to tears readily, and always being on edge may tell us many things about our inner self as well as our physical self. We are, however, more than a mass of biological laws and processes. We are made to love and be loved, to discover knowledge and to live in community. These natural inclinations cannot be reduced to the physical alone.

We are human beings, reflecting on the many experiences of what it means to be truly human; and this process is how we discover the natural law. The Church document dealing with human life, *Instruction on Respect for Human Life in Its Origins and the Dignity of Procreation*, expresses it this way:

> The natural law expresses and lays down the purposes, rights and duties which are based upon the bodily and spiritual nature of the human person. Therefore this law cannot be thought of as simply a set of norms on the biological level; rather it must be defined as the rational order whereby man is called by the Creator to direct and regulate his life and actions and in particular to make use of his body.

Let us now return to our example of donating a kidney to another person who will die without the transplantation. Our natural inclination to preserve another life, to live in solidarity with, and out of love for, another is totally natural. In other words, the physical, biological laws and functions of the human body may give us some indication of the natural law, but they cannot simply be equated with it. We must reflect on more than the purely biological inclinations or purposes. In this case, we reflect on the natural inclination to live in solidarity and charity and can conclude that following such an inclination can be practically expressed by the donation of one of my healthy kidneys.

5. The Content of the Natural Law: Primary and Secondary Principles

While Saint Thomas would claim that the primary insight of the natural law, namely, doing good and avoiding evil, is self-evident to all, he also stresses that there are similar self-evident principles and other secondary principles, which are based on them.

PRIMARY PRINCIPLES

Primary principles are universally valid. A primary principle which particularizes "do good and avoid evil" is "one should do no evil to another person" (*Summa Theologiae*, I–II, q. 100, a. 3; see also *The Splendor of Truth*, §50). Notice, however, that this statement is still a general principle. Similarly, one could say "love God and your neighbor" is a primary principle of natural law. These admit of no exception. At no time could one say that it is right to do evil to another person nor a time when one could morally stop loving God and neighbor. Primary principles are more general and are universally held.

SECONDARY PRINCIPLES

Secondary principles, as we have indicated, are derived from primary principles and specify more clearly what reason demands in specific cases. However, the more particular the circumstances become, the more difficult it is for us to interpret and apply the natural law or natural inclination. Saint Thomas himself made this point when he wrote that secondary principles would be valid "in the majority of cases...yet in some few cases it may fail" (*Summa Theologiae*, I–II, q. 94, a. 4).

As an example, certain commandments that express the natural law, such as "do not kill," can be known after a little consideration. Killing innocent people readily goes against our natural inclination and our reason as it reflects on the value of human life. But what about capital punishment? Is it against the natural law? Do we and should we have a natural inclination to terminate guilty human life? Or, is it against the natural law to remove feeding and hydration tubes from a person who is in a permanent vegetative state after a severe accident? These cases require remote conclusions from the natural inclination to preserve life. To put it another way, we know that the preservation of human life is generally a good to be done, but can circumstances or the preservation of other goods overrule this basic inclination? We enter a thick forest here. As we have said, Saint Thomas acknowledges that some decisions respecting our human nature require long and careful reflection by the wise. Since natural law has been the foundation of so much of Catholic moral theology, and at times the almost exclusive source of moral reflection, even to the extent of wrongly side-stepping the Scriptures, the wise have reflected and argued much over the more remote moral conclusions we can reach from the natural law.

Attitudes to slavery, torture, and religious persecution in the moral tradition will illustrate this point well. No Catholic theologian would argue today that slavery, torture, and the persecution of non-Christians are in accord with the natural law, but it has not always been this way. It has taken centuries of time and reflection to outrightly condemn such barbaric practices and attitudes. What went wrong in the thinking? Perhaps, in the past, those classified as human and made in God's image were falsely limited to those with a particular physical appearance or a particular religious belief. It was also not uncommon for theologians to claim that when criminals performed certain crimes they ceased to be human, or they forfeited their human dignity and so could be treated like animals. Perhaps a claim was made that the truths of Christianity are rationally self-evident; anyone who did not accept them must be irrational and therefore not fully human; and as a result they would be liable to persecution. These and other examples raise the question of what is called the immutability of the natural law. Put simply, can the natural law change, does our human nature change, and what reasonable change is good for us? Saint Thomas makes a decisive distinction at this point. Change, he argues, can occur through addition or subtraction. In regard to addition, he argues that nothing hinders the natural law from being more fully known by us. A more profound reflection on, and investigation into, human nature and experience may well uncover insights that have escaped previous generations, as with the cases of torture, slavery, and religious persecution. Regarding subtraction, could we say that something that was once in accord with natural law is no longer in accord with natural law? Here he answers in the negative, for otherwise we would be admitting that the natural inclinations and yearnings of the human mind and heart simply change as the centuries roll on. We cannot hold that what is truly natural in one generation, part of our human nature and part of God's design for us, ceases to be so for the next.

6. A Contemporary Insight Into Natural Law

We have already considered some of the goods we seek; namely, the preservation of life, taking a spouse and raising children, living together in a society, and the search for truth. We seek these goods because they are the objects or ends of our natural inclinations, and these natural inclinations point us in the direction of human fulfillment. While Saint Thomas briefly outlines some of these inclinations and the goods to which they point us, some contemporary theologians identify other goods to be pursued that correspond to our natural inclinations.

One such example is our human inclination for justice and friendship. In other words, deep within us, a natural longing exists to have right relationships in our lives, not only a right relationship with someone with whom we have much in common, such as a friend, but also with others not as intimately close to us. It is not just a matter of survival, as we stressed earlier. Justice springs from that inner longing to live in harmony with other human beings, and living in harmony requires that we respect persons and give them what is their due. To live in peace and harmony with others is part of the natural law, part of God's design for us. Of course, the inclination toward harmony does not reach its fulfillment only in relationships with other human beings, for we are made to be in harmony with our God too. Thus, religion is a good to be pursued, a good which springs from our natural inclination to enjoy a harmonious life, especially with the One who made us.

If you have ever been astounded by a masterpiece of art, by the beauty of song, or by the thrill of dance, you will also know that beauty somehow fulfills a natural inclination in us. On the more practical side, to have acquired a skill to a degree of excellence, such as in cooking, sewing, building, or healing, brings with it a sense of fulfillment. These activities or skills fulfill another natural inclination we have in our search for wholeness as human beings. In fact, we do not have to be divas, or maestros, or champions in our skills, or even in our play, to be able to appreciate the satisfaction and sense of purpose that comes from doing a job well or striving for a touch of excellence in our lives, however small or apparently insignificant. These endeavors enrich us because they are natural to us.

7. The Teaching Church and the Natural Law

The teaching Church claims authority not only to interpret the Sacred Scriptures but also to interpret the meaning of the natural law. Pope Pius IX, in the *Syllabus of Errors*, argued that the indissolubility of marriage was based on the natural law; Pope Leo XIII wrote that the right to private property and ownership was based on a correct understanding of human nature and on the most holy law of nature; Pope Pius XII used natural law argumentation to condemn direct sterilization and artificial insemination; and Pope Paul VI's teaching on artificial contraception relies heavily on interpreting the natural law.

The authority of the Magisterium extends also to the specific precepts of the *natural law*, because their observance, demanded by the Creator, is necessary for salvation. In recalling the prescriptions of the natural law, the Magisterium of the Church exercises an essential part of its prophetic office of proclaiming to men what they truly are and reminding them of what they should be before God (CCC §2036).

In fact, as the chapters on specific ethical issues will illustrate, the Church appeals frequently to both Scripture and natural law to give guidance in the area of sexual morality, bioethics, environmental ethics, and justice. In so doing, the Church can appeal to all men and women of good will who search for the truth, whether Christian or not, and hopefully demonstrate that faith and reason, rather than working in opposition to one another, are, in the words of Pope John Paul II, like two wings on which the human spirit rises to the contemplation of the truth.

8. Two Wings for the Human Spirit

Saint Augustine, and many of the Fathers of the Church, referred to these two complementary modes of assessing God's wisdom and his plan for us, namely, the Scriptures and the natural law. Both reveal the image of God. In fact, before Saint Augustine, Saint Paul spoke of the unwritten law that is present in everyone, even the Gentiles, that is, those who did not believe and did not have the written law of God. "When Gentiles, who do not possess the law, do instinctively what the law requires, these, though not having the law, are a law to themselves. They show that what the law requires is written on their hearts, to which their own conscience also bears witness" (Rom 2:14–15).

However, because of sin, our reason, which can discover this unwritten law, has to struggle to gain this moral knowledge. According to the Fathers, this is why the Scriptures also reveal in written form what is unwritten in our hearts. They often refer to the golden rule as it is presented in the Gospel of Matthew, "You shall love your neighbor as yourself" (Mt 22:39), or to its negative formulation as it is found in the Old Testament, "Do not do unto others what you would not want them to do to you." This fundamental written commandment or golden rule corresponds with what is already there unwritten within us, from the mere fact that we are made in God's image. This general rule, according to the Fathers, is spelled out in more detail in other parts of the Scriptures, especially the Decalogue, the Ten Commandments. Thus, they would draw parallels, for example, between our inclination to have a spouse and children with the Genesis command, "Be fruitful and multiply" (Gen 1:28).

The actual Ten Commandments are more specific translations of the general command to do unto others as we would want them to do unto us. The point is that, as people of faith, we are supported by two wings of knowledge, the unwritten natural law and the written word of the Scriptures. Saint Thomas also explained that the moral teachings of Jesus in the New Testament are an expression of the virtues that pertain to all human beings and in theory can be found in the natural law. Scripture and natural law do not fight against each other; rather, both reveal how we are to touch and live out those inclinations towards the good, inclinations we have because we are created in the image of God. The Scriptures also help us to identify other inclinations, such as aggression, jealousy, domination, and anger, that need to be subordinated and directed by our human reason so as to bring about the good and avoid what is evil.

9. The Natural Law and Moral Education

Returning to our case of the doctor who directly shortens the life of the sick and elderly, we would argue that moral education and development is urgently needed. The truth of the sanctity of life founded on the natural law will only be grasped if a person remains open to further reflection and wider human experience. We need to ask the following penetrating question: Are such people, even when they ask for their lives to be terminated by a physician, really yearning for something else? Perhaps proper palliative care to relieve pain, perhaps a sense that they are not a burden on family and society, perhaps a sense that someone still cares for them and loves them would stop this sad request from even entering their minds. How many of the elderly, frail, and seriously ill are really dying from loneliness and a lack of human affection? Is this what drives them to underestimate the innate value of their own lives and tempts the healthy to do the same in their regard? As the conscience can be erroneous, so can our interpretations of human inclinations and yearnings, and so we have an obligation to learn, to listen, to reflect, to change, and to be open.

10. Conclusion

Like the commandments, the natural law is not exterior to us. It does impose obligations on us, and obligations are important in the moral awareness and growth of the person. As with the Ten Commandments, however, the dictates of the natural law really correspond to our deepest and most intimate yearnings and hopes. The more we reflect on this experience of being human, being made in God's image, the more this interior wisdom will unfold itself. Furthermore, when we open ourselves to the Word of God in the Scriptures, we have two wings with which to fly towards our true selves and our calling.

CHAPTER 8

The Magisterium As Authoritative Teacher

(CCC §§888–892; §§2032–2040;
see also *The Dogmatic Constitution on the Church*, §§18–25)

In 1987, the Vatican's Congregation for the Doctrine of the Faith published a brief work entitled *Instruction on Respect for Human Life in Its Origins and on the Dignity of Procreation*. It dealt with contemporary reproductive technologies, such as *in vitro* fertilization and surrogate motherhood, and offered a moral evaluation of them for the Roman Catholic community and for anyone else who should choose to read the document. The text was subtitled: "A Response to Certain Questions of Our Day." It was written in answer to queries from the Catholic community around the world, requests for guidance to navigate these unchartered waters of new technologies in reproduction.

As we conclude this second section of the book on avenues to moral truth, we look to a particularly rich resource that Catholics possess in the teaching office of the Church, what is commonly called the magisterium. First, we will examine what we mean by the magisterium. Second, our attention will turn to the authoritative teaching ministry of the magisterium and its varieties of expression. Third, we will study the different types of teaching that the magisterium offers to the Roman Catholic community and the nature of assent required in each case. Finally, we will consider the possibility of withholding assent from a non-dogmatic teaching of the Church if and when a person comes to a judgment of conscience which differs from the teaching of the pastoral magisterium.

1. What Is the Magisterium?

The word "magisterium" comes from the Latin word "*magister*" which means "teacher," or even closer, "master," in the sense of one who is highly competent in a particular area. Within the Christian community of the first two centuries emerged an authoritative body which was responsible for ensuring the integrity of the faith and practice of the Christian community; in other words, for making sure that what people believed and how they acted was consistent with the life and teaching of Jesus. Today, as then, the bishops of the Church comprise the magisterium; they are the authoritative teachers in the community.

The bishops in the Church have the threefold ministry of sanctifying, governing, and teaching the People of God. Our focus is on the teaching ministry. Giving "an authentic (authoritative) interpretation of the Word of God, whether in its written form or in the form of Tradition, has been entrusted to the living teaching office of the Church alone. Its authority in this matter is exercised in the name of Jesus Christ" (*Dogmatic Constitution on Divine Revelation*, §10).

Note that the magisterium interprets Scripture and Tradition for the community. In doing so it requires other avenues to moral truth, such as natural law and the human sciences. In fact, much of the teaching of the magisterium within the moral tradition rests on its interpretation of natural law. As "expert in humanity," the Church is particularly equipped to interpret natural law and to offer an authentic vision of the human good (cf., PAUL VI, Message to the United Nations, October 4, 1965: Insegnamenti di Paolo VI, Vol. III (1965); *Gaudium et spes*, #4). But the magisterium's principal competency is Scripture and Tradition. The magisterium interprets these two avenues to moral truth in a way that is faithful to them and strengthening for the People of God. The Tradition is the ongoing development of the Church's understanding of the mystery of revelation within which stands the Word of God as the normative text for the Christian community and the magisterium as its servant. For this reason, the bishops themselves at the Second Vatican Council wrote that the "magisterium is not superior to the Word of God but, rather is its servant. It teaches only what has been handed on to it. At the divine command and with the help of the Holy Spirit, it listens to this devoutly, guards it reverently, and expounds it faithfully" (*Dogmatic Constitution on Divine Revelation*, §10). The magisterium stands within the Roman Catholic Tradition and furthers it as it interprets the Sacred Scriptures in our world today.

The Roman Catholic Tradition traces a connection from the bishops of today back to the apostles and to Christ himself. The Second Vatican Council teaches that bishops "have by divine institution taken the place of the apostles as pastors of the Church in such wise that whoever hears them hears Christ and whoever rejects them rejects Christ and Him who sent Christ (cf. Lk 10:16)" (*Dogmatic Constitution on the Church*, §20). Such a claim underscores, first, the care and humility with which bishops must exercise their teaching office, aware that they are shepherds of the Church and successors to the apostles. It also highlights the respect and humility with which the People of God ought to listen to and receive the teachings of the magisterium.

2. Varieties of Expression of the Magisterium

Within the Church, the magisterium fulfills its task as authoritative interpreter of Scripture and Tradition in a variety of ways. These range from a single letter written by a bishop in his diocese to a statement by a national conference of bishops to a document approved by the bishops gathered with the pope in Ecumenical Council to a statement made by the pope alone. All of these are voices of the magisterium. They fall, however, under two main categories, the extraordinary magisterium and the ordinary magisterium, depending on the nature of the teaching and who is proposing it.

THE EXTRAORDINARY MAGISTERIUM

The extraordinary magisterium proposes teachings infallibly to the Church. This teaching may be done by the whole college of bishops, who only have authority if they are in communion with the pope. The pope alone, as the head of the college of bishops and universal head of the Church, may also propose teachings infallibly (*Dogmatic Constitution on the Church*, §22). An individual bishop, an episcopal conference, a gathering of bishops without the pope, or any other group apart from the two mentioned above may not propose teachings infallibly to the Catholic community; only the college of bishops in union with the pope or the pope alone as head of the college of bishops may so act.

We will say more in a moment about the specific character of teachings, that is, definitive dogma, definitive doctrine, and authoritative non-definitive doctrine. For the moment, we simply make a distinction between the ordinary magisterium and the extraordinary magisterium. The extraordinary magisterium is exercised rarely.

THE ORDINARY MAGISTERIUM

As the title itself suggests, the ordinary magisterium refers to the common or usual teaching of the bishops of the Church. When the bishops of the Church, gathered in Rome in the 1960s for the Second Vatican Council, offered sixteen documents ranging in topic from the liturgy to the mission of the Church in the modern world, it was an exercise of the ordinary magisterium. Similarly, when a conference of bishops from a particular country offers a teaching unanimously confirmed by the conference or approved by two-thirds of the conference with subsequent approval by the Vatican, it is an exercise of the ordinary magisterium. Any teaching offered by a bishop or bishops in his or their official capacity as pastors of the People of God falls under the category of the ordinary magisterium.

So, exercises of the ordinary magisterium may include a statement by the pope alone, the pope teaching with bishops, a conference of bishops, or an individual bishop. They offer or reaffirm a teaching for the good of the community in order that the implications of the faith for understanding and Christian practice may be more clearly comprehended.

3. Teaching With Authority

Before moving to a consideration of the nature and type of assent required to teachings of the pastoral magisterium, we say a word about teaching itself and how this service of the magisterium is to be exercised. The bishops teach with an authority which comes to them as successors to the apostles who were entrusted with the ministry of teaching by Jesus. How the bishops teach and learn, however, is critical so that their exercise of authority genuinely mirrors the authority with which Jesus spoke and acted.

MODELS OF TEACHING

Teachers can approach their task in a variety of ways. One teacher may enter a classroom presuming that he is the sole source of knowledge and that everyone else in the room, whether they are first-graders or candidates for a doctoral degree, is there to listen to him. The students have nothing to contribute, it is presumed; they are there to listen and to learn. This approach to teaching focuses not so much on the subject matter as on the teacher as master of the material. The teacher is indispensable and may be seen as the only way to understand the subject matter.

Some people would prefer that the magisterium teach in this manner where it approaches its task as the sole possessor of the truth and teaches it authoritatively to a passive People of God. This model, however, is not consistent with what the magisterium is nor how it should teach.

In another model, the "teacher" is akin to a group facilitator who starts a discussion and then sits on the sidelines, allowing the students to "carry the ball" wherever they wish. In this instance, although one would presume that the teacher knows the subject matter, she is given little opportunity to demonstrate her knowledge. Rather, her skills would be more evident in formulating a good question to begin the discussion.

Those who favor this model of teaching might wish that the magisterium would have little to say at all about moral matters in the Church. Perhaps they would prefer that the magisterium simply remind people of general Gospel principles and then leave individual members of the Church community to work out the particulars on their own. This model, too, is inconsistent with what the magisterium is within the Church.

In yet another approach to teaching, teachers do not enter the classroom believing that they have a monopoly on truth or knowledge nor do they abandon their students to their own whims. Rather, these teachers are aware of the particular expertise that they bring to the learning process. In their approach to teaching, they realize that the focus ought to be not on themselves as the teachers but on the subject matter. They know that the students should be drawn to the subject matter both by what they, the teachers, say and how they say it. They also acknowledge that good learning occurs when a student can be involved actively in the process of learning, where the student is even encouraged to speak about what he or she already knows of the subject matter.

The function and place of the magisterium in the Church is similar to this third model. It is so because all members of the Church are first the People of God. The magisterium and the faithful are baptized into the same Church and together are entrusted with the faith. The "subject matter" of our joint study, if you will, is first and foremost the revelation which is Jesus Christ and the way the person of

Christ and his Good News have been made manifest to the Church through Sacred Scripture and Tradition. The fathers of the Second Vatican Council put it this way:

> Tradition and scripture make up a single sacred deposit of the word of God, which is entrusted to the Church. By adhering to it the entire holy people, united to its pastors remains always faithful to the teaching of the apostles, to the communion of life, to the breaking of bread and the prayers....So, in maintaining, practicing and professing the faith that has been handed on, there is a unique interplay between the bishops and the faithful (*Dogmatic Constitution on Divine Revelation*, §10).

The image presented previously, then, captures the joint effort of all members of the Church in discerning the significance of the Gospel for moral practice today. The *Catechism of the Catholic Church* reiterates this joint effort when it reminds us that in the task of transmitting and applying the teachings of Catholic morality, the Church requires the contribution of its pastors, the expertise of theologians, and the support of all people of good will. It goes on to say: "Faith and the practice of the Gospel provide each person with an experience of life 'in Christ,' who enlightens him and makes him able to evaluate the divine and human realities according to the Spirit of God. Thus the Holy Spirit can use the humblest to enlighten the learned and those in the highest positions" (CCC §2038).

The Holy Spirit is at work in the whole Church as it strives to live the Gospel in always new and challenging times. There is an optimism about the effect of the Spirit in the Church. The *Dogmatic Constitution on the Church* from the Second Vatican Council assures the Church of the Spirit's guiding presence. It states: "The whole body of the faithful who have received an anointing which comes from the

Holy One...cannot be mistaken in belief. It shows this characteristic through the entire people's supernatural sense of the faith, when, 'from the bishops to the last of the faithful,' it manifests a universal consensus in matters of faith and morals" (§12).

We offer this rather lengthy comparison of models of teaching because it places the role of the magisterium within the context of the entire Church's mission to plumb the mysteries of the faith and their implications for Christian practice. The magisterium's particular gift in this teaching process, however, is the charism of the truth. This charism is not supernaturally infused knowledge, but a gift of the Spirit to discern and recognize apostolic faith. This competence of the magisterium is evident in its long tradition of sorting out what is consistent or not with the Gospel and enriched by the international character of the body which is the magisterium of the Church.

4. The Nature of Church Teaching and Assent Required of the Faithful

One of the earliest references in the Christian Tradition to a teacher indicating varying degrees of authority to his teaching comes in Saint Paul's First Letter to the Corinthians, chapter 7, where he addresses the Corinthian community about marriage. He states at one point, "I give this command—not I but the Lord" (1 Cor 7:10); he forbids divorce. Shortly thereafter Paul writes: "To the rest I say—I and not the Lord" (1 Cor 7:12). Paul goes on to speak of marriages between believers and nonbelievers. Realizing the significance of his voice as an apostle, Paul clearly distinguishes what is of the Lord and what is his best grasp of what he believes is consistent with what the Lord would want. He is careful, however, to note the difference.

The magisterium acts similarly when proposing teachings to the Roman Catholic community. Although it does not state it in the same way as Saint Paul, it categorizes different types of teaching, each with a particular binding force on the faith community.

The Roman Catholic Tradition makes a distinction technically between dogma and doctrine. Dogma refers to the basic tenets or creeds of our faith; they are presumed to be divinely revealed. Doctrine is a broader term than dogma and refers to those teachings of the Church, some presumed to be divinely revealed, others less directly connected to divine revelation but still important for the faithful. Dogma, then, is subsumed into the larger category of doctrine. Doctrines may be divinely revealed or not; dogmas are always presumed to be so.

The three principal categories of teaching, each anticipating a particular kind of assent or reception on the part of the faithful, are as follows: definitive dogma; definitive doctrine; authoritative nondefinitive doctrine.

DEFINITIVE DOGMA

Definitive dogma refers to teachings "proposed by the church—whether in solemn judgment or in the ordinary and universal magisterium—as divinely revealed and calling for faith" (*Profession of Faith*, Congregation for the Doctrine of the Faith, in "Doctrinal Congregation Publishes Faith Profession and Oath," *Origins* 18/40 [March 16, 1989]: 663). Under this category would fall the statements in the creeds of the Church, such as the Nicene Creed where we profess that we believe in one God, the Father almighty, and so forth. Also contained here would be the belief in Jesus' humanity and divinity and the belief in the Virgin Mary's Immaculate Conception and Assumption into heaven, among other dogmas.

To declare a dogma definitive the Church is saying that the truth expressed in the dogma is unchanged and unchangeable; one may also say that the truth is irreversible. Its particular expression may change, but the truth will never change. For example, we believe that Jesus is both human and divine. We have used terms borrowed from Greek philosophy to attempt to explain this wonderful mystery. We speak of Jesus having two natures, one divine and one human. Should we find another way to communicate this truth we may do so, but we may not do so at the expense of the truth. Our expression could not lead one to doubt the divinity and humanity of Jesus. More importantly, a definitive dogma may not be expressed in such a way that following it will lead us away from the path to salvation. So, to declare a dogma definitive, the Church says that the truth expressed there is unchanged and unchangeable. Sometimes definitive dogmas are the result of solemn definition; other times they are not.

Dogma taught definitively by solemn judgment: The *Profession of Faith*, published by the Congregation for the Doctrine of the Faith in 1989, notes that some dogmas are proposed in solemn judgment. This exercise of authority belongs to the extraordinary magisterium. Recall that the extraordinary magisterium comprises the college of bishops teaching in communion with its head, the pope, or the pope, speaking *ex cathedra*, as head of the college of bishops. When the Church declares a definitive dogma infallibly, or in solemn judgment, it binds the members of the Church community to accept the teaching in faith. In this case, the teaching office is really saying that this dogma is "of the Lord." One does not automatically presume that any and every authoritative teaching of the Church has been taught infallibly as a dogma. It must be "manifestly demonstrated."

Dogma taught definitively by the ordinary and universal magisterium: The extraordinary magisterium's proposal of a teaching as irreformable is very clear. As the Code of Canon Law says, it must be manifestly demonstrated. Less clear in the Roman Catholic Tradition is how a dogma may be taught infallibly by the ordinary and universal magisterium. *The Dogmatic Constitution on the Church* states that the ordinary and universal magisterium may teach infallibly when the bishops around the world, in union with the pope, are consistent in their teaching and agree that a particular issue of faith and morals is to be held as definitive (*Dogmatic Constitution on the Church,* §25; *Code of Canon Law,* canon 749, §2). Recently, Pope John Paul II has offered another way of recognizing when the bishops have taught something by the ordinary universal magisterium. He has, in several instances, such as in *Evangelium vitae,* offered a "papal confirmation" that the bishops have in fact taught a particular teaching infallibly in the ordinary and universal magisterium.

Perhaps it is worth pointing out here that often the dogmas of the Church have been defined in solemn judgment at times when their truth has been questioned. For example, the real presence of Christ in the Eucharist was always a belief of the Christian community. Over the centuries, however, there were those who questioned the truth of this teaching. In several Church councils, the teaching of the real presence of Christ in the Eucharist was defined, most notably in the Council of Trent in the sixteenth century.

There are dogmas, however, that have never been solemnly defined. For example, Sunday after Sunday we recite the Creed and say, "we believe in the communion of saints." We also commonly believe in Jesus' bodily resurrection even though we know from Scripture stories that his resurrected body must have been different in some way. These beliefs have not been defined in solemn judgment but are commonly held beliefs in the Roman Catholic Tradition.

Scholars writing on the infallibility of the ordinary and universal magisterium suggest that this exercise of infallibility is evident when, in the course of their teaching, bishops from around the world continue to teach and hold as definitive the dogmas and doctrine of the Church which have not been solemnly defined but are still held as true. The two examples cited previously support this view.

As with any exercise of the charism of infallibility, the magisterium must use its authority cautiously and humbly. It would seem critical to verify the mind of the bishops and the People of God throughout the world and not to presume that there is unanimity in a particular area, especially one that is controverted. Pope Pius IX and Pope Pius XII set a precedent in this regard when they queried the bishops regarding the faith of the Church before solemnly defining the dogmas of the Immaculate Conception and the bodily Assumption of Mary. Obviously this was not juridically demanded for a valid exercise of papal infallibility, but it reflects the pope's determination to ensure that they were teaching the faith of the Church.

Nature of assent required for definitive dogma: The *Profession of Faith* and subsequent documents note that definitive dogma is to be received by the faithful with an assent of faith, that is, they are to be accepted "as divinely revealed and calling for faith" (*Profession of Faith*). Should one find oneself in persistent doubt about a definitive dogma one might reasonably wonder about one's communion with the Roman Catholic community.

For example, in our pastoral ministry we have met people who confessed to doubting the real presence of Christ in the Eucharist. We encouraged them to align their faith with the faith of the community and to continue to go to Mass and receive Communion. After a period of time, their doubts decreased and they once again could profess their faith in the real presence.

However, if a central tenet of the faith is belief in a triune God and I cannot, persistently and with integrity, accept this dogma in faith, I may have to withdraw from the community out of fidelity to my own conscience and out of respect for the community of faith and its beliefs.

Whereas in the past, the Church might have actively sought out those who did not accept dogmas central to the faith and excommunicated them, the emphasis here is on the individual's exercise of conscience and her own act of integrity regarding membership in the community. We noted that this would be in the case of doubts that are "persistent," not passing. Definitive dogmas whether taught by the magisterium infallibly or not are to be received with an assent of faith because they are divinely revealed.

DEFINITIVE DOCTRINE

The 1989 *Profession of Faith* and *Oath of Fidelity* are to be professed by those who "are called to exercise an office in the name of the church." Those professing their faith are to say: "I also firmly accept and hold each and every thing that is proposed by that same church definitively with regard to teaching concerning faith or morals" (*Profession of Faith*). This category of doctrine first appeared in the *Profession of Faith* of 1989.

Whereas the subject matter of definitive dogma is presumed to be part of divine revelation, the same is not true of definitive doctrine. Pope John Paul writes that the truths of definitive doctrine, however, are a "deeper understanding of some truth concerning faith or morals" (*Ad Tuendam Fidem*, §3). They are "required for the sacred preservation and faithful explanation of the...deposit of faith" (*Code of Canon Law*, canon 750, §2). For example, the teaching of the Church on euthanasia is definitive, as reiterated in the *Gospel of Life*. There is no explicit condemnation of euthanasia in the revealed Word of God, yet it would seem that an opinion contrary to this teaching would in some way compromise the deposit of faith, specifically the scriptural themes of God as Creator and Author of all life and ourselves as stewards of life. These scriptural themes support the Church's teaching. Other arguments are offered as well, but we point out the connection to Sacred Scripture as a way of showing how a particular teaching of the magisterium may be taught definitively not because it is part of divine revelation but because it is "required for the sacred preservation and faithful explanation of the same deposit of faith."

In sum, the magisterium's use of the term "definitive" indicates that it believes that the subject matter of the teaching, either in faith or morals, is understood with sufficient clarity in the Church and that the teaching on it is irreversible or irreformable. It will not change in substance.

Nature of assent required for definitive doctrine: Pope John Paul II writes that definitive doctrine must be "firmly embraced and maintained" (*Ad Tuendam Fidem*, §4; *Code of Canon Law*, canon 750, §2). The *Profession of Faith* says, "I also firmly accept and hold" teachings proposed definitively.

Whereas definitive dogma is to be received by the faithful with an act of faith, believing that what is taught is truly divinely revealed, definitive doctrine does not presume an act of faith on the part of the believer. Rather, these teachings are to be firmly accepted and held as true, trusting in the working of the Holy Spirit in the teaching office of the pastoral magisterium.

AUTHORITATIVE NON-DEFINITIVE DOCTRINE

A third type of teaching referred to in the *Profession of Faith* is non-definitive doctrine. The document refers to teachings proposed by the pope or the college of bishops "even if they proclaim those teachings in an act that is not definitive." In offering moral wisdom to the Roman Catholic community, the magisterium attempts to understand God's revelation better, to connect certain teachings with more fundamental truths of the faith, and/or to caution the community about certain ideas which run contrary to the truths of the faith. These may be theological opinions or wisdom about the morality of particular issues.

When teaching in an authoritative but non-definitive and non-infallible way, the magisterium offers wisdom to the community as its best grasp on the truth of the matter under consideration. Aware of the difficulty of overstating our capacity to know the truth in very particular matters, the magisterium teaches authoritatively but not definitively. The community presumes the assistance of the Holy Spirit in these teachings of the magisterium as well.

Nature of assent required for non-definitive doctrine: The *Profession of Faith*, following the teaching of the *Dogmatic Constitution on the Church* from the Second Vatican Council, says that the faithful are to receive non-definitive doctrine with a "religious submission of will and mind" (§25). Others translate the Latin term in this text, *obsequium religiosum*, as a "religious deference of will and mind." In any case, the faithful are to receive this teaching and to make it their own to the best of their ability. They do so, again, confident that the Holy Spirit is working in the ministry of the pastoral magisterium and out of respect for the teaching office.

5. Conclusion: A Common Task: Tending Toward the Good for the Fullness of Life

In John's Gospel, Jesus says, "I came that they may have life, and have it abundantly" (Jn 10:10). Jesus promises us that following him will lead us to the fullness of life. The task of the magisterium and the task of individual believers is a common one in that we seek to know how to follow the Lord in today's world so that we may have the fullness of life.

While the teaching office of the Church must do this at a level for the whole Church community, individual believers must do so in the context of their own life within the Christian community. The tasks are not in opposition but in need of each other. The teaching office learns from the experience of the believers of the community, and the community learns and is shaped by the teaching office of the magisterium.

Individual believers must recognize their own limitations as they strive to understand the truth and to make good moral judgments in their lives. We are all called to ongoing conversion and have many blind spots in our vision of the truth. We are in need of others, the community at large, and the teaching office in particular, to guide us in the pursuit of the fullness of life.

The teaching office must also recognize its limitations regarding the ability to know the truth and articulate it in a way that is appropriate for the community. Precisely for this reason, the Church articulates different categories of teaching with varying degrees of assent required for them. The Church recognizes humbly that moral truth may not always be grasped fully by us, even with the assistance of the Holy Spirit. So, the Church offers moral wisdom to the community to assist it in the formation and exercise of conscience, firmly believing that those who follow the teaching will come to the fullness of life.

The experience of history has shown both that the teaching office of the Church has learned by being attentive to the *sensus fidelium*, the sense of the faithful, and the faithful have learned by being attentive to the teaching office of the Church. The gospel and the Roman Catholic community are served best when this relationship of mutual enrichment is nurtured and mined so as to grasp more fully the Good News in today's world.

Specialized Moral Theology

Introduction

If you were to hold a prism up to a light, you would see diverse reflections of that same light, brilliant colors depending on the way that the light hits the prism. Although each reflection is beautiful, none captures the fullness of the light, but only redirects the light in pleasing colors, in a limited way. Jesus Christ is the fullest revelation of God. Yet, our grasp of Jesus, the light of the world, and of the God he reveals is incomplete. It is limited because of our humanity, both personal and communal. The notion of Tradition and the development of our understanding of who Jesus is indicates that even the Church is always learning and delving more deeply into the mystery of God. Despite, yet precisely because of, this reality, we continue to approach God in faith and to study theology. As we mentioned earlier, theology is an attempt to systematize, to categorize, what we learn about God and our faith.

DIVISIONS OF THEOLOGY

In the process of writing theology, however, we have necessarily divided up the material studied in various subdivisions or aspects of theology, depending on what particular part of revelation we were exploring. Consequently, we speak of dogmatic theology or systematic theology to refer to the central truths of our faith, such as a study of the Trinity, or the person of Christ, and so forth. Sacramental theology studies the way that the sacraments are particular manifestations, "outward signs," of God's life and our lives coming together.

We also have historical theology, liturgical theology, moral theology, pastoral theology, and other subdivisions according to the material appropriate to that aspect of theology.

There is always a danger when we categorize or subdivide theology that we will forget that it is really a unified whole, attempting to give greater insight into the mystery of our Triune God. The subdivisions of theology are merely necessary for its study and dissemination.

MORAL THEOLOGY AND ITS SUBDIVISIONS

What is said of theology as a whole is true of moral theology as well. We have spoken of moral theology as that discipline of theology which studies the implications of our faith for the type of people we are to become as well as the kinds of actions that we should do. If the moral life is our response to God's many acts of love on our behalf, moral theology guides us in that response. Moral theologians, however, have created further divisions in the discipline of moral theology to address particular dimensions of our response in the moral life. In this third and final section of the book, we will offer brief overviews of four subdivisions of moral theology: biomedical ethics, sexual ethics, social ethics, and environmental ethics.

TENDING TOWARD THE GOOD/GOD

A theme repeated throughout this book so far is that the moral life consists in our "tending toward the good," tending toward God. In particular, we have noted that the habitual tending toward the good is the substance of the virtuous life. As we review these specializations of moral theology, we will be looking at the "good" from the particular vantage point of the biomedical good, the sexual good, the social good, and the environmental good. Although we believe that there are particular specifications of the good in each of these areas, some overarching goods are at work in each of them. Rather than treating them in each chapter, we present them here in more general terms. Their specific character should become evident as we look more closely at moral theology through the prism of its distinct disciplines.

Human life (CCC §2258 and following; Gospel of Life): We begin with human life itself. Human life is *the* foundational human good because without it we cannot enjoy any other good thing in this world. If we enjoy our family, travel, education, sports, song, dance, whatever it may be, unless we are alive we can experience none of it. Human life is the foundational human good. More importantly, our human life is the condition for our being able to come to know and love God. Unless we are born into this world, we are not invited into relationship with God and called to the fullness of life with him. In the various branches of moral theology that we will examine, then, we presume an unconditional respect for human life as the foundational human good.

To speak of human life as a foundational good does not mean that it is an absolute good, that is, that it may never be sacrificed. We believe that one may never directly attack the good of innocent human life. For this reason, we understand murder, abortion, euthanasia, and suicide to be morally evil. However, our Tradition also honors martyrs and, of course, the person of Jesus himself, who died that we might have life. So, while our earthly life is of inestimable value, it is not our ultimate destiny. Rather, we are destined to be with the God who made us in his own image (see *Gospel of Life*, §2).

When we discussed the criterion for right and wrong action in moral theology, we underscored the teaching found in Pope John Paul II's encyclical letter, *The Splendor of Truth*, in which he states that actions are morally right or wrong depending on whether they contribute to or detract from authentic human good. In all of the subdisciplines of moral theology, then, tending toward the good will include an unconditional respect for the human person and for his or her life.

Dignity of the human person (CCC §357; §1881; §§1928–1933): A second overarching good may well seem inseparable from the first, but merits attention on its own, that is, the dignity of the human person. The Roman Catholic Tradition points to the origin of human dignity in our Creation in the image and likeness of God (CCC §357). Simply because we exist, we are people of dignity. Dignity is ours precisely because we are sons and daughters of God. Becoming fully the image and likeness of God would be the highest expression of our dignity, its greatest manifestation.

Human dignity cannot be taken away: This inherent or intrinsic dignity which we possess cannot be taken away from us. This affirmation stands in sharp contrast to other uses of the term "dignity." In some societies, the dignity attributed to a person corresponds to his rank in society; one might expect people of royalty to possess greater dignity than a commoner. The British philosopher Hobbes measured dignity according to the public worth of a person. Popular language speaks quite easily of people losing their dignity for a variety of reasons. People might refer to an unreformed alcoholic who spends much of his time on the streets as "undignified," suggesting that he has lost his dignity as a human person. In debates over physician-assisted suicide, many people argue that the terminally ill lose their dignity when they can no longer care for themselves or make decisions for themselves. They argue for the right to "die with dignity." These notions of dignity suggest that human beings are somehow bestowed dignity based on their reputation, what they have accomplished, and the like. The Roman Catholic Tradition disputes this position and states quite clearly that people have dignity simply because they *are.*

To say that we always have dignity does not suggest that we always live in a manner consistent with our dignity. If we are created by love for love, lives of vice rather than virtue and every sinful act compromise our dignity as a child of God. On the contrary, a virtuous life expressed in loving actions toward God and others enhances our dignity precisely because it makes us more like the God in whose image we have been made.

Reflection in moral theology guides our actions so that the dignity of the person is respected, protected, and offered an environment where the person may flourish. A fundamental principle is that a person must never be used as a means to achieve some other end. Persons are always valued for themselves and not instruments to be used for some other gain. Among other areas, then, social ethics would argue for a just wage for workers and for decent working conditions; otherwise, workers might be simply pawns in the hands of employers. Sexual ethics touches on a core of our humanity as relational and social persons. Any abuse of another person, sexual or otherwise, degrades them and attacks their human dignity. Biomedical ethics will ensure that each person is treated as worthy of the utmost care and respect, that individuals are offered whatever medical attention is appropriate to their illnesses, and people are always honored until their last earthly breath. Environmental ethics sees the human person as the culmination of God's creative act and consequently ensures that the good of the human person is a priority, even as we attempt to discern how to be good stewards of God's Creation. These brief examples indicate how the good of respect for the dignity of the human person is at work in the various subdivisions of moral theology.

The human person as social/relational (CCC §§371–372; §376; §§1878–1880): People made in the image and likeness of a Triune God resemble God in their relationships "in truth and love" (CCC

§1878). We will be most truly ourselves when our relationships are in harmony, that is, the fourfold relationships with God, with others, with oneself, and with all of Creation. This third overarching good will be at work in all the specific areas of moral theology that we will discuss.

In the sections that follow, we might be tempted to think that social ethics and environmental ethics are "public" moral issues, while decisions about healthcare and one's sexual life are "private." This classification is not the case, however. Because the human person is relational and because our moral lives shape us as persons, it is on target to say that there is really no such thing as a private moral act. Whether we are discussing issues of the relationship between developed and developing countries, the choice for new reproductive technologies, responsible parenthood, or the impact of a new housing development on local wildlife, underneath all of these issues is the question of harmonizing those fourfold relationships.

Goodness of Creation (CCC §339; §§364–365): A final general good which we call attention to is the goodness of Creation. We are familiar with the text from the first book of the Bible, Genesis, where God the Creator looked upon all that he created and saw that it was good. This basic claim of the goodness of Creation also impacts our moral reflection across the board. While one might immediately tend to associate this good with environmental ethics, it is applicable to the other three areas that we will examine as well.

If our first overarching good is the goodness of the human person, this claim of the goodness of Creation affirms the goodness of the human person as body-soul (CCC §§364–365). The goodness of the human body *as well as* the soul underscores the moral obligation to care for our bodies and to attend to how we use them. Thus, both biomedical ethics, which concerns above all the health of the person, and sexual ethics, which guides our sexual relationships as embodied people, presume the goodness of all of Creation, the human body in particular. Social ethics and environmental ethics will attend to the goodness of all that exists as well as the obligation to be good stewards of the goods of the earth, ensuring that people have what they need to flourish as human beings and to enhance their dignity as children of God.

We could cite other "goods" as we begin this final section on the specific areas of moral theology. Let these suffice, however, to serve as the "umbrella" goods which will appear explicitly or implicitly in the areas that follow. Tending toward the good in the moral life will always include a profound respect for these goods both in attitude and in action.

CHAPTER NINE

Bioethics: Safeguarding Human Life, Human Dignity, and Health

1. Introduction

Daily headlines announce breakthroughs in technology which hold the promise of extending both the quantity and quality of life. Yet it comes as a surprise to no one that these "breakthroughs" often leave us with as many questions as hopes. As we discover more and more about the genes that make up the human person and the possibility of altering genes to produce the kind of person we would like, we naturally ask the question: "How much change is too much?" Should we choose blue eyes if we want them for our child? What about gender? Height? Weight? Rid them of potential diseases?

Other questions are: "How much medical treatment should I use to deal with my sickness?" "When is it legitimate to withdraw medical treatment that does not seem to be keeping my mother alive but only prolonging her death?" "What measures should my spouse and I take to have our own biological child?" All of these questions highlight the importance of clear thinking and analysis about issues of life; this is the concern of bioethics.

Bioethics is that branch of moral theology which deals with questions of life, its protection, and enhancement. Consequently, a central concern of bioethics is issues in healthcare. In the pursuit of the fullness of life to which we are called, bioethics considers the moral quality of our responses to questions surrounding conception, death, and the many life issues between the two.

2. Historical Overview

It is difficult to pinpoint a "birth" of bioethics since its subject matter has been considered for centuries. However, we can surely speak of a boom in bioethics beginning in the mid-twentieth century. One of the horrific discoveries about the Nazi regime during the Nuremberg Trials was that doctors had performed experiments on people without their consent. Purportedly to advance scientific knowledge, people were used as guinea pigs with little or no attention to their well-being. Reaction was strong against using people for medical advancement without their consent. Further, questions were raised about the conditions under which scientific knowledge may be obtained, a matter of bioethics.

Later developments in the twentieth century underscored the need for focused reflection on issues affecting human life and health. The promise of organ transplants, reproductive technologies, and other advances in technology to assist the normal functioning of human organs, such as renal dialysis, all raised questions about their ethical legitimacy. The possibility of keeping patients alive on respirators, feeding tubes, and the like further complicated end-of-life issues and raised new questions about when people had ethical obligations to use medical treatment and when they could refuse it. Unfortunately, discoveries in medical technology have also been used to terminate life, as in abortion and euthanasia.

The result of these advances and questions was a flourishing of literature to assist reflection in these complex scientific, medical, and moral issues. In addition, centers dedicated specifically to issues in bioethics began to appear around the world. The sheer wealth of material and distinctiveness of issues merited the designation of another area of moral theology which we refer to as bioethics.

3. Tending Toward the Good in Bioethics

Throughout this work, we have raised the issue of what it means to be virtuous in the moral life, that is, how to tend toward the good. Attaining human flourishing in cooperation with God's grace in the area of bioethics will entail tending toward particular goods which promote human life, the dignity of the person, and each individual's integral good as body/soul people.

In the introduction to this third section of the book, we spoke of three goods which are relevant here: human life, human dignity, and the relational nature of the human person. We address them with a particular nuance as they relate to the good in bioethics. Further, we call attention to three other goods which arise in bioethics. First, we mention the good of the unity of body and soul, faithful to an incarnational principle, and so important for considerations of advances in technology and medicine. Second, we examine the good of health itself, whose pursuit is the driving force behind much of the scientific research and advances in technology. Finally, we mention the virtue of compassionate presence to the ones who are suffering as a particular sign that medical personnel and pastoral ministers tend toward the good in bioethics.

RESPECT FOR HUMAN LIFE

When does human life begin? Throughout this book, we have underscored that human life is the foundational good for human beings; it is the human good without which no other good can be enjoyed. No doubt exists that the questions raised in the field of bioethics concern legitimate ways of bringing about and sustaining life and of how to act responsibly with those who are dying.

A critical question operative in issues such as abortion, reproductive technologies, embryonic stem cell research, and other issues is this: "When does human life begin?" The complex scientific response to this question cannot be dealt with adequately here. The Church, basing itself on sound scientific evidence, consistently teaches that "human life must be respected and protected absolutely from the moment of conception. From the first moment of his existence, a human being must be recognized as having the rights of a person—among which is the inviolable right of every innocent being to life" (CCC §2270).

Some people propose that there should be gradations in respect and protection given to human life according to its various stages of development. For example, they might suggest that a fetus of eight weeks merits greater respect than a newly fertilized egg. Official Church teaching, however, considers human life so important and inviolable that it takes the most strict and morally safe position regarding the beginning of human life. "The terms *zygote, preembryo, embryo,* and *fetus* can indicate in the vocabulary of biology successive stages of the development of a human being." Church teaching, however, attributes "to them an identical ethical relevance, in order to designate the result (whether visible or not) of human generation, from the first moment of its existence until birth" (*Instruction on Respect for Human Life in Its Origin and on the Dignity of Procreation,* "Introduction"). Or, as the *Catechism of the Catholic Church* states that the newly fertilized egg must be treated as a person from its very inception, protected, nurtured, aided, and respected insofar as possible as we would treat any other human being (CCC §2274).

Another expression of the question "When does human life begin?" is "When is someone a person?" or "What constitutes personhood?" Attempts to answer this question are many and varied. Although this moral question is a significant one, the Church has really placed it in the shadow of a more fundamental respect for all human life. The Church does not define in its official documents when someone is a person but declares that all human life must be treated "as a person" from conception. Since the criterion for right and wrong actions focuses on the effect of actions on the good of the person, one must consider any endangerment of innocent human life from conception to natural death as a morally illicit action, an abuse of human freedom.

When does human life end? If the Catholic Tradition calls for respect for human life from the womb to the tomb, the determination of when someone is ready for the tomb is critical. Determining the moment or imminence of death is significant from a moral standpoint on a number of fronts. Families who are trying to decide whether to initiate, continue, or withdraw medical treatment will need a solid medical opinion on the condition of their loved ones. Successful organ transplants require "healthy" organs—those harvested as soon as possible after death occurs. Of course, death involves much more than a medical judgment. Although clear medical information about the imminence of death or its occurrence will give objective information to family members and friends, the emotional dimension of saying good-bye to a loved one is a significant factor in making judgments about healthcare. Pastoral care and medical personnel must be aware of all these factors when dealing with a dying patient and his or her loved ones.

Progress in science has assisted us greatly in understanding the process of the beginning of life. Humanity's search for earthly immortality and the advances in technology to pursue it have prompted questions about when earthly life ends. The only definitive answer, most probably, is the onslaught of bodily decomposition. We do not wait that long, however.

If in former days the cessation of the heartbeat was a determination of death, today we have the technology to keep a human heart beating. If in the past the detection of breath, symbolized by condensation on a mirror held to a person's nose or mouth, indicated the presence of life, today we have the technology to keep human lungs breathing "beyond death." These technologies are most helpful when people need temporary assistance with their heart or lungs until the organs are capable of functioning on their own again. At other times, however, technology prolongs death, not life.

How do we determine the moment of death? The Pontifical Council for Health Care Workers writes: "Death is seen and experienced by people as a decomposition, a dissolution, a rupture. It comes when the spiritual principle which governs the unity of the individual is no longer able to exercise its functions on and in the organism and the elements of the latter, left to themselves, dissociate" (Pontifical Council for Pastoral Assistance to Health Care Workers, *Charter for Health Care Workers*, §128). More specifically, the Council writes: "A person is dead when he has irreversibly lost all ability to integrate and coordinate the physical and mental functions of the body." Second, with regard to the precise moment of death: "Death comes when: (a) the spontaneous functions of the heart and breathing have definitively ceased, or (b) the irreversible arrest of all brain activity" (§129). In reality, "brain death is the true criterion of death, although the definitive arrest of cardio-respiratory activity very quickly leads to brain death" (§129). In the final analysis, the Pontifical Council advises listening to sound medical counsel on the matter. Determining the moment of death "is not a matter for faith or morals but for medical science....Moral theology, in fact, cannot but acknowledge the biomedical determination as the decisive criterion" (§128).

From a moral standpoint, the value of human life is not lessened because of death. Death is a natural part of our spiritual lives. As one preface for funeral liturgies states: "Lord, for your faithful people, life is changed, not ended." Faith brings another dimension to the reality of death, offering hope in the midst of darkness, the hope of resurrection while suffering the cross (see also CCC §1012).

Tending toward the good in biomedical ethics is expressed concretely, then, when human life is respected and protected from the womb to the tomb, from conception to natural death. We will discuss the implications of this specific moral stance later in this chapter.

HUMAN DIGNITY:
BALANCING AUTONOMY AND RELATIONALITY

The horror of experimentation on prisoners in concentrations camps during the Nazi regime drew swift condemnation and a commitment to respect the dignity and in particular the autonomy of the human person. Autonomy comes from Greek words meaning "self" (*auto*) and "law" or "norm" (*nomos*). Autonomy implies that a person should be able to set for himself or herself the laws of their lives. In the language that we used in Chapter Two, autonomy is linked to people's responsibility to exercise freedom to shape their own lives in accordance with God's call to fullness of life in Him. A danger in interpreting autonomy as "self-rule" is that this interpretation might suggest that people are free to do whatever they wish. This view is an inaccurate one of genuine autonomy in the Christian Tradition.

Bioethics upholds certain essentials that are necessary to ensure that the freedom and autonomy of the individual are respected. Whether treating a patient medically or experimenting with new drugs on patients, the free and informed consent of the patient, or of the person of his or her choosing, must be sought in order to proceed. This informed consent respects the dignity of human beings, recognizing that they have been given freedom to shape their lives in the image and likeness of God. Decisions which will have a significant impact on their lives, medically, relationally, and spiritually, cannot be made without receiving sufficient information to make a judgment. The reason for this principle is that people must be informed in order to make a responsible judgment of conscience. Consequently, this emphasis on informed consent presumes an atmosphere of trust and truth-telling between a patient and his or her caregivers, so that human dignity and autonomy are respected.

A critical question that arises in ongoing reflection in bioethics is this: "Are there limits to autonomy?" In other words, what should guide a person's use of freedom? In this regard, we refer the reader back to Chapter Two and the responsible use of freedom. Freedom and autonomy are not characterized primarily by freedom from constraints, although this characterization is central to the concept of both, but rather by a freedom for excellence; that is, freedom to choose that which promotes authentic human good.

The complement, then, to an emphasis on autonomy is the focus on the relational nature of the human person. Let us take an example to see how these two dimensions might interact. Suppose Jack, a married man with three children under the age of fifteen, is diagnosed with a brain tumor. Jack's doctor describes several options, among them radiation to shrink the tumor or immediate surgery. When absolute autonomy is upheld, Jack would be free to make a judgment about his treatment without informing or consulting with anyone, his spouse and other family members included. If Jack's autonomy is balanced with the recognition of his relationality, he would most surely exercise his conscience and come to a judgment about medical treatment after talking with his spouse and other significant people in his life. Doing so recognizes the interdependence of people on one another while recognizing that Jack must ultimately make the judgment himself. An even broader, but more difficult, question to raise is whether and to what extent money should be spent on, perhaps even overusing, available means in a world where many lack basic care.

Autonomy highlights the dignity and good of the individual person, ensuring that a person is not used as a means to an end. Human relationality reminds moral agents that their exercise of freedom always affects others and should be used bearing in mind our fundamental call to give and to receive love. In the chapter on social ethics, we see this same relationship in the balance and tension between individual human rights and the common good. Tending toward the good in bioethics will be marked by autonomy exercised in relationality.

UNITY OF BODY AND SOUL (CCC §§362–368)

In our reflections on issues in biomedical ethics, we underscore the unity of body and soul as a human good which figures into our consideration of what is morally right and wrong. Human beings are both "corporal and spiritual. By virtue of its substantial union with a spiritual soul, the human body cannot be considered as a mere complex of tissues, organs, and functions, nor can it be evaluated in the same way as the body of animals; rather, it is a constitutive part of the person who manifests and expresses himself through it" (*Instruction on Respect for Human Life in Its Origin and on the Dignity of Procreation*, "Introduction," section 3).

The practical consequences of this unity of body and soul is the realization that what affects the body affects the soul, and vice versa. Shortly, we will examine briefly the experience of suffering. Sufferers of prostate cancer or breast cancer do not find themselves focused narrowly on a particular section of their bodies. They do not say "my prostate has cancer" or "my breast has cancer." "I have cancer," they say. Disease affects the whole person.

Similarly, it is not the body alone that suffers, but the spirit of the person as well. It is not uncommon for people suffering tremendous stress to manifest physical ailments ranging from acne to ulcers. Recognition of, and respect for, the unity of body and soul is another value which we bear in mind in our reflections in bioethics.

HEALTH (CCC §§2288–2291)

A final good which we address is that of health itself. In light of what we have mentioned previously regarding the unity of body and soul, we understand health in a holistic manner, reflected in the Charter for Health Care Workers: "The term and concept of health embraces all that pertains to prevention, diagnosis, treatment and rehabilitation for greater equilibrium and the physical, psychic and spiritual well-being of the person" (*Charter for Health Care Workers*, §9).

Why care for our health? We have mentioned that the basic human good, the primary one without which no other good can be enjoyed, is human life. To be good stewards of the gift of life which we have received, we must take responsible and reasonable attention and solicitude of it, taking the needs of others and the common good into account (CCC §2288).

COMPASSIONATE CARE FOR THOSE WHO SUFFER

In the Middle Ages, an aphorism was used to guide those in medical care. It said: Cure sometimes, relieve often, comfort always. Whether this advice was carried out in practice, it indicated a priority: compassion toward the sufferer. In the hustle and bustle of today's technological and medical world, one can get the impression that the sole emphasis is on cure. Yet, reflection in bioethics over the past thirty years in particular has highlighted care rather than cure as the overarching goal in healthcare. Tending toward the good in bioethics reminds us of the dignity of the human person and that compassionate care for people is a fundamental value in healthcare and bioethics.

4. Suffering: Absence of These Goods in Varying Degrees

When the goods that we have mentioned above are threatened or even temporarily endangered, people suffer. Bearing in mind that health affects body, mind, and soul or spirit, we can understand that one suffers in each of these areas as well.

We have often given lectures on human suffering and have invited those present to articulate feelings that they or people they know have experienced due to suffering. Anger, guilt, confusion, loneliness, despair, alienation, and fear name just a few of the feelings expressed. What seems nearly universal, however, is that suffering leaves one in a situation previously unknown and floundering, trying to find one's way again. The experience of suffering throws us into a tailspin, and we are not sure what to do or how to respond.

The most commonly asked question of the one who suffers is "Why?" Answers range from an inadequate "It is God's will" to "Fate." Neither response is satisfactory. We do not believe that there is a single response to why people suffer. Unable to grasp the "why" of suffering, people often attempt to make sense of it. They sometimes think that they are being punished; others hope to learn from their suffering; and some people endure suffering believing that something better will come to them.

In the Christian Tradition, we have been reminded often that our suffering can be redemptive, or saving. A phrase that we may have heard was "offer it up," suggesting that we should endure our suffering for the good of others. How might our suffering be redemptive, though?

In light of the theme that we have reiterated frequently in this book, we would suggest that suffering may help us, in some way, to give and to receive love. If it does, it is truly redemptive. If we are able to admit our dependence on others, as difficult as that may be for us, we are learning to receive love. If we continue to love in the midst of our suffering, we unite our suffering to the suffering of Christ who loved even as he was being nailed to the cross. On the other hand, if our suffering moves us to strike out against others and to become more self-absorbed, it is hardly redemptive but rather destructive.

The simple measure of how redemptive our suffering may be is the degree to which we continue to love others. No matter what meaning we may give to suffering, if it does not lead us to give and to receive love, it is not as redemptive as it might have been.

RESPONSE TO SUFFERING

How might we and others respond to suffering? We would like to examine briefly one's personal response, the response of the pastoral minister, and, finally, the medical response.

Personally, it would seem that the most adequate response to suffering is to try to integrate it into our lives and move ahead. Left with more questions than answers, we would hope that our experience of suffering does not embitter us but, at some point, becomes an occasion for us to acknowledge our limitations, our dependence on God and others, and to continue to love in spite of our suffering.

Pastorally, the appropriate response to the sufferer is simply prayerful accompaniment, being with the person who suffers. If we were to summarize the feelings that people describe as theirs when they suffer, we might speak of a loss of a sense of belonging, both to oneself and to others. People who are suffering no longer feel connected to themselves or others. Think for a moment about how uncomfortable it is at times to be with someone who is suffering, physically or mentally. People sense our discomfort and feel their difference. The best pastoral response, then, is to simply be with people who are suffering, to restore, to some degree, their sense of belonging to a community. The compassionate care of the hospital chaplain, the physician, and the nurse are all critical in this regard.

The medical response to suffering is to seek its cause and to cure and/or to relieve it. A word of caution or a reminder is in order, however; the search for the cause and cure must be done within the context of respect for the good of the whole person, recognizing that compassionate care of a suffering patient requires more than the proper medical technology. We do not suggest that physicians and nurses and other medical personnel assume the role of chaplain or psychotherapist or family member but that they recognize the multifaceted experience of suffering and ensure that those with expertise in body and soul work in harmony with one another for the good of the patient.

The natural limitations of the human condition guarantee that there will be suffering in our lives. Tending toward the good in bioethics includes compassionate care for those who suffer. The branch of moral theology known as bioethics pays particular attention to the moral quality of responses to suffering in medicine and technology. Before examining particular issues in bioethics, we look to principles which have developed in the Roman Catholic Tradition to guide deliberations in these matters. We will see the principles at work in the analyses that follow.

5. Principles: Aids to Moral Reasoning in Bioethics

In the following discussion, we highlight principles that should guide responses to human suffering, both regarding specific responses to real suffering patients and experimentation to seek cures for disease. We review certain principles which have developed in the Roman Catholic Tradition as guides to the reasoning process.

As we study these principles, it is important to remember that a principle is formulated as a result of reflection on a good judgment. Principles are not created out of nothing and then applied to specific situations. They arise from reflection on experience. For example, although one could argue that bioethical theorists could have easily created a principle which argues for free and informed consent on the part of patients regarding their illness, the experience of experimentation on people without their consent gave rise to an emphasis on autonomy and informed consent. Thus, the principle of autonomy arose. Similarly, other principles are "created" by reflecting on wise judgments that we have made previously. Theorists try to examine what made the decision wise and formulate a principle to guide us in future similar situations. Sometimes, principles will serve us well in this regard; at other times, the uniqueness of a particular situation may suggest that the principle is not relevant. Nonetheless, principles have served us well in the Tradition, and we examine three such principles briefly: the principle of double effect, the principle of cooperation, and the principle of totality.

THE PRINCIPLE OF DOUBLE EFFECT

The principle of double effect begins with a recognition of the complexity of moral action. Sometimes we are presented with responses to human suffering which seem to combine good and evil. For example, suppose your great uncle is in severe pain due to advanced cancer throughout his body. The best medical advice is to keep him comfortable since nothing can be done to rid him of cancer. However, the pain medication may well weaken him and hasten his death. Faced with the desired good of pain relief and the sad truth that the very medication used to help him may quicken his death, how should we act? Using the four points of the principle of double effect as a guide for our moral reasoning, we could conclude that we may give Uncle Bob the pain medication to comfort him even if it hastens his death.

The principle of double effect recognizes that one may not do evil to achieve good. It also presumes, however, that some actions are accompanied by both desirable and undesirable consequences: some good, some bad. One may not directly harm a person in order to bring about some good. The four guidelines for the principle are as follows:

(a) The action that one is contemplating must be either morally good or morally neutral. In this case, giving pain medication to a suffering patient is a good moral act.

(b) One cannot intend the evil effect of the action, even though it is foreseen. The doctors have told us that giving pain medication to Uncle Bob will most likely quicken his death. This effect is not our intention which is only to keep him comfortable and out of pain.

(c) The good achieved cannot be the result of the evil. The relief from pain for Uncle Bob is a result of the pain medication not the hastening of his death.

(d) There must be a proportionate reason for allowing the evil to occur.

As we examine Uncle Bob's condition, we must consider whether keeping him out of pain or as comfortable as possible is a good enough reason to run the risk of hastening his death, as undesirable as that is. It would seem that this reason does justify using the pain medication (see also Congregation for the Doctrine of the Faith, *Declaration on Euthanasia*; United States Conference of Catholic Bishops, *Ethical and Religious Directives for Catholic Health Care Services*, *Origins*, 31/9 [July 19, 2001], §47, p. 160).

In the course of reflection in bioethics, many other moral evaluations concur with the reasoning demonstrated in the principle of double effect. For example, one may provide necessary medical treatment to a pregnant woman which might result in the death of the unborn child (United States Conference of Catholic Bishops, *Ethical and Religious Directives for Catholic Health Care Services*, §47, p. 160); or one may employ procedures which are used to treat a medical condition but which might result in sterility (*Ethical and Religious Directives for Catholic Health Care Services*, §53, p. 160). In the area of social ethics, people have justified the bombing of military arsenals in time of war even if noncombatants might be killed as a result of the destruction of the arsenal.

The principle of double effect reflects prudential judgments where good and evil are present in a given action. It guards against direct choices for evil while recognizing the reasonableness of judgments for the good where evil may be an unintended and indirect result.

THE PRINCIPLE OF COOPERATION

Old gangster movies would often present a group of men seated around a table plotting a bank robbery. After the basics of the plan were laid out, the boss might be heard saying, "You in or you out?" asking the others whether they were going to take part in the bank heist or not. The responses and consequent tasks of the members of the mob varied.

The principle of cooperation recognizes that many and diverse players participate in bringing about evil, in harming people. The principle of cooperation attempts to guide us in our moral reasoning so that we do not knowingly and willingly (both are important) assist in bringing about evil.

When we discussed sin in Chapter Four, we mentioned two types of sin: formal and material. Material sin violates the moral order and brings about wrong. It is an objective description of sin and its effects. Formal sin, on the other hand, refers to the subjective state of the person who commits the sin, whether he is culpable or not.

Similarly, we speak of formal and material cooperation in evil. Formal cooperation presumes that I align my will to the evil of the principal moral agent; material cooperation presumes that I do not, although it does not excuse culpability.

To clarify how the principle works, let us use an example of assisting someone in committing suicide. We begin with the presumption that taking one's life and assisting another to do so is morally wrong, intrinsically evil as the Catholic moral tradition would say. Let us presume that the person who wants to take his life needs your help to obtain sufficient painkillers. He asks you to go to the pharmacy, to pick up a new prescription. You know that he wants the medication to kill himself.

Formal cooperation suggests that you not only go to the pharmacy but also that you approve of the man's action of taking his life. You align your will with the one doing the wrongful deed. Material cooperation suggests that you do not approve but that, because of some other factors, such as duress, a false sense of loyalty to the person, or some other factor, you choose to cooperate in obtaining the medication. You do not approve, but you decide to perform some helpful action. Unknowingly, the pharmacist has also cooperated materially, in that she has provided the medication. However, she has no idea that it will be used to take someone's life. Your cooperation, however, because it is closer and almost essential for the action, is more grave and borders on being formal cooperation in evil.

The principal of cooperation attempts to assess how closely one aligns one's own intention with another person's to do evil. One may never cooperate formally in evil. Under certain circumstances, one may cooperate materially, but never, as in the case we have presented, if one's cooperation is indispensable in bringing about evil.

THE PRINCIPLE OF TOTALITY

A final principle which we address is called the principle of totality. Again, this principle reflects prudential judgments which have been made in the past. Right moral action promotes authentic human good. We have mentioned earlier that health, and consequently authentic human good, concerns biological, social, spiritual, and psychological integrity. The principle of totality recognizes that one may at times sacrifice a part of oneself for the good of the whole, as long as the choice one makes is not intrinsically evil, that is, harmful to authentic human good.

A person who suffers with a gangrenous leg may justifiably have the leg amputated so that the whole person may survive. One may temporarily lose consciousness through anesthesia so that one may undergo an operation. A part is sacrificed, even temporarily, for the whole. More broadly speaking, a kidney may be donated for the good of another. As with the principle of double effect, however, we must repeat that an action which is intrinsically evil, such as sterilization, may not be chosen directly as a means to safeguard the good of the whole person. As with the principle of double effect, the action chosen must be either morally good or neutral.

6. Issues in Bioethics: Morality of Certain Responses to Suffering

All we have said so far serves as the context for a consideration of specific issues in bioethics. Two overarching statements which will help to summarize the conclusions of the Roman Catholic Tradition on many of the issues to be discussed are these: even with the best of intentions, persons may never be used as a means to an end; their dignity requires this prohibition; second, human beings are stewards of their lives and of all Creation, not masters. The *Catechism of the Catholic Church* puts it this way: We are not owners of the life God has given us, but we are stewards and caretakers. Life is not ours to discard as we wish (CCC §2280). We will see these two overarching values challenged again and again as we examine specific issues.

ISSUES AT THE BEGINNING OF LIFE

The issues that touch on the respect for, and protection of, human life from the moment of conception are many: *in vitro* fertilization and other reproductive technologies, cloning, embryonic stem cell research, and genetic interventions. In one way or another, the Church has judged that human life and/or dignity is threatened or outright harmed by most of these technological and medical procedures. Genetic interventions must be investigated further. Consequently, in some cases, as we shall see, the Church has judged them harmful to human life and immoral.

Key points from Church teaching concerning the beginning of life: As we examine these issues, two key points should be kept in mind. The Church teaches that new life should be the result of sexual intercourse between spouses, respecting the unitive and the procreative dimension of human sexual expression. To remove the creation of new life from this setting risks treating new life as the product of technology and not the self-gift of loving spouses. Further, both the sacredness of conjugal love and the dignity and life of this new creation may be endangered.

Reproductive Technologies (CCC §§2374–2377): The Church teaches that reproductive technologies may be morally acceptable when they assist but do not replace the natural way of bearing children, that is, through sexual intercourse between spouses. Most of the technologies that are widely used today, however, replace and do not assist reproduction.

In vitro *fertilization and artificial insemination: In vitro* fertilization involves the union of sperm and egg outside of the womb, in a petri dish, with subsequent transfer of the fertilized egg into the uterus of the woman bearing the child. Often, the procedure requires the fertilization of several eggs, all of which may not be implanted in the uterus at the same time. Some may be frozen or simply discarded. Some variations in *in vitro* fertilization include the donation of sperm or egg from a third party. Surrogate motherhood, where a woman other than the egg donor bears a child, is also an option offered to couples in our day.

In addition to *in vitro* fertilization, there is also artificial insemination in which the sperm of the biological father is inserted into the woman's vagina. The sperm may be that of the husband or of a donor.

The Church teaches that all of these reproductive procedures are morally illicit because they do in fact replace and not assist the natural process of procreation through the marital act. They separate the procreative dimension of human sexuality from the unitive. This reason, and not the artificiality of the procedure itself, renders these reproductive technologies morally wrong (CCC §§2375–2378). The use of third parties, such as donor sperm, egg, or even uterus in the case of surrogate motherhood, affects even the unitive nature of the marital act (CCC §2376).

Cloning: The media were abuzz with excitement when, in 1997, it was announced that a sheep had been cloned successfully; her name was Dolly. Immediately, speculation and questions rose about human cloning. The logic of the Church's teaching regarding human cloning is similar to that of her teaching in regard to *in vitro* fertilization. In the process of human cloning, the procreative dimension of human sexuality is separated from the unitive dimension. The Vatican's Pontifical Academy for Life calls cloning "an asexual and agamic reproduction meant to produce individuals biologically identical to the adult which provided the nuclear genetic inheritance....It represents a radical manipulation of the constitutive relationality and complementarity which is at the origin of human procreation in both its biological and strictly personal aspects" (Pontifical Academy for Life, *Reflections on Cloning*, Libreria Editrice Vaticana, 1997). The Pontifical Academy recognizes this split between human lovemaking and generation which cloning entails. There is also a lack of respect for the new life coming into existence, not only in the manner in which conceived but also with seemingly little regard for the psychological, spiritual, and perhaps physical challenges which lie ahead of the new life produced in this way. Cloning seems to treat new life as a market item more than someone deserving profound respect.

Embryonic stem cell research: Almost daily the media present us with reasons for greater hope in medicine. One such hope has been the promise of the use of stem cells to treat ailments such as Parkinson's disease and Alzheimer's disease, and to restore damaged bodily organs. Although still in embryonic stages itself, scientists are promising great advances.

Stem cell research on animals has been conducted for many years now. Only fairly recently has attention turned to the use of human stem cells to address disease. Ordinarily, we speak of two kinds of stem cell research: embryonic stem cell and adult stem cell research.

The moral difficulty which arises in embryonic stem cell research is that embryonic human life is being experimented upon and used in order to make medical advances. "The Church has always taught and continues to teach that the result of human procreation, from the first moment of its existence, must be guaranteed that unconditional respect which is morally due to the human being in his or her totality and unity in body and spirit" (*The Gospel of Life*, §60). Embryos which are created and utilized for stem cell research are not afforded this respect.

The Church does not oppose experimentation in and of itself. It expects, however, that those who are the objects of experimentation give free and informed consent to the experimentation. This consent is clearly not possible with embryos. Further, the Church expects that experiments conducted without the consent of the person should at least contribute to their good in some way. Again, this is not the case in embryonic stem cell research.

The Church views embryonic stem cell research as a violation of the dignity of new human life and opposes its manipulation even for the best of purposes. "*No end believed to be good*, such as the use of stem cells for the preparation of other differentiated cells to be used in what look to be promising therapeutic procedures, *can justify an intervention of this kind.* A good end does not make right an action which in itself is wrong" (Pontifical Academy for Life, *Declaration on the Production and the Scientific and Therapeutic Use of Human Embryonic Stem Cells*).

The Church at this time does not take a similar stance regarding adult stem cells. These do not require the production and/or destruction of a human embryo and, consequently, "represent a more reasonable and human method for making correct and sound progress in this new field of research and in the therapeutic applications which it promises" (Pontifical Academy for Life, *Declaration on the Production and the Scientific and Therapeutic Use of Human Embryonic Stem Cells*).

Genetic interventions: Scientists have found, and continue to hope, that a greater understanding of the genetic structure of human beings will lead not only to a better grasp on how we "tick," so to speak, but also will lead to discovering the connection between genes and disease. The morally significant question is what we do with the scientific knowledge and the particular information that we learn in specific cases. Should technological interventions be judged morally acceptable, for example, if they are done to choose the sex of a new child, or eye color, or similar traits? Apart from the issue of separating the procreative dimension of reproduction from the unitive, one must wonder if the potential child is not being treated like a product, being shaped or predetermined according to the designs of the parents and technicians. For this reason, the Church teaches that these "manipulations are contrary to the personal dignity of the human being and his or her integrity and identity" (*Instruction on Respect for Human Life in Its Origins and on the Dignity of Procreation*).

Greater sympathy is in order for attempts to discover the genetic links to disease and to attempt to eradicate them; however, this may never be done at the expense of another person or by harming the dignity of a human life. There have been many positive and morally acceptable advances in this regard. The discovery alone of the gene linked to cystic fibrosis has brought rapid advances in its treatment. Further study may bring even more hope and promising results.

Another question involves what is called genetic screening of those who are already alive to see if they might be disposed to a particular disease. Sometimes screening and/or prenatal diagnosis is done on a developing fetus with the intent to abort if defects are found. The Church would judge abortion as a morally wrong response to this situation (CCC §2274). Other times, however, people may wish to know if they are likely to develop a certain disease, based on their genetic makeup. This information may be helpful for people to prepare for their future care and for those for whom they are responsible.

Many people have suggested that technological advances in and of themselves are not particularly meritorious if they are not accompanied by moral advances. Knowledge in genetics could promote a drive for the "perfect" individual where certain standards, not necessarily respecting the dignity of the human person, would dictate genetic interventions. Many groups of disabled persons fear that this eugenics would endanger and demean them. As study and application of newly gained knowledge continues in the area of genetic intervention, attention must continue to be paid to the dignity of all human life and our role as stewards, not creators of life.

Abortion: In his encyclical letter, *The Gospel of Life*, Pope John Paul II describes procured abortion as "the deliberate and direct killing, by whatever means it is carried out, of a human being in the initial phase of his or her existence, extending from conception to birth (§58). It is a direct taking of innocent human life, an act of injustice to the newly developing life (§13). The Church also recognizes that there are many motives for procuring an abortion, such as protection of the mother's health, the welfare of other family members, and even the belief that the new child should not be born into a desperate situation (*The Gospel of Life*, §58). Despite these pressures, the Church teaches that abortion is not the morally right response.

Perhaps it is important to point out as well that part of Church teaching is to remind people to provide environments of support for those who might consider an abortion so that their burden is lightened through the compassionate care that they receive from others.

ISSUES AT THE END OF LIFE

If new discoveries in science and technology have presented ethical challenges at the beginning of life, the same is true at the end of life. The Congregation for the Doctrine of the Faith points out in its *Declaration on Euthanasia* that "medicine has increased its capacity to cure and to prolong life in particular circumstances, which sometimes gives rise to moral problems." We will consider briefly criteria for withholding and withdrawing medical treatment at the end of life and the specific issues of euthanasia and physician-assisted suicide.

Neither vitalism nor disregard for life: The discussion of these issues might be set between two extremes: prolonging life at all costs and a disregard for human life. As Christians, we believe that our earthly life is a wonderful gift from God but one which will end as we move from earthly life to eternal life. For this reason, as we have said many times, earthly life is the fundamental human good, but not an absolute good. It may be sacrificed; we must not cling to it as if this life were all we have. For this reason, we reject the first position which might be called "vitalism," keeping someone alive at all costs. However, as we have noted before, we are stewards of life, not masters of it. Therefore, we have a responsibility to care for the life and health of ourselves and of others. We must reject any cheapening of human life or any disregard for it, in particular the direct taking of innocent human life. As we know, however, the judgments as to when to hold on and when to let go of our own lives or that of a loved one are never easy. This difficulty is evident in the complex issues of withholding and/or withdrawing medical treatment and in the debate over euthanasia and physician-assisted suicide.

Withholding and/or withdrawing medical treatment (CCC §2278): We knew of a man who was referred to as the "miracle man" for all the times he was at death's door but seemed to bounce back miraculously, even by the accounts of medical personnel. Whenever he was asked whether he wanted the doctors to try whatever was available to keep him alive, he replied "Yes!" We recall another friend, however, who was terminally ill with cancer and suffering from kidney failure. She was told that by having recourse to renal dialysis she could live a bit longer. She refused the treatment saying, "My time has come." In both instances, the patients were in a position to make decisions for themselves. The former wanted aggressive treatment; he was a fighter. Our other friend simply resigned herself to her impending death and chose to live her remaining days accepting her physical condition and allowing the disease to run its course. Both acted responsibly, it would seem. Why?

Extraordinary/disproportionate and ordinary/proportionate moral obligations (CCC §2278): Many Catholics will be familiar with the terms ordinary and extraordinary means, with the understanding that one is obliged to use ordinary means but is not obliged to use extraordinary means. The common misconception among people, however, is that ordinary and extraordinary refers primarily to the type of procedure. For example, in 1975 open-heart surgery was a relatively new practice requiring a rather lengthy hospital stay. By 2000, people could be in and out of the hospital after open-heart surgery within a week. Some would suggest that in 1975 open-heart surgery was an extraordinary means, but in the year 2000 it had shifted to an ordinary means. This shift in classification is not necessarily the case.

Ordinary and extraordinary qualify the type of moral obligation that one has in the face of medical procedures. In the above example, the woman who chose not to pursue renal dialysis for her kidney ailment rejected what is a relatively simple, though time-consuming, medical procedure. In her case, she perceived her obligation to make use of renal dialysis as an extraordinary ethical obligation. It appears that she is correct. The same might not be said of a twenty-five-year-old who has no other medical complications. In his case, as far as we could tell, he would have an ordinary ethical obligation to undergo dialysis in order to maintain his health.

The Congregation for the Doctrine of the Faith offered new language to speak of this reality in its 1980 document, *Declaration on Euthanasia*. It speaks of proportionate and disproportionate means. Criteria are offered for the judgment of what is proportionate or disproportionate: "the type of treatment to be used, its degree of complexity or risk, its cost and the possibilities of using it, and comparing these elements with the result that can be expected, taking into account the state of the sick person and his or her physical and moral resources." Later, the document even includes expense to the family and community among factors which figure into the judgment of continuing or withdrawing medical treatment.

This analysis is often referred to as the benefit/burden analysis wherein one tries to examine the benefit of continuing a medical procedure in light of the burdens that will accompany it. Those burdens may be physical, psychological, and/or spiritual for the patient and/or his or her family and community. It must be stated clearly that one may never directly take someone's life because they feel burdened or believe themselves burdensome to their family and community. However, one is not obligated to pursue every means at one's disposal. The *Declaration on Euthanasia* summarizes its wisdom as follows: "Such a refusal is not the equivalent of suicide; on the contrary, it should be considered as an acceptance of the human condition, or a wish to avoid the application of a medical procedure disproportionate to the results that can be expected, or a desire not to impose excessive expense on the family or the community (*Declaration on Euthanasia*, section IV: Due Proportion in the Use of Remedies).

Nutrition and hydration: A particularly thorny issue in bioethics today is withholding and/or withdrawing nutrition and hydration. The debate revolves primarily around how to define nutrition and hydration and whether it must always be used. Some suggest that nutrition and hydration is a medical procedure which must be used according to the criteria mentioned above. Others argue that giving food and water to a patient is not a medical procedure at all, but normal, ordinary patient care. The latter do not emphasize the medical procedures necessary to provide nutrition and hydration in these often tragic cases. They argue for its use in almost all cases.

There is no definitive Catholic teaching on this issue as of this writing, but documents speak of a presumption in favor of using nutrition and hydration, though even this presumption is qualified. In 1992 the Pro-Life Committee of the National Conference of Catholic Bishops of the United States issued a document entitled *Nutrition and Hydration: Moral and Pastoral Reflections*. They wrote: "We reject any omission of nutrition and hydration intended to cause a patient's death. We hold for a presumption in favor of providing medically assisted nutrition and hydration to patients who need it, which presumption would yield in cases where such procedures have no medically reasonable hope of sustaining life or pose excessive risks or burdens."

One can note that the members of the committee are walking a fine line between respecting the dignity and life of the patient and recognizing that there is no obligation to sustain earthly life at all costs. Of course, these judgments are always rendered more complex because of the emotions experienced by the sick and their loved ones.

Euthanasia and physician-assisted suicide (CCC §§2276–2283): Recent times have seen the legalization of euthanasia and physician-assisted suicide under certain circumstances. *"Euthanasia in the strict sense* is understood to be an action or omission which of itself and by intention causes death, with the purpose of eliminating all suffering. Euthanasia's terms of reference, therefore, are to be found in the intention of the will and in the methods used" (*The Gospel of Life*, §65; see also *Declaration on Euthanasia*). Media reports over the past two decades have told stories of "angels of death" who deliberately deliver overdoses of medication to bring about the death of a patient. In more recent years, we have seen the rise and legalization of physician-assisted suicide where medical personnel provide fatal doses of drugs to bring about a person's death. Despite the best of motivations, these direct attacks on human life are morally wrong (CCC §2277). As stewards of life and not its masters, we attempt, within reason, to care for our own life and health and that of those entrusted to our care.

Killing and letting die: Pope John Paul II speaks of an action or omission which "of itself and by intention causes death." Although the claim is disputed, the Church holds for a legitimate distinction between killing and letting die. Administration of an overdose to bring about a person's death clearly fits the description of euthanasia outlined above. So, too, does the case where medical personnel refuse resuscitation to a patient who has requested it because they believe it to be undesirable. Although they may be right from a purely medical perspective, they are acting contrary to the wishes of the patient and so choosing death by allowing the patient to die. Their omission brings about the patient's death.

Not all letting die, however, fits the description of euthanasia as described by Pope John Paul II, remembering that euthanasia could be defined as an omission which in itself and by intention causes death. Medical personnel who do not resuscitate someone who is terminally ill and who, for morally acceptable reasons, has requested a "do not resuscitate" order, do not commit euthanasia by allowing the person to die. Rather, they honor the wishes of the patient who accepts that her earthly life has come to an end and who does not wish to prolong it by any medical interventions that are disproportionate to the benefits received.

Simply put, all direct killing of the innocent is morally wrong. Some "letting die" is morally wrong; some is morally right. In cases of "letting die," attention to the intention of the moral agent is critical. Reference back to the principle of double effect earlier in this chapter may help us in our analysis. If we directly intend the death of the patient, our action is morally wrong. On the other hand, if our action is morally good or neutral with a positive and a negative side effect, we may proceed with the action, that is, omitting a particular medical intervention and allowing the person to die.

7. Guidelines for Consideration of Issues in Bioethics

This chapter has necessarily dealt with specific issues in bioethics in a brief manner. As new issues arise and we reflect further on the rightness or wrongness of new discoveries in science, technology, and medicine, we will want to keep in mind the goods we have outlined as contributing to authentic human good. We recall the four overarching goods which are always operative in moral theology, that is, the value of human life, the dignity of the human person, the social nature of the human person, and the goodness of all Creation. Focusing on the bioethical good, we highlighted further balance of autonomy and relationality, the unity of body and soul, health itself, and compassionate care for those who are suffering. With these as a context, we might use the following questions as guidelines to remind us of the fundamental values at stake and to examine the issues in light of them.

1. Is human life itself threatened by the matter under consideration? In our response to this issue are we stewards or masters of Creation? Are we avoiding the extremes of vitalism and the cheapening of human life?
2. Is the dignity of the human person compromised by this issue? Are the rights of the individual being denied? Are human beings used as a means or an end? Would approval of this issue present an obstacle to the individual's exercise of freedom that would enhance his or her dignity?
3. Do we respect the unity of body and soul? In issues of reproductive technology, does the procedure under question assist or replace the natural process of reproduction? Is the unitive and procreative dimension of human sexual expression maintained?
4. How is the social dimension of the human person affected by this issue? Is there a proper balance between autonomy and relationality, between the individual and the common good?
5. Is our response to suffering marked above all by compassionate care for the one who is suffering?

8. Conclusion

We subtitled this chapter: "Safeguarding Human Life, Human Dignity, and Health. The driving force behind so many discoveries in science, technology, and medicine is to alleviate suffering and to offer people a better quality of life. In our efforts to do so, however, we must never lose sight of the meaning of life which is giving and receiving love.

In this chapter, we have held out the goods of human life, human dignity, unity of body and soul, health, and compassionate care for the suffering as particularly important in the field of bioethics. Noting that human suffering arises when these goods are absent, we named the various types of response to suffering, underscoring the importance of accompaniment for those who may feel abandoned and lost. Responses to human suffering must respect these aspects of authentic human good. We offered some principles which have surfaced in the Roman Catholic Tradition to guide our reflection on appropriate and inappropriate responses. Our cursory analysis of issues took us from issues at the beginning of life to those of the dying. One can see the profound respect for human life and the dignity of the person throughout these issues. Abuses occur and harm is done to human life when, in our zeal for further advances, we forget our responsibility to all human life, especially the weakest. Pope John Paul II once said: "The quality of a society and a civilization is measured by the respect shown to the weakest of its members" *(Statement for the International Year of Disabled Persons, 1981).*

Even as the Church offers clear teaching on these matters, it also stands as a channel of God's mercy for those who sin and fail in their efforts to give and to receive love. It recognizes, as we discussed in Chapter Two, that we do not always act with complete freedom and knowledge in our moral lives. Consequently, a judgment by the Church of the moral gravity of these issues does not imply a condemnation of those who for one reason or another act contrary to these teachings. Rather, they are entrusted to the God of life who first gifted us with life and calls us to be stewards of one another.

9. Selected Bibliography of Church Teaching on Bioethics

Congregation for the Doctrine of the Faith. *Declaration on Euthanasia*, 1980.

_____. *Declaration on Procured Abortion*, November 18, 1974.

_____. *Instruction on Respect for Human Life in Its Origin and on the Dignity of Procreation (Donum Vitae)*, 1987.

Pontifical Academy for Life. *Reflections on Cloning,* 1997.

Pontifical Academy for Life. *Declaration on the Production and the Scientific and Therapeutic Use of Human Embryonic Stem Cells,* August 25, 2000.

Pontifical Academy of Sciences. *Declaration on the Artificial Prolongation of Life and Determining Exactly the Moment of Death,* 1989.

Pontifical Council for Pastoral Assistance to Health Care Workers. *Charter for Health Care Workers,* 1995.

Pope John Paul II. *The Gospel of Life (Evangelium Vitae),* 1995.

United States Conference of Catholic Bishops. "Ethical and Religious Directives for Catholic Health Care Services," *Origins* 24/27 (December 15, 1994): pp. 450–462.

United States Conference of Catholic Bishops. "Ethical and Religious Directives for Catholic Health Care Services," *Origins* 31/9 (July 19, 2001): pp. 153–163.

CHAPTER TEN

Male and Female, God Created Them: The Catholic Tradition and Human Sexuality

(CCC §§2331–2400, §§2514–2533)

A t the mere mention of sexuality, people often think of sexual acts, whereas in fact sexuality refers to much more. It is that fundamental component of ourselves which is the grounding of our capacity to relate, to foster friendships, to love, to feel, to procreate, and to experience intimacy. Drawing from this dimension of our personality, two people can be capable of committing themselves to each other exclusively and for life in marriage. Our very identity, both psychological and spiritual, flows from our sexuality in its never-ending struggle to reach human maturity.

This chapter begins with the assumption that one's growth in understanding human sexuality does not somehow end with puberty or even marriage, but rather, like the Christian call to love and be loved, it continues to unfold throughout our lives with reflection, experience, and God's grace. So our discussion of human sexuality in the Catholic Tradition will not be limited to specific sex acts and their moral evaluation, although this will certainly be part of our goal. Our approach proceeds from the belief that our sexuality is part of the mystery of what it means to be human, and being human is intimately bound to the God who created us and calls us to love him, ourselves, and others.

1. The Gift and Power of Sexuality

It is because our sexuality touches all the vital areas of our lives that it is so powerful and precious a gift from the Creator. First, it touches the relational aspect of being human. We all relate as sexual beings; it is not as if we suddenly can become neutral when we, as males or females, relate to other males or females. Our sexuality, thus, is part of our identity, that is, who we are, together with all our desires, longings, hopes, fears, and limitations. Since relationships determine how we communicate or fail to communicate, and vice versa, the way we understand and accept our sexual selves will play an important part in our quest to be communicating and fulfilled Christians. These relationships are essential to the Christian because they provide the context in which we become who God wants us to be, namely, people who can give and receive love, to and from God, to and from each other. This goal of giving and receiving love is how we fulfill our calling to mirror the Trinity in whose image we are made.

In the chapter on "The Community of Mankind" in the *Pastoral Constitution on the Church in the Modern World*, we read:

Furthermore, the Lord Jesus, when praying to the Father "that they may all be one...as we are one" (Jn 17:21–22), has opened up new horizons closed to human reason by indicating that there is a similarity between the union existing among the divine persons and the union of God's children in truth and love. It follows, then, that if human beings are the only creatures on earth that God has wanted for their own sake, they can fully discover their true selves only in sincere self-giving" (§24).

John Paul II reaffirms this insight of the Second Vatican Council. "Sexuality is an enrichment of the whole person—body, emotions, and soul—and manifests its innermost meaning in leading a person to the gift of self in love" (Apostolic Exhortation *On the Family*, §37).

2. I Call You Friends

Both ancient philosophy and the Genesis account of Creation ponder the fact that we are somehow not whole or contented by ourselves. We need and long for the other to complete us. We are, as it were, only half of ourselves; and only relationships with others and the Other will bring us wholeness. One of the relationships we learn to treasure in this life is that of friendship. Friendship requires trustworthiness, the mutual willingness to share joys and frailties, self-disclosure, and an eagerness to put the happiness of the other high on the list of our priorities. Friendship is also closely linked to our attitude to, and dealings with, loneliness, that sense of not being whole. Our friendships with people of the opposite or the same sex draw on the need to be intimate. This very longing to be intimate with another human being, to have affections for them, and desires for their happiness, springs from our sexuality. We are really speaking here of what is known as "affective sexuality," that is, we draw on feelings and needs that flow from our sexual selves; and these feelings and needs enhance friendship and communion between people. This affective sexuality is to be distinguished from genital sexuality, another expression of sexuality reserved for marriage and in the marriage context closely linked to the affective.

In the gospels we find ample witness to the friendships of Jesus. We can recall the stories about Mary, Martha, Lazarus, Peter, James, and John, "the beloved disciple." Jesus trusted these people, revealed his power and his fears to them; he encouraged them and received their support; he loved them and was loved in return. He did all this as God incarnate, God-made-flesh, not as a neutered being but as a man like us in all things but sin. We may also recall the great affection between David and Jonathan in the Old Testament, and Saint

Francis and Saint Clare of Assisi. Listen to the depth of affection that Saint Augustine had for one of his close male friends who had died.

> I marveled that other men should live, because he, whom I had loved as if he would never die, was dead. I marveled more that I, his second self, could live when he was dead. Well has someone said of his friend that he is half of his soul. For I thought that my soul and his soul were but one soul in two bodies. Therefore, my life was a horror to me, because I would not live but as a half (Saint Augustine, *The Confessions of Saint Augustine*, trans. by John K. Ryan, Book IV, Chapter 6 [New York: Doubleday Image Books, 1960], p. 100).

The very fact that God made us in his own image, the interrelation of three persons, and chose the Word to become flesh, raises our human sexuality to a new dignity and goodness.

3. Sexuality and Sex

Perhaps we have already sensed that there is a difference between sexuality and sex. Sex refers either to the biological aspects of being male or female, as when a questionnaire asks us what sex we are. On the other hand, it can refer to particular expressions of sexuality, in common parlance, usually genital actions, such as intercourse that can result in orgasm. Sexuality is far more encompassing, as the following quotations from recent Church teaching indicate.

> The human person is so profoundly affected by sexuality that it must be considered as one of the factors which give to each individual's life the principal traits that distinguish it (Congregation for the Doctrine of the Faith, *Declaration on Certain Questions Concerning Sexual Ethics*, §1).

> Sexuality is a fundamental component of personality, one of its modes of being, of manifestation, of communicating with others, of feeling, of expressing and living human love. Therefore it is an integral part of the development of the personality, and of its educative process (Congregation for Catholic Education, *Educational Guidance in Human Love*, §4).

> Sexuality concerns the intimate nucleus of the person (The Pontifical Council for the Family, *The Truth and Meaning of Human Sexuality*, §11).

Thus, from the beginning of our reflection on human sexuality, it is imperative that we start with a positive attitude to our bodily selves, desires, and attractions. Naturally, such a power within us, with its desires and attractions, can be used for good or for the destruction of self and others. Nevertheless, our starting point is that God saw all that he had made, including our sexual selves, and found it very good. This opinion has not been held consistently by all. A story is told that when the old Latin manuals of moral theology were first translated into English, the sections dealing with the sixth and the ninth commandments (those commandments dealing with material of a sexual nature) were left in Latin so that young seminarians would not be scandalized by their content. The presumption was that the new generation of seminarians could not read Latin. The presumption was half right. The titles for the two tracts took the Latin names for the sixth and the ninth commandments, namely "De sexto" and "De nono." It seemed obvious to the new students of moral theology that it simply meant that "sex is a no no" in Catholic teaching. This perception is certainly a distortion of the living and developing Catholic Tradition.

4. Sexuality and Pleasure

While we are discussing misconceptions of Catholic teaching on sexuality, let us say a word about pleasure. It is true that over the centuries the Christian attitude toward sexual pleasure has often been one of suspicion. One heresy known as Manichaeism in the early Church went so far as to try to deny the importance of the body and all the pleasure associated with it. This heresy was just one manifestation of the struggle that humans have in dealing with the fact that we are composed of both body and soul. In other centuries, philosophers and even Christian believers, have taken the other extreme, pretending that the body is all-important as are its pleasures. There is always the temptation to split the human person into two separate parts, body and soul, and human experience into pleasure versus the spiritual, denying one part and exalting the other. We are not angels, and we are not mere bodies. We strive for integration. To highlight the inseparability of the body and soul, an elementary-school teacher of our acquaintance used to write "body" on the blackboard and "soul" right on top of the word "body." The message was clear: we are embodied souls or ensouled bodies, but they cannot be separated permanently.

Pleasure can be good, just as it can be inordinate. Inordinate and inappropriate pleasure can reduce a person to a mere seeker of the carnal, a pleasure seeker, at the expense of others and despite the cost. On the other hand, Saint Thomas Aquinas confirms that not only can the taking of pleasure in sex be sinless (he is speaking here of sexual pleasure that accompanies sexual intercourse in marriage); but it is meritorious, in other words, it is a part of the integrated virtuous life. A person is supposed to enjoy sexual pleasure in marriage insofar as it is bound up with human well-being. The saint even goes so far as to state that deliberately frustrating this pleasure would run counter to nature, and one could develop a vice of *insensibilitas* or unfeelingness (*Summa theologiae*, II. II, q. 142, a. 1).

Obviously, we seek a wholesome integration of the physical and the spiritual, of pleasure and self-control, of giving and receiving. It would be a mistake to overlook the fact that pleasure, even sexual pleasure in marriage, cannot satisfy all the unlimited needs in the human heart, for the soaring moments of plenitude vanish and the thirst always reappears. Equally, it would be a mistake to pretend that sexual pleasure in marriage is of no consequence.

5. The Sexual Virtue

In Chapter Two, we discussed the virtues of the Christian life. Virtue, we said, tends toward the good and expresses itself in right feeling, thinking and judging, choosing, and eventually acting. There is also a sexual virtue; it is called chastity. Many people immediately think of chastity as a special virtue reserved for vowed religious, be they sisters, brothers, or priests. This narrow view is not how the Church understands this virtue.

The *Catechism of the Catholic Church* says that true chastity involves the internal unity of a person's spiritual and bodily existence. It successfully brings together as a whole sexuality and the person (CCC §2337). Further the Congregation for Catholic Education says that "chastity consists in self-control, in the capacity of guiding the sexual instinct to the service of love and of integrating it in the development of the person" (*Educational Guidance in Human Love*, §18).

Thus, chastity is the virtue by which one integrates one's sexuality according to the moral demands of one's state of life. It is the integrating, relating, communicating, feeling, desiring, enjoying, believing, acting, and ultimately loving dimensions of our sexual selves. A married man and woman are called to the virtue of chastity just as is the single person or a nun in an enclosed convent. All strive for this integration according to the moral demands of their state of life. Chastity channels the human sexual drive in appropriate ways. For example, even though we all seek friendship and relationships, it may be inappropriate for a lawyer who tries cases regularly in a particular courtroom to befriend the judge who often hears those cases. Even though the desire for friendship is legitimate, prudence and chastity might dictate that this particular relationship is not good. The same may be said regarding friendships that married men and women develop. Chastity warrants particular vigilance regarding appropriate and inappropriate friendships. That being said, one cannot deny that:

> The virtue of chastity blossoms in *friendship*. It shows the disciple how to follow and imitate him who has chosen us as his friends…Chastity is expressed notably in *friendship with one's neighbor*. Whether it develops between persons of the same sex or opposite sex, friendship represents a great good for all. It leads to spiritual communion (CCC §2347).

All Christians, therefore, are called to the virtue of chastity, just as all are called to the virtue of justice. It is a mistake to equate chastity with the suppression of all things sexual, the "no, no" approach to human sexuality. We will examine in more detail what right feeling, thinking, judging, choosing, and acting means for different people in different states of life in the area of sexuality.

Closely linked to the virtue of chastity is the habit of modesty. Modesty in the context of sexuality is the habit of seeing other people as persons and not as sexual objects to be used. The other half of modesty is to help others see us as human persons, not sexual objects. We do this by behaving, speaking, and dressing in ways that are sensitive to the emotions and desires of others. Of course, in practice, what modesty means will vary from culture to culture and from situation to situation, yet at its core the *Catechism of the Catholic Church* says that modesty defends the inner core of a person, keeping hidden what should remain hidden and protects the dignity of the person by guiding how one looks at and behaves toward other people (CCC §§2521).

6. The Christian Virtue

As Christians, we approach the virtue of chastity with the eyes of faith. "Human sexuality is a gift understood in the light of faith" (The Pontifical Council for the Family, *The Truth and Meaning of Human Sexuality*, §3). While the virtue of chastity has been highly esteemed throughout human history, this natural virtue takes on a supernatural dimension with faith. Chastity becomes a gift from God with a power that enables the will not to suppress the sexual but rather to make the sex drive part of the Christian personality (Congregation for Catholic Education, *Guide to Formation in Priestly Celibacy*, §27). All this can happen through the power of the Holy Spirit, evoked by prayer, who enables us to integrate the sexual dimension of ourselves, so that we can develop the capacity for self-giving in the vocation of our own life.

We did not begin our reflection on human sexuality with a consideration of sins of impurity, carnal desires, or lust. Following recent Church teaching, we acknowledge that Catholic sexual morality is never to be limited to teachings about sexual sins. We have started by acknowledging the goodness of the gift of human sexuality and recognizing that we are called to the positive virtue of chastity, that is, a sacred and mysterious part of our lives that brings with it true joy (*The Truth and Meaning of Human Sexuality*, §122). In a nutshell, it is all about relating our sexual nature with its desires, urges, feelings, and power to the Christian call to love and be loved.

7. The Sexes: Male and Female

Each of us experiences our sexual selves within certain limitations. One obvious limitation is our sex, namely, we are either male or female because of the structure of our chromosomes. There should be no doubt in the Catholic mind that males and females are equal because both are made in the image of God.

The *Catechism* points out that both men and women are representatives of the tender care and powerful love of God. Each are equal in dignity but in a different way (CCC §2335). The Congregation for Catholic Education states that "the sexes are complementary: similar and dissimilar at the same time; not identical, the same, though, in dignity of person; they are peers so that they may mutually understand each other, diverse in their reciprocal completion" (*Educational Guidance in Human Love,* §22).

8. The Equality of Women

In all honesty, we must admit that the sexes have not always been treated equally. This fact has been attested to by the teachings of John Paul II. He has written more than any other pope in the defense of the dignity and equality of women. In his *Letter to Women,* the pope reflects:

> Women's dignity has often been unacknowledged and their prerogatives misrepresented, they have often been relegated to the margins of society and even reduced to servitude...Certainly it is no easy task to assign blame for this...And if objective blame, especially in particular historical contexts, has belonged to not just a few members of the Church, for this I am truly sorry (Pope John Paul II, *Letter to Women,* §3).

In the lengthy reflection on the Genesis account of Creation in his Apostolic Letter, *Mulieris Dignitatem* (*The Dignity of Women*), the pope states: "Yet your desire shall be for your husband, and he shall rule over you" (Gen 3:16), in their proper context, and explains that such an attitude of men to women is the result of sin and not how the relationship should be. At the same time, he wants to safeguard the difference between the sexes.

Consequently, even the rightful opposition of women to what is expressed in the biblical words, "He shall rule over you," (Gen 3:16) must not under any condition lead to the "masculinization" of women. In the name of liberation from male "domination," women must not appropriate to themselves male characteristics contrary to their feminine originality (*The Dignity of Women*, §10).

Many issues of justice are based on a proper understanding of human sexuality. One such issue is the difference between sexism and complementarity. Sexism is the belief that the sexes are unequal and expresses itself in prejudice and unjust discrimination while complementarity holds that the sexes are equal in God's sight but are different. The road to liberation from sexism is a long and complicated one, but a road that must be traversed energetically by those called to the virtue of chastity. In his 1995 World Day of Peace Message, Pope John Paul II, commenting on the process of women's liberation, gives us encouragement.

The journey has been a difficult and complicated one and, at times, not without its share of mistakes. But it has been substantially a positive one, even if it is still unfinished, due to the many obstacles which...still prevent women from being acknowledged, respected, and appreciated in their own special dignity (John Paul II, *Women: Teachers of Peace,* 1995 World Day of Peace Message, *Origins,* 24/28, [December 22, 1994]: §4, p. 467).

GENDER ROLES

The previous quotation from Pope John Paul II's *Women: Teachers of Peace* raises the interesting distinction between our sex (male or female) and social expectations of maleness and femaleness. The question arises: What is truly masculine and what is truly feminine?

Certain conventions and appropriate behavioral patterns are set for boys and girls, men and women, by a society. Many of these conventions and behavioral patterns can change from society to society and within the same society over time. Anthropologists may argue that men in primitive societies, because of their size and musculature, were the hunters and fighters while the women were the bearers, and the carers of the young. However, in many contemporary Christian societies, men and women do not wish to make such sharp divisions of roles and qualities. We just have to compare what young parents do today compared with what our grandparents or great-grandparents did. Fathers bathe their children, feed them, and clothe them, they cook meals and reveal a talent for nurturing. Mothers have responsible jobs and make important familial decisions. False dichotomies between the passive female and the dominating active male are continually challenged in Christian households today. It is not that males and females are identical, they are not; it is a recognition that their complementarity is more complex and fluid than often once thought.

The lives of the holy ones in our Roman Catholic Tradition bear witness to the expression of Saint Paul in his letter to the Galatians, that in Christ there are no slaves and free, Jews and Greeks, males and females. Women saints, like Saint Perpetua, revealed a courage and physical strength in the arena with the savage beasts that would rival any male. Saint Thecla cut off all her hair and dressed as a man so that she could travel without molestation to continue her works of charity. The gentleness of a Saint Francis of Assisi and the nurturing qualities of many of the founders of male religious orders confirm our belief that both male and female are created as images of God with equal dignity expressed in a different way" (CCC §2335).

9. Married Love and Life

In reflecting upon the Genesis accounts of Creation (Gen 1:1—2:3, 2:23–25) and the meaning of the natural law, the Church has continually focused on two particular insights into married love and life. First, it is not good for the human person to be alone (Gen 2:18), and second, our first parents are commanded to be fruitful and multiply (Gen 1:28). Not being alone and having children has implications: "Therefore a man leaves his father and his mother, and clings to his wife, and they become one flesh" (Gen 2:24). The "becoming one flesh" indicates a unique union of man and woman that has a profound depth of relationship and commitment. The becoming "one flesh" includes sexual union, and this sexual expression is reserved for a man and woman who are no longer alone, and who are open to the gift of procreation in the lifelong and exclusive relationship which is marriage.

10. Conjugal Unity

What are the characteristics of this union? In the Second Vatican Council document, *Pastoral Constitution on the Church in the Modern World,* the bishops together with Pope Paul VI encapsulated the Church's teaching on marriage and sexuality.

> The intimate partnership of married life and love has been established by the creator and qualified by God's laws. It is rooted in the conjugal covenant of irrevocable consent. Hence, by that human act whereby spouses mutually bestow and accept each other, a relationship arises, which by divine will and in the eyes of society, too, is a lasting one. For the good of spouses and their offspring as well as of society, the existence of this sacred bond no longer depends on human decision alone (§48).

So the married life is an intimate partnership of love, an irrevocable covenant, for the good of the couple and for their offspring and society. The document goes on to stress that this special union of man and woman is for their mutual sanctification and for the glory of God. Marital love is a mutual and free gift of self made by each spouse to the other in the one spirit and the one flesh.

Perhaps now we can understand the central teaching of the Church regarding sexual intercourse or genital sexual expression. Only marital commitment, fidelity, and love is the proper context for sexual intercourse, for only in this setting does sexual intercourse have its true meaning, namely, an act of loving union, and an act open to procreation. The Church is saying that there is something about genital sexual expression that makes it reserved for marriage. It is not just a biological act as performed by other animal life; it is ordained by the Creator to be an intimate action that expresses total self-giving with a respect for, and openness to, procreation. In the 1930s, the theologian Dietrich von Hildebrand said that the act of sex, as contrasted with other aspects of bodily experience, is essentially deep, that it involves the soul deeply in its passions and longings and touches the spiritual and psychological core of ourselves.

No sexual act between humans really leaves them untouched. They can be touched deeply in a positive way or touched deeply in a destructive and negative way. Whatever the way, they are touched. We have read about, no doubt, and perhaps experienced personally, the deplorable damage done to human lives and futures through sexual abuse. This abuse of another person, especially minors, scars not only the victims and their futures but also the families of the victims and those associated with the abuser.

The Church teaches that the Creator has inscribed in sexual intercourse two inseparable meanings: the first meaning is love and the second meaning is new life. The more technical language of some of the documents of the Church refer to the inseparable link between the two aspects of human sexual intercourse, namely, the unitive and the procreative. Sexual intercourse is the language or symbol of total self-giving and loving, not a giving for the moment or a loving of this particular person just for now. Pope John Paul II expresses this insight of the Catholic moral tradition as follows: "The only place in which this self-giving in its whole truth is made possible is marriage, the covenant of conjugal love freely and consciously chosen, whereby man and woman accept the intimate community of life and love willed by God himself" (*On the Family*, §13).

11. The Fecundity of Marriage (CCC §§2366–2379)

This giving of the whole self does not end with the married couple, but is linked to the Creator who cooperates with them in giving life to a new human person. Married couples share in the creative power and the fatherhood of God (CCC §2367).

> Married couples should regard it as their proper mission to transmit human life and to educate their children; they should realize that they are thereby cooperating with the love of God the Creator and are, in a certain sense, its interpreters. They will fulfill this duty with a sense of human and Christian responsibility (*Pastoral Constitution on the Church in the Modern World*, §50).

Children, then, spring from the very heart of a couple's mutual self-giving; they are its fruit. For this reason the Church constantly teaches that "each and every marriage act must remain open to life" (*On Human Life*, §11). "This particular doctrine, expounded on numerous occasions by the Magisterium, is based on the inseparable connection, established by God, which man on his own initiative may not break, between the unitive significance and the procreative significance which are both inherent to the marriage act" (*On Human Life*, §12).

We will continue our reflection on this particular doctrine when we treat specific issues in sexual morality, especially the Church's teaching on artificial contraception.

12. Everyday Struggles

Of course, married couples struggle with the ideals of total self-giving, loving, and the procreative dimension of sexual intercourse. This struggle requires patience, learning, changing, and listening. It will involve mistakes and regrets, as well as joys. Despite the struggles, sexual intercourse remains one important way for couples to foster this marital love and gift of self.

> This love is uniquely expressed and perfected through the marital act. The actions within marriage by which the couple are united intimately and chastely are noble and worthy ones. Expressed in a manner which is truly human these actions signify and promote the mutual self-giving by which spouses enrich each other with a joyful and thankful will (*Pastoral Constitution on the Church in the Modern World*, §49).

13. Sexual Intercourse Outside of Married Love

To limit sexual intercourse to marriage may seem both unpopular and unreal. The United States Conference of Catholic Bishops in 1991 quotes statistics that indicate that more than half of America's teens have experienced sexual intercourse by the time they are seventeen, and that more than one million unwed teenage girls in the U.S. become pregnant each year. It also claims that more than 400 thousand teenage girls have abortions each year (*Human Sexuality: A Catholic Perspective for Lifelong Learning*, §35). Obviously, feeling, thinking, judging, and acting in a responsible manner in the area of sexuality, that is, the promotion of chastity, does not come easily. It takes education, good example, self-discipline, prayer, and an awareness of the suffering and tragedy that can result from a lack of integration of the sexual dimensions of our lives. We will briefly discuss some instances of this lack of sexual integration, what the *Catechism of the Catholic Church* terms offenses against the dignity of the sacrament of marriage (CCC §§2380–2391), in the second part of this chapter.

14. Sexual Orientation and Sexual Behavior

We need to consider two other aspects of sexuality before reflecting on specific sexual issues, namely, sexual orientation and sexual behavior. Sexual orientation refers to which gender (male or female) of other people attracts and arouses another person sexually. Adults can be heteroerotic, that is, it is the opposite sex that attracts them and is the major source of their sexual desires. They can be homoerotic, in which people of the same sex attract them and are the major source of their sexual desire. Some adults can be bierotic, that is, they find both sexes sexually attractive and both sexes are the source of their sexual desire. Speaking of a person's sexual orientation, we commonly refer to people as being heterosexual, homosexual, or bisexual. Sexual behavior, on the other hand, refers to the actual sexual actions of a person, and it does not necessarily have to correspond with their sexual orientation. For example, a person may be heterosexual by orientation but choose to engage in homosexual behavior. Likewise, a person may be homosexual by orientation but choose to engage in heterosexual behavior. Often, particular circumstances may propel persons to behave in a way that is different from their orientation. Notice that in these explanations we are reducing sexual behavior to sexual actions, whereas in fact we are sexual in all dimensions of our lives. We are suggesting that one's sexual orientation influences more than sexual attraction and action. People's orientation may well influence the way they think, respond, create, and structure their lives and their world.

Modern psychology would also indicate that we cannot simply

divide the whole human population into sheep and goats, meaning people are of 100 percent heterosexual orientation and others of 100 percent homosexual orientation. We humans are complex creatures and what attracts and arouses some people may be equally complex.

15. The Christian Family

Marriage and the family are two of our most precious institutions. Pope John Paul II refers to the family as the first community to announce the Gospel to a person and to bring them to full human and Christian education. The family can help us to discern our own vocation, to accept our responsibility in the search for greater justice, and to teach us the meaning of love in our interpersonal relationships (*On the Family,* §2). Since parents are the first educators of their children, the family will play a vital role in an education of young people in human sexuality. In fact, parents have the primary role. The example, the patience, the affirmation, and the faith of a family are the solid foundation stones on which persons can hope to build an integrated sexuality and right relationships in their lives.

Thus, family forms that primary community of persons, where we learn to love and to receive love, to trust and to have faith. It is often from this familial community that a person gains the confidence, the desire, and the skills to participate in the larger community of human society, and to share in the very life and mission of the Church.

16. Some Specific Issues in Sexual Morality

In the first part of this chapter, we have outlined some of the basic attitudes and principles that form the foundation of the Church's teaching on human sexuality. We are now in a better position to consider some specific issues. Obviously, the issues to be considered have to be limited in number; however, it should become clear that the foundational attitudes and principles can be applied to many specific questions about human sexuality.

St John C does not agree !

ARTIFICIAL CONTRACEPTION

Pope Paul VI's encyclical, *Humanae Vitae* (*On Human Life*), is usually remembered as a document that caused so much controversy in the Church because of its teaching on methods of contraception. His teaching in this encyclical, which also reflected on the beauty of marriage, continued that of Pope Pius XII and Pope Pius XI before him, as well as the constant teaching of the Church on contraception. Pope John Paul II in his apostolic letter, *On the Family*, 1981, offers further reflection on the teaching. Still, in 1968, just before *On Human Life* was published, many Catholics, including laity and theologians, predicted a change in the teaching, which, as we know, did not occur. Given the history of the teaching's high profile during the last thirty-five years, let us examine the doctrine in some detail.

The meaning of marriage: The overall context for the teaching on methods of contraception is the meaning and nature of marriage. Marriage is understood as part of God's plan because it reflects the Creator's love in us. In order for marriage to truly reflect God's love, a total union of body and spirit is needed between husband and wife, a union that is exclusive, lifelong, and fecund. This last attribute of married love, fecundity, is a cooperation with the Creator in the generation and education of new lives (*On Human Life*, §8). As we have already mentioned, these two purposes of marriage, namely, the exclusive, lifelong union of husband and wife, and the procreative, have an inseparable link. The encyclical argues that the inseparable connection is willed by God (*On Human Life*, §12) and God's will is expressed through the natural law (*On Human Life*, §11). In other words, by reflecting on the nature of the marriage act, sexual intercourse, one can discern that there are inherent meanings in its

oral sex

Aids ext

60 years Civ agree ? do not Many

very structure, namely, the unity of husband and wife and the openness to new life. It is on this basis that the Church teaches that to interfere with these purposes or to separate them is against the natural law and the meaning of the marriage act according to the Creator. It further implies that to artificially contracept would be damaging to the married couple, harming them personally.

Nature as a moral teacher: It would seem that the physical make up of our bodies has a moral significance for understanding the purpose of sexual intercourse in marriage. The nature of the physical act itself tells us that it is meant for two people who are dedicated to each other in an exclusive, lifelong union of marriage. The act also tells us that it is for the procreation of new life as well as for the growth of the union. To have the physical union of intercourse without the openness to procreation, or to have an openness to procreation without the union, does damage to the very meaning of the conjugal act of intercourse. To have sexual intercourse in marriage without the openness to procreation damages the mutual and total self-giving of the spouses to each other in the act. In other words, sexual intercourse has the power to express mutual, total self-giving, which is the ideal of marriage, only when it is open to new life (*On the Family,* §32). For this reason "each and every marriage act must remain open to the transmission of life" (*On Human Life,* §11).

Acts to be excluded: Based on the preceding understanding of sexual intercourse, the encyclical draws the conclusion that the following is to be excluded: "Every action which, either in anticipation of the conjugal act, or in its accomplishment, or in the development of its natural consequences, proposes, whether as an end or a means, to render procreation impossible" (*On Human Life,* §14). In this statement, Pope Paul VI is referring to acts of sterilization, both permanent and temporary, that are directly willed, procured abortion (*On Human Life*, §14), and other methods of artificial birth control (*On Human Life*, §17). He considers the contraceptive act an "intrinsic disorder" and "hence unworthy of the human person, even when the intention is to safeguard or promote individual, family, or social well-being" (*On Human Life*, §14).

Family planning: Pope Paul VI anticipates an objection to his teaching:

> ...the objection is made...that it is the prerogative of the human intellect to dominate the energies offered by irrational nature and to orientate them toward an end conformable to the good of the human person. Now some may ask: in the present situation, is it not reasonable in many circumstances to have recourse to artificial birth control, if thereby, we secure the harmony and peace of a family and better conditions for the education of the children who are already born? (*On Human Life,* §16).

The response to the question is twofold. First, the pope acknowledges that our human intelligence should be applied to sexual intercourse and procreation. If there are serious reasons to space out births, the serious reasons may spring from the physical or psychological conditions of the husband or wife or from external conditions, "the church teaches that it is then licit to take into account the natural rhythms immanent in the generative functions for the conjugal act during infertile periods only and in this way to regulate birth without offending the moral principles which have been recalled earlier" (*On Human Life*, §16). The encyclical argues that there is an essential difference between contraceptive practice which is natural and that which is artificial.

Pastoral directives conclude Pope Paul VI's encyclical. Pastors are reminded that in this matter they are to be like the compassionate Redeemer, and this teaching must be accompanied by patience and goodness and an echo of the loving voice of that same Redeemer.

Summary: The Church teaches that the conjugal act of sexual intercourse has a special purpose given to it by the Creator. It binds the couple in mutual and total self-giving and enables this self-giving to express itself in the generation of new life. These two aspects of conjugal sexual intercourse both reflect God's love and enable couples to collaborate with the Creator in the generation and education of new life. The human person, therefore, must always respect and never nullify the inseparable connection willed by God between the unitive and procreative values of conjugal sexual intercourse. The knowledge and use of natural biorhythms of fertility can be used as a means for responsible parenthood and do not contradict the meaning and purpose of conjugal intercourse. Whereas artificial contraception is intrinsically dishonest because it does contradict the meaning and purpose of conjugal sexual intercourse willed by God.

PREMARITAL SEX AND COHABITATION

Despite the growing number of people who engage in sexual activity before marriage, it will not surprise the reader, having read what we have said previously, that the Church continues to teach that all sexual activity between persons, including sexual intercourse, is reserved for marriage. Why? Because genital sexual expression between two people is meant to be a sign that they are ready to give to each other not only their bodies and pleasure, but all of themselves. They are to share their hopes and their dreams, their disappointments, good health, ill health, fears, failures, bad moods, their futures, and their joys. This is to be lived in a lifelong exclusive covenant of love.

Current statistics indicate that many engaged couples live together in a sexual relationship before making a permanent commitment in

¿ Higher for those Catholics marrying outside the Church?

marriage. Some claim that nearly 50 percent of couples who present themselves for marriage in the Catholic Church in the United States have been cohabiting. These figures naturally are of great concern to the Church. Why are so many couples deciding to live together before their marriage? Perhaps, many delay marriage for economic or social reasons; others feel they need to test the relationship; or there could be a fear of a longterm relationship. For others, the importance of marriage has changed, and the public and Church recognition of their union has little significance.

A teaching moment: Many pastors believe that when such couples present themselves to the Church for marriage we have a significant teaching moment. In other words, rather than scolding the couple or denying the Church's stance on this matter, the sensitive pastor can use this encounter to encourage the couple to reflect on their present situation and the meaning of marriage. With the right questions and gentle guidance, the man and woman can come to appreciate the concerns of the Church, the teaching of the Church on human sexual expression, and the purpose and meaning of a Christian marriage. "Marriage between two baptized persons is a real symbol of the union of Christ and the Church which is not a temporary or trial union, but one which is eternally faithful" (*On the Family*, §81).

SEXUAL ABUSE

In the past twenty years, there has been a marked increase in the number of reported cases of sexual abuse in our communities at large. We are no doubt aware of the increasing number of such cases within the Church itself which has been a cause of great anguish and scandal.

The term, sexual abuse, describes precisely the immorality of these kinds of actions. They are literally an abuse of one's sexuality, an offense to the dignity of the victim. Rather than using sexuality for mutual self-gift in marriage, it used as a manipulation of the other, often involving violence of some kind. The mutuality between adults which ought to characterize genital sexual expression is missing. Abusers are commonly in some position of authority or power in the eyes of the victim. Startlingly, statistics often note that most victims know their abusers. They also suggest that, in the United States, one in six boys is abused before the age of sixteen; one in four girls experiences sexual abuse before the age of sixteen.

Shame is so closely tied to sexual abuse that instances of abuse often go unreported for years. Some studies today indicate increases in sexual abuse, but it is difficult to assess whether there is an increase in criminal behavior or an increase in the reporting of cases. No matter what the truth may be, sexual abuse is a pressing moral issue in today's society and Church—an issue which merits ongoing attention, most especially because of the lasting harmful effects it can have on its victims.

Enough stress cannot be laid on the pastoral responsibilities of the Church regarding this attack on a person's well-being and dignity, especially attacks of this nature on children and youth. Although Church leadership and clergy do not bring any particular competency to the psychological healing which is needed for victims and abusers, they can call on the skilled members of the community to address the issue and to offer their expertise in any way possible. In doing so, the pastoral response of the Church counts on the clinical expertise of its members and the ongoing spiritual care of the whole Christian community.

Instances of abuse within the Church itself require a more particular pastoral response. There are at least two obligations, the first is an obligation to provide for healing, and the second obligation pertains to prevention.

In terms of healing, the Church must offer understanding and treatment or therapy to the victims of sexual abuse so that scars may begin to heal. The families of sexual abuse victims as well as the community will need assistance to deal with hurt, anger, and confusion, while the abuser should be referred to legitimate civil authorities and, if feasible, required to undergo appropriate medical evaluation and intervention.

In terms of prevention, the Church must do all that is possible to ensure that all, especially children and youth, are protected from being victimized. Prevention will also include relieving the alleged offender of ministerial duties when allegations are supported by sufficient evidence.

The Church must continue to struggle so as not to be part of the problem but, rather, part of the solution to the wider crime of sex abuse.

PERSONS WITH A HOMOSEXUAL ORIENTATION (CCC §§2357–2359)

A significant number of men and women discover that their sexual inclinations are oriented chiefly towards people of the same sex. Sometimes, in our enthusiasm to make judgments about such an orientation, or the actions that could flow from such an orientation, we can forget another central teaching of the Church. Namely, that every person has an inherent dignity because he or she is created in God's image and therefore:

The Christian community should offer its homosexual sisters and brothers understanding and pastoral care" (NCCB, *Always Our Children*, 1997–1998); "every sign of unjust discrimination in their regard should be avoided" (CCC §2358); "homosexual persons have the same rights as all persons, including the right of not being treated in a manner which offends their personal dignity" (Congregation for the Doctrine of the Faith, *Responding to Legislative Proposals on Discrimination Against Homosexuals,* 1992, §3), and "homosexual persons, like all other persons, are called to chastity" (CCC §2359).

While the Church acknowledges that the causes of homosexuality, be they genetic, hormonal, psychological, or social, are still unclear, the Church is very clear about the moral evaluation of homosexual genital acts. Drawing on the Scriptures (Gen 19:1–29; Rom 1:24–27; 1 Cor 5:10; 1 Tim 1:1–10) and the interpretation of the natural law, the Church teaches that such acts are "intrinsically disordered" (CCC §2358). This teaching is consistent with the Church's understanding of marriage, namely, that only in heterosexual marriage is the sexual act not only a means of uniting the married couple in love and total self-giving but is also always open to the gift of new life.

Official Church documents have also commented on the homo-sexual orientation itself, stating that while the orientation itself is not a sin, the inclination itself is "objectively disordered." To under-stand what is meant by this description of the orientation, it is worth quoting in full from the document, *Letter to the Bishops of the Catholic Church on the Pastoral Care of the Homosexual Person.*

> Here two things must be noted. To speak of the homosexual inclination as "objectively disordered" does not mean that the homosexual person as such is evil or bad. Furthermore, the homosexual person is not the only one who has disordered tendencies or inclinations. All human beings are subject to some disordered tendencies (The Congregation for the Doctrine of the Faith, *Letter to the Bishops of the Catholic Church on the Pastoral Care of Homosexual Persons*, §3).

Summary: In summary, we may say that the goods the Church pro-poses to uphold in its teaching on homosexuality are as follows: (a) the dignity of all human beings regardless of their sexual orientation, including the recognition of human rights and responsibilities; (b) that genital sexuality has its true meaning only in the covenant of heterosexual marriage, which entails the complementarity of the sexes and an openness to the transmission of new life; (c) and love can be shared, nurtured, rejected, and even lost. The family with a homosexual member or members has an added opportunity to share and accept love as does the homosexual person himself or herself.

17. Conclusion: The Need For, and Obligation Of, Pastoral Care

In all these specific areas of human sexuality, the Church's teaching must be accompanied by pastoral care and sensitivity. Concern for married couples and families, for homosexual persons, for single people in general, and for those who have suffered sexual abuse, obviously must go beyond the publication of encyclicals and pastoral letters. In their efforts to live up to the ideals of the teaching of the Church, people need practical support systems and structures, as well as a sense of care from their spiritual leaders, pastors, and fellow believers.

After the publication of *On Human Life*, the National Conference of Catholic Bishops of the United States, in their pastoral letter, stressed the need for proper preparation of future spouses, the establishment of diocesan family life centers, a valid and modern theology and spirituality of marriage, and an encouraging and compassionate attitude of pastors (*Human Life in Our Day*, 1968, §§55–60). Pope John Paul II, in his Apostolic Exhortation *On the Family*, calls for pastoral programs to support those whose marriage has ended in separation or divorce. Concrete pastoral suggestions are always made in Church documents dealing with homosexuality. For example, the establishment or promotion of authentic pastoral programs that will assist homosexual persons at all levels of the spiritual life (*Letter to the Bishops of the Catholic Church on the Pastoral Care of Homosexual Persons*, §15), support groups for the parents and family of gay and lesbian people (NCCB, *Always Our Children*), effective preaching, teaching, and counseling that springs from a sound knowledge of homosexuality and Church teaching (NCCB, *Always Our Children*). No one now doubts the pressing need for pastoral care for the sexually abused. Within the Church, honesty, apologies, healing, and well-thought-out policies are imperative when it comes to sexual abuse.

Pastoral care is for the good and dignity of the person, so that he or she can reach the goals and fulfillment for which they were created as sexual human beings. While such care is the mission of the structured Church, it is also our mission to care for ourselves and for others, because we are called to intimacy, holiness, commitment, chastity, new life, and joy as sexual people.

18. Guidelines for Consideration of Issues in Sexual Ethics

No doubt the reader could raise many issues in sexual ethics not specifically treated in this chapter. We have only attempted to draw attention to some of the basic values that form the foundation of a Christian sexual ethic. These values, upheld by the Roman Catholic Tradition, cause us to ask these questions:

1. Do we accept our human sexuality as part of God's good Creation and as an integral component of our very identity?
2. Have we mistakenly equated sexuality with sex acts, thinking that control of our sex acts alone will bring an integrated sexuality?
3. Every Christian is called to the virtue of chastity. What concrete form should chastity take for my state of life?
4. Do we use or abuse others as objects of sexual pleasure, reducing them from persons worthy of respect to objects without dignity?
5. Have sexist attitudes in the surrounding culture become part of my way of thinking and behaving, and do I unjustly discriminate against a person because of his or her sexual orientation?
6. What is my response to the teaching of the Church that marital commitment, marked by fidelity and love, is the proper context

for sexual expression, and that sexual intercourse has two inseparable meanings, namely, the mutual love of the spouses and an openness to new life?

7. Do I treasure and nurture my friendships, as the Lord himself did, so that my affections give life and encouragement to others, and my friendships help to mold me into the image of Christ?

19. Selected Bibliography of Church Teaching on Sexual Ethics

Pius XI, *On Christian Marriage (Casti Connubii)*, 1930.

Vatican II Documents, *Pastoral Constitution on the Church in the Modern World (Gaudium et Spes)*, 1966.

Paul VI, *Priestly Celibacy (Sacerdotalis Caelibatus)*, 1967.

Paul VI, *On Human Life (Humanae Vitae)*, 1968.

Congregation for the Doctrine of the Faith, *Declaration on Certain Questions Concerning Sexual Ethics (Persona Humana)*, 1975.

Congregation for Catholic Education, *A Guide to Formation in Priestly Celibacy*, 1976.

John Paul II, *On the Family (Familiaris Consortio)*, 1981.

Congregation for Catholic Education, *Educational Guidance in Human Love: Outlines for Sex Education*, 1984.

Congregation for the Doctrine of the Faith, *Letter to the Bishops on the Pastoral Care of Homosexual Persons*, 1986.

Congregation for the Doctrine of the Faith, *Instruction on Respect for Human Life in Its Origins and on the Dignity of Procreation (Donum Vitae)*, 1987.

John Paul II, *On the Dignity of Women (Mulieris Dignitatem)*, 1988.

United States National Conference of Catholic Bishops, *Human Sexuality: A Catholic Perspective for Education and Lifelong Learning*, 1991.

Congregation for the Doctrine of the Faith, *Some Considerations Concerning the Response to Legislative Proposals on the Non-Discrimination of Homosexual Persons*, 1992.

Pontifical Council for the Family, *The Truth and Meaning of Human Sexuality: Guidelines for Education Within the Family*, 1996.

United States Conference of Catholic Bishops Committee on Marriage and Family, *Always Our Children: To the Parents of Homosexual Children*, 1997.

CHAPTER ELEVEN

Social Ethics

(§§CCC 1877–1948; §§2207–2213; §§2234–2246;
§§2263–2267; §§2306–2317; §§2401–2414; §§2419–2449)

1. Introduction

Social ethics refers to that area of moral theology which deals with the implications of our faith for the type of persons we should be and the kind of actions we should perform, particularly in the political, economic, and social realms. Some people might suggest that this area of moral theology lies outside the concerns of the Church. We are not social workers; we are not politicians; we do not have a lasting city on earth. From the outset of this book, however, we have spoken of our response to God as making God's loves our own; a God who is not distant and unconcerned with his Creation. We may or may not be social workers or politicians, but the good of the human community is our concern as followers of Jesus. This concern for the world was noted so eloquently in the document from the Second Vatican Council in which the bishops reflected on the role of the Church in the modern world. They wrote: "The joys and hopes, the grief and anguish of the people of our time, especially of those who are poor or afflicted, are the joys and hopes, the grief and anguish of the followers of Christ as well" (*Pastoral Constitution on the Church in the Modern World*, §1).

Catholic social teaching focuses on the social dimension of the gospel. It is generated by the magisterium, guided by the Holy Spirit, as it interprets current events in the context of the whole of the revelation of Jesus Christ. "The Church's social teaching proposes principles for reflection; it provides criteria for judgment; it gives guidelines for action (CCC §§2423).

2. Historical Overview

Many people date the beginning of modern Church teaching in the area of social ethics to the late nineteenth century, in particular to Pope Leo XIII's encyclical, *On the Condition of Labor*, an encyclical letter that focused in particular on the situation of the worker in the late 1800s (CCC §2421). Since then, popes from Pius XI to John Paul II have written encyclicals commemorating the publication of *On the Condition of Labor,* using its anniversary as an opportunity to interpret the signs of the times and to offer teaching to the Church in response to the pressing social needs of the day. The social teaching has been developed in other documents as well, at the level of both the universal and the local Church.

3. Seeking Justice

The obvious goal of the social teaching of the Church is the promotion of justice, particularly the change of structures to ensure that justice is realized. Although we discussed the virtue of justice in Chapter Two, it is worth repeating the fundamental understanding of justice here as well.

4. Types of Justice: Legal, Commutative, Distributive

Justice consists in giving to God and to neighbor their due (CCC §1807). The challenge, of course, is determining what is due and how the demands are to be met. The Roman Catholic Tradition has used the common categories of commutative, legal, and distributive justice (CCC §2411). Commutative justice refers to honoring contracts or agreements between persons, corporations, institutions, and the like. To be just, one must follow through on what one has agreed to. For example, if I borrow money from a friend, I must pay it back. Commutative justice requires that I pay my debt, honor contracts, and fulfill obligations that were agreed upon. Legal justice includes the obligation of individuals to the community, perhaps more strictly, the duties of citizens to their state. Individual members of a community or society are just when they adhere to the norms regulating life in that society. Finally, distributive justice governs the obligation of the community or state to the individual. The community is just when it gives citizens their due in response to the legitimate needs of the individual or based on merit.

While these descriptions of justice help us to determine one's "due," we must remember that the overriding notion of justice is right relationships among people. Sometimes, the minimum requirements of justice—while technically meeting the demands of commutative, legal, or distributive justice—may not fulfill completely what justice, understood as right relationship, might require of followers of Christ. At the core of the social teaching of the Church is the dignity of the human person in community and a concern that political, economic, and social conditions facilitate one's growth as a child of God and not present obstacles to human flourishing.

5. Tending Toward the Social Good

As we study further what social justice means within the Roman Catholic Tradition, we point to four areas in particular which merit attention. The social teaching of the Church proposes that if people are to reach their full stature as persons, if human dignity is to be respected and nurtured, attention must be paid to the virtue of solidarity, the common good, a preferential option for the poor, and the good of the individual secured by human rights. Attending to these will underscore two of the overarching human goods that we spoke of in the introduction to the chapter on the subdivisions of moral theology: the dignity of the human person and his or her social nature. These two goods are really at the heart of social ethics in the Roman Catholic Tradition.

SOLIDARITY AMONG ALL PEOPLE (CCC §§1939–1942; §§2437–2449; SEE ALSO *ON SOCIAL CONCERN*, ESPECIALLY §§38–42)

One of the miracles of modern technology is that we can watch events around the world from the comfort of our living room. Millions, if not a billion, people watch the international Olympic games as they are played out in various countries of the world. Midnight Mass from the Vatican is broadcast, and we can see the liturgy better than if we were in Saint Peter's Basilica. However, it is not just sporting events or religious celebrations that are transmitted into our homes. We also witness the ravages of natural disasters, terrorism, and war. Day after day, newspapers tell of tragedy that touches the human community throughout the world.

How do we respond to the "joys and hopes, the grief and anguish" of people, whether in our family, neighborhood, country, or on the other side of the world? Do we make them our own, as the Second Vatican Council announced? The response called for by the Church's social teaching is to cultivate the virtue of solidarity in our moral lives.

Solidarity "is a firm and persevering determination to commit oneself to the common good; that is to say, to the good of all and of each individual, because we are all really responsible for all" (*On Social Concern*, §38). Pope John Paul II's description contains both the virtue and the expression of solidarity. The social teaching of the Church begins with a presumption that we are a human family. As such, we are entrusted to one another's care. Aside from any concrete action on behalf of one another, the social teaching of the Church addresses what lies in our hearts. Pope John Paul II describes an attitude of solidarity as "a commitment to the good of one's neighbor with the readiness, in the Gospel sense, to 'lose oneself' for the sake of the other instead of exploiting him, and to 'serve him' instead of oppressing him for one's own advantage" (*On Social Concern*, §38). Solidarity is at work when society's "members recognize one another as persons" (*On Social Concern*, §39); or, again, "everyone should look upon his or her neighbor (without any exception) as another self" (*Pastoral Constitution on the Church in the Modern World*, §26; see also CCC §1931).

Solidarity presumes a mutual interdependence among the members of the human family. As the definition of solidarity offered by Pope John Paul II suggests, solidarity is closely linked to the common good.

COMMON GOOD (CCC §§1905–1912)

The *Pastoral Constitution on the Church in the Modern World* describes the common good as "the sum total of social conditions which allow people, either as groups or as individuals, to reach their fulfillment more fully and more easily" (§26; see also *On Christianity and Social Progress*, §65). As such, the common good serves as a corrective to the extremes of individualism and collectivism. Whereas individualism overemphasizes the autonomy of the individual at the expense of the obligations of individuals to the wider human community, collectivism might well sacrifice the good of the individual for society.

We could imagine the extreme of individualism represented by a chief executive officer (CEO) who cares little for the well-being of his workers, as long as the business is productive. The people who work for him are merely easily disposable cogs in his business machine. The CEO is preoccupied with himself and sees nothing wrong with doing whatever needs to be done to ensure that he is wealthy and comfortable. The extreme of collectivism might be seen in a state which takes a legitimate business away from a creative entrepreneur in order to keep all members of society at a relatively even economic level, appropriating to the government the hard-earned resources of a good person.

The Roman Catholic Tradition's focus on the common good recognizes the social nature of the human person and acknowledges reciprocal rights and responsibilities between the individual and the community and or society.

Speaking of the virtue of solidarity in the international community, Pope John Paul II writes: "An essential condition for global solidarity is autonomy and free self-determination, also within associations such as those indicated. But at the same time solidarity demands a readiness to accept the sacrifices necessary for the good of the whole world community" (*On Social Concern*, 45). Once again we see the twofold focus of the common good: the good of the individual in balance with the good of the larger community, whether that be a small local community or the broad community that is the human family.

Three essential elements of the common good: The *Catechism of the Catholic Church* points to three essential elements which the common good includes and which capture the twofold focus of the common good, that is, the individual and the community: respect for the person, social well-being and development, and peace (CCC §§1907–1909). First, the common good must recognize the dignity of the person and work towards all that will foster the growth of the person; at the same time, the *Catechism* recognizes that there is a duty to ensure the development of society as a whole. In this case, the legitimate authorities may have to discern when the wishes of individuals must yield to the good of society, never, of course, doing so at the expense of the dignity of the person. Finally, the common good requires an atmosphere of peace where this mutual development may occur.

Participation in the common good (CCC §1914): The common good rightly requires the participation of the members in the common endeavor. The contribution of individual members of society to the common good occurs both on the personal and public level.

Personally, members of society participate in and enrich the common good by attending to their own development and to those in their care. Included here would be one's pursuit of a good education, suitable employment, charitable works, and any other involvement of the individual in the common life. By doing so, they enhance the good of all.

Participation in public life is also an important contribution that individual members of society make to the common good. This participation is most evident in democratic societies where citizens may be involved in the political life of their land. As we have said before, the common good includes both society's commitment to and action on behalf of the human person and the individual's obligation to society.

Both the virtue of solidarity's invitation to a sense of responsibility for others and the common good's emphasis on structures which provide an environment for human flourishing invite a particular attention to the disadvantaged, the marginalized of society, particularly the poor.

PREFERENTIAL OPTION FOR THE POOR (CCC §§2443–2449)

The first explicit statement from the magisterium about a preferential option for the poor came from Latin American bishops in a document following a meeting in Puebla, Mexico, in 1979. Scandalized by the poverty in which the majority of the people lived, the spiritual pastors called on the Church as a whole to make a preferential option for the poor. The bishops implicated themselves in their challenge to the Church:

Not all of us in the Latin American Church have committed ourselves sufficiently to the poor. We are not always concerned about them, or in solidarity with them. Service to them really calls for constant conversion and purification among all Christians. That must be done if we are to achieve fuller identification each day with the poor Christ and our own poor (Latin American Bishops' Conference, *Evangelization in Latin America's Present and Future: The Final Document*, [Maryknoll, NY: Orbis Books, 1980], p. 264).

Pope John Paul II further elaborated on the poor, expanding those included under its umbrella. Whereas the Latin American bishops' prophetic call came as a result of their exposure to the economic poverty of so many of their people, Pope John Paul II sees the poor as including not only those who are materially deprived, but culturally and spiritually as well (see *On One Hundred Years of Catholic Social Teaching*, §57).

If one of the principal goals of the social teaching of the Church is to ensure that the political, economic, and social environments are such that human beings flourish, it makes sense to have a particular concern for those who are without the means necessary to participate fully in their own development and to take steps on their behalf. We do this not primarily out of charity, but of justice. It is Saint John Chrysostom who said: "Not to enable the poor to share in our goods is to steal from them and deprive them of life. The goods we possess are not ours, but theirs."

Closely linked to both solidarity and the common good, the preferential option for the poor marks followers of Christ who see Christ in the poor and see in them "another self." A preferential option for the poor is a third condition for respect for the dignity of the person in the social order.

THE GOOD OF THE INDIVIDUAL SECURED BY HUMAN RIGHTS

A final presupposition of social ethics and the social teaching of the Church focuses on the good of the individual, especially as that is secured by human rights. We noted earlier that the common good entails a balance between society's obligation to the individual and each member's duty to society. The virtue of solidarity, the common good, and the preferential option for the poor have focused, not exclusively, on the good of the community and the individual's obligations there. Here we focus on the claims of the individual members of society. Since we have addressed the respect due to the human person because of his or her dignity in the introductory remarks to these chapters, we focus here on the human rights which are the concrete way in which a society honors and protects human dignity.

Ideally, the virtue of solidarity and a sense of oneness among the members of the human family should be enough to ensure that people have the proper environment in which to grow as children of God. However, in our sinful world, this is often not the case. Even though created by love for love, we often fail in living to our fullest potential; as history and current events attest, people suffer at the hands of one another. The social teaching of the Church has given considerable thought to those rights which should be accorded to all people so that they might flourish and live in accordance with their dignity. Naming these rights, of course, does not ensure that people will flourish anymore than insisting on the dignity of the human person guarantees that people will in fact live up to their dignity. It simply sets up the structure and names the conditions under which people should live so as to be afforded the possibility of full development as persons.

Human rights to be guaranteed: The *Catechism of the Catholic Church* notes that respect for the dignity of the human person involves acceptance and respect for those rights that proceed from his dignity as God's creation. "It is the Church's role to remind men of good will of these rights and to distinguish them from unwarranted or false claims" (CCC §1930). In Catholic social teaching, Pope John XXIII was the first pontiff to articulate a list of rights which society should guarantee for its people. In his 1963 encyclical letter, *Peace on Earth*, Pope John listed and elaborated on rights and duties of people in society. Foundational, of course, was "the right to life, to bodily integrity, and to the means which are necessary and suitable for the proper development of life. These means are primarily food, clothing, shelter, rest, medical care, and finally the necessary social services" (*Peace on Earth*, §11). Pope John spoke further of rights pertaining to culture, worship, and one's social, economic, and political life. Little more than fifteen years later, Pope John Paul II, in a speech to the United Nations, provided an expanded list of rights which the Church holds out to humanity as essential for human development. He mentioned these:

> …the right to life, liberty and security of the person; the right to food, clothing, housing, sufficient health care, rest, and leisure; the right to freedom of expression, education and culture; the right to freedom of thought, conscience and religion; the right to manifest one's religion either individually or in community, in public or in private; the right to choose a state of life, to found a family and to enjoy all conditions necessary for family life; the right to property and work, to adequate working conditions and a just wage; the right of assembly and association; the right to freedom of movement, to internal and external migration; the right to nationality and residence; the right to political participation and the right to participate in the free choice of the political system of the people to which one belongs (John Paul II, *Address to the Thirty-Fourth General Assembly of the United Nations*, October 2, 1979, §13).

If one recalls that the purpose of rights is to ensure that people are afforded the proper conditions to flourish as human beings, one can see the reasonableness of the list provided by Pope John Paul II and may even think of other rights to add.

We have focused in this section on the importance of respect for human rights. As our discussion of the common good and solidarity reminds us, however, there is always an ongoing balance between the needs of the individual and the good of the community. Although in the Roman Catholic Tradition, we believe that these goods are never opposed to one another it is always a delicate task requiring prudence to discern the rights and duties of individuals in community.

With these four areas as a context, we move to a consideration of three areas which receive the bulk of attention in the social teaching of the Church: public/political, economic, and social dimensions of life.

6. Public/Political Dimension of Life

Catholic social teaching presumes that human beings live in and need community or society. Society is necessary for the development of human beings. It is part and parcel of human nature (CCC §1879).

The *Catechism of the Catholic Church* notes that the societies of family and the state correspond most to the nature of the human person (CCC §1882). We will address these two societies briefly. In doing so, we should keep in mind the four marks of tending toward the social good mentioned previously and note the ongoing need to keep in balance the individual and the community's good.

FAMILY: THE ORIGINAL CELL OF SOCIAL LIFE
(CCC §§2201–2213; §1882)

The family, according to the *Catechism of the Catholic Church,* is the basic unit of society precisely because it is the means by which family members are admitted and oriented to social life (CCC §2207). It is not uncommon for us to presume that a troubled family life accounts in part for people who have difficulties in adjusting to society or who clash with the law. Similarly, we often presume that people who are well-adjusted are the product of a good family background. These presumptions are true sometimes, but it is not always the case. The phrase "the apple doesn't fall far from the tree" still rings true because we acknowledge the influence of parents on children. Noting this link between family life and social life, the *Catechism* states that "authority, stability, and a life of relationships within the family constitute the foundations for freedom, security, and fraternity within society" (CCC §2207). It is the first place where socialization occurs.

Once one understands the Church's vision of marriage and family life, one can comprehend more fully the concern that the Church has that this *original cell of society* be safeguarded and that social conditions foster its development. The chapter on sexual ethics covers these areas more completely, but a brief summary here will enable us to move ahead regarding the family in society.

Marriage and family in Church teaching: The Church's teaching on marriage is that it is a sacrament marked by the mutual gift of spouses to one another. This mutual gift of love is particularly marked when the love of the couple issues forth in new life, a concrete sign of the love of the spouses. The mutual sharing of life and love between spouses is now widened to include the child, the family (see especially Paul VI, *On Human Life,* and John Paul II, *On the Family*).

One might imagine a pebble dropped into a still pond. Little by little concentric circles emanate from the area where the pebble was dropped. In the Church's view, the love of a married couple gives way to the love within a family, which gives way to a sharing of love in a wider circle of family and friends (for example, a parish community) and, finally, into society as a whole. Logically, if the giving and receiving of love is unobstructed along the way, there will be positive ramifications for life in society; blocking the flow of love within the family and the outer circles of love is like a cancer attacking the cell of society and society itself.

We are aware that few families fully model this image of expanding circles of love. Human sinfulness and weakness present many obstacles to harmony in familial relationships. Family members, parents in particular, have an obligation to work toward the common good at the local level, attending to the same three areas mentioned earlier: respect for the individual, concern for the good of the whole family, and an environment of peace.

The Church's social teaching, however, asks those with civil authority to ensure that social structures support the good of the family as well (CCC §2210). Specifically, it calls on the "political community" to ensure the freedom to start a family, to bear children, and to raise them according to one's religious beliefs (CCC §2211). It also reiterates some of the rights that we have mentioned earlier regarding private property, healthcare, and the like. It is precisely because the family is so crucial in society that the Church calls for its protection and support (CCC §2210).

THE STATE: INSURER OF THE COMMON GOOD

The second society which is so important for humanity and which builds on the first is the state, the political society. Interestingly, Church teaching does not endorse one particular form of government over another. However, one criterion must be met for morally legitimate governance: "The diversity of political regimes is morally acceptable, provided they serve the legitimate good of the communities that adopt them" (CCC §1901). "It is the role of the state to defend and promote the common good of civil society, its citizens, and intermediate bodies" (CCC §1910), remembering that the human person is "the beginning, the subject and the object of every social organization" (*Pastoral Constitution on the Church in the Modern World*, §25; CCC §1881).

Legitimate authority in the state (CCC §§1897–1904; §§2234–2246): Although the social teaching of the Church does not favor any particular political configuration (CCC §1901), it does insist on the need for authority in human communities. Authority's purpose is to keep unity in the community and to order society to the common good of its members. It must provide opportunities for participation in the common good. Its moral legitimacy is based on how well it fulfills this task. The power of the state, says the *Catechism of the Catholic Church,* is legitimate only when it fosters and protects the common good of its citizens and only if it exercises morally permissible means to achieve this power (CCC §1903).

We can imagine instances where abuses of authority would undermine individual and common good. Consider a civil authority who is upset over homeless people who bother tourists visiting his city. In an effort to ensure the beauty and attractiveness of the city, he orders police forces to transport the homeless to a section on the fringe of the city where they will be out of view. Although seemingly promoting the common good, the authority steps on the good of the individual homeless people to achieve it. The best of intentions cannot legitimate this abuse of authority. Similarly, a civil authority who appoints people to positions of public service based on friendship or political motives and not on the competency of the individual puts the common good at risk while seeming to attend to the good of an individual.

Citizens have a duty to speak out when abuses of authority occur (CCC §2238). In fact, they are obliged to follow their consciences if they believe that the directives of civil authorities contradict the moral good (CCC §§2241–2242). Just as civil authorities must attend carefully to the means that they use to promote the common good, never utilizing immoral means, citizens in their response to abuses of authority must do the same (CCC §2243).

Balancing the individual and the common good and doing so with morally acceptable means marks a wise exercise of civil authority. Those who do it well serve the citizens in justice.

Two principles to guide the state (CCC §§1883–1885; §2209): We take for granted that the goal of the common good and of societies as such is to provide an atmosphere where people can flourish and manifest the dignity which is theirs. As we noted in our discussion of the common good, a presupposition at work in the social teaching of the Church is that people must have the opportunity to participate actively in society. The *Catechism of the Catholic Church* notes that "to promote the participation of the greatest number in the life of a society, the creation of voluntary associations and institutions must be encouraged 'on both national and international levels, which relate to economic and social goals, to cultural and recreational activities, to sports, to various professions, and to political affairs'" (CCC §1882; see also Pope John XXIII, *On Christianity and Social Progress*, §60).

Participation in society promotes both the good of the individual who is social by nature and the good of the community which can only be enriched by the generous contribution of the gifts and skills of its members.

Another point must be made here: we cannot flourish or develop fully as persons on our own. We require one another even to enjoy certain fundamental human goods such as health and education. Thus, Church teaching presumes that one's ability to give and receive love and to be involved in the public/political dimension of life is enhanced and can only be achieved through good organizations in the political, economic, and social spheres. We can think of the United Nations as a political body, international finance organizations, and on the local or national level a healthcare system, an educational system, social service organizations, and the like.

It is in part the responsibility of civil authorities to attend to these structures for the good of the citizens. Catholic social teaching has proposed principles or norms to guide the exercise of authority in the state in securing the common good: socialization and subsidiarity.

Socialization: Socialization addresses precisely what we have noted above. The state will make sure that certain associations and institutions exist for the welfare of its citizens. Many nations felt the need for an international body like the United Nations after the First World War of the twentieth century. At national levels, we expect the state to have a system of education, institutions for healthcare, associations for people with special needs, and so forth. As part of their responsibility for members of society, civil authorities must see to these kinds of associations among the people they serve so that the common good and individual good are respected.

Subsidiarity: The second norm, subsidiarity, was elaborated by Pope Piús XI in his encyclical on the fortieth anniversary of Pope Leo XIII's *On the Condition of Labor*. Pope Pius XI described subsidiarity as a principle by which "a community of a higher order should not interfere in the internal life of a community of a lower order, depriving the latter of its functions, but rather should support it in case of need and help to co-ordinate its activity with the activities of the rest of society, always with a view to the common good" (*On Reconstruction of the Social Order*).

If the common good finds itself always trying to balance the individual good and the common good, careful not to sacrifice the freedom and autonomy of the individual to the good of the community, the principle of subsidiarity serves as a way to ensure that the freedom and autonomy of smaller communities are not denied, even by well-intentioned motives of the larger community.

For example, as good as a state system of education might be, it would be wrong for the state to insist that all citizens must go to a state-run school if others have banded together to provide other means of education. Also, one would expect national educational associations to respect the autonomy of local associations, and the like. Similarly, the state could not require that all medical care be sought at a state-sponsored institution if others provided a similar service. While it is the prerogative of parents to raise their children, and one would not expect the state to interfere in this responsibility of parents, one can attest to interventions on the part of the state to safeguard children from abusive parents. The same might be true regarding educational and healthcare institutions.

The principle of subsidiarity cautions against excessive centralization of authority. The autonomy of the local level should always be respected. Any interventions from a higher authority must be proportionate and measured in light of incompetence at the lower level.

One notes again the tension and need for balance between a government which respects the freedom and autonomy of the individual while establishing structures where they can be exercised to the greatest benefit of the whole community.

Catholic social teaching affirms the role of the state in promoting social justice for citizens, beginning with a realization that we are one human family bound together as stewards for one another. Within this society, there is a need for legitimate authority to promote participation in the common good by all its citizens.

7. Economic Dimension of Life (CCC §§2426–2449)

A second area occupying attention in the social teaching of the Church is the economic dimension of life. Perhaps one of the most countercultural statements that Catholic social teaching can make in today's world is that life is about more than money. Any theory or approach to economics "that makes profit the exclusive norm and ultimate end of economic activity is morally unacceptable....A system that 'subordinates the basic rights of individuals and of groups to the collective organization of production' is contrary to human dignity" (CCC §2424). Just as the role of the state is to uphold human dignity and to establish structures which facilitate human development, so too all economic activity has as its end the good of the human person. Consequently, the Church does not endorse any particular economic system but is wary of any system that puts the person at risk.

No one, of course, makes money simply to look at it. People buy things. The importance of the economy in Catholic social teaching is the intimate link that the teaching makes between the economy and human development. If the focus of the economy is not on the human person but on the accumulation of goods and the like, then human dignity is in danger. Pope Paul VI noted that "the acquisition of worldly goods can lead men to greed, to the unrelenting desire for more, to the pursuit of greater personal power. Rich and poor alike— be they individuals, families or nations—can fall prey to avarice and soul-stifling materialism" (*On the Development of Peoples*, §18). In other words, it can dehumanize rather than humanize people.

This seemingly obvious placement of economic life within the context of the good of the person is not always apparent in economic practices. Newspapers report with some frequency on the effect of multinational businesses on peoples in developing nations where labor is cheaper than in the developed world. We have heard of chief executive officers of floundering companies bailing out with huge sums of money while leaving middle managers and workers jobless and without a pension. When economic practices are marked more by ruthless self-promotion than by solidarity, when they lose sight of the common good in favor of individual rights, they become destructive of both the individual and the community. Contrary to these abuses and what many experience, economic life is not an end in itself, but the Church considers it very important.

RIGHTS ASSOCIATED WITH WORK (CCC §§2427–2436)

Pope John XXIII surprised readers of his encyclical, *Peace on Earth*, when he went beyond an articulation of political rights and spoke of economic rights. Among the rights that he listed are "the natural right to free initiative in the economic field and the right to work" (*Peace on Earth*, §18). He also listed good working conditions, the right to work according to one's capacity and competence, the right to a just wage, and the right to private property (*Peace on Earth*, §§19–22).

One can easily see how much attention human work receives in the listing of rights and in the social teaching of the Church. This attention is merited because the Church links work to human dignity. Pope John Paul II points out that unlike any other creature, human beings work. We might say that a beaver builds a dam or a robin a nest, but their activity is not the same as human work.

He writes that "there is no doubt that human work has an ethical value of its own, which clearly and directly remains linked to the fact that the one who carries it out is a person, a conscious and free subject, that is to say, a subject that decides about himself" (*On Human Work*, §6.3). Why do we find "sweat shops" degrading? Not because of the type of work that people do, but because the dignity of the person is not being respected. In these instances of injustice, the product is more important than the person. Persons are being treated as a means to an end, not respected as persons, as ends in themselves. It is precisely for this reason that Pope John XXIII emphasized not simply the right to work but the right to do so under conditions which are respectful and not demeaning of the person. The most menial jobs or the most coveted can enhance the dignity of the person.

A concomitant concern along with the right to work is that one be compensated justly. Two factors are to be considered: merit and need. Interestingly, the *Catechism of the Catholic Church* suggests that there are objective standards to a just wage. So, agreement between parties to a particular wage does not guarantee that the wage is in fact morally just (CCC §2434). Rather, the wage should be sufficient "to provide a dignified livelihood" for the person and his or her family (*Pastoral Constitution on the Church in the Modern World*, §67; CCC §2434).

Returning momentarily to the overarching common goods and the particular concerns of social ethics, we can see a convergence of concerns both in the political and economic spheres that the dignity of the person be upheld, that the interdependence of peoples be recognized, and that political and economic activity promote the common good while never trampling on the individual good. Honoring these goods ensures an environment for human flourishing and sound political and economic policies.

8. Social Dimension of Life (CCC §§1886–1889)

Before moving on to a consideration of specific issues in social ethics, we draw attention to another responsibility of society as addressed in the *Catechism of the Catholic Church*, one which we include as the social dimension of life. The *Catechism* states: "Society is essential to the fulfillment of the human vocation. To attain this aim, respect must be accorded to the just hierarchy of values, which 'subordinates physical and instinctual dimensions to interior and spiritual ones'" (CCC §1886; see *One Hundred Years of Catholic Social Teaching*, §36).

Pope John Paul II writes in *One Hundred Years of Catholic Social Teaching* that "a given culture reveals its overall understanding of life through the choices it makes in production and consumption" (*One Hundred Years*, §36). What meaning of life might we grasp from our culture? To what is our energy directed? It might be all about beauty, or fame, or fortune. If these are the dominant images and messages conveyed in a culture we can anticipate an "understanding of life" different from "giving and receiving love."

Beyond production and consumption, however, what does the prevailing culture say about the dignity of the person? Are women and men treated equally? Is there subtle or not so subtle unjust discrimination based on race, creed, gender, sexual orientation, education, financial status, and the like? Again, what messages are given about the meaning of life?

Catholic social teaching falls back again and again on the dignity of the person as a member of the human community. We are stewards of one another, destined for life in the kingdom. Any culture which demeans the human person or places obstacles to his or her authentic development is itself in need of conversion. "Charity is the greatest social commandment. It respects others and their rights. It requires the practice of justice, and it alone makes us capable of it. Charity inspires a life of self-giving" (CCC §1889).

9. Specific Issues in Social Ethics

In this final chapter, we will examine fairly briefly three issues in social ethics where we might see the principles and teachings elaborated above worked out in practice. We will focus on an issue from each of the above areas, that is, political, economic, and social.

PUBLIC/POLITICAL LIFE:
LEGITIMATE PROTECTION FROM AGGRESSORS:
CAPITAL PUNISHMENT AND JUST WAR
(CCC §§2263–2267; §§2307–2317)

The principal concern of Pope John Paul II's 1995 encyclical, *The Gospel of Life*, is the value of human life which is repeatedly called "sacred" and "inviolable" throughout the document. Yet the Roman Catholic Tradition has allowed for legitimate self-defense on the part of both individuals and the state, even to the point of taking lives if necessary. The Holy Father writes that "to kill a human being, in whom the image of God is present, is a particularly serious sin. *Only God is the master of life!* Yet from the beginning, faced with the many and often tragic cases which occur in the life of individuals and society, Christian reflection has sought a fuller and deeper understanding of what God's commandment prohibits and prescribes" (*The Gospel of Life*, §55). He quotes the *Catechism of the Catholic Church* which says that "legitimate defense can be not only a right but a grave duty for one who is responsible for the lives of others" (CCC §2265).

The starting point within the Christian Tradition, of course, is a presumption against violence. If and when violence must be used, however, it should be sufficient to the task, but not more than is needed. Accepting the paradox and allowing for the legitimacy of defense, then, a word of caution must be issued regarding the means used to defend oneself or the state. The means of defense should be bloodless if possible because they better correspond to the "concrete conditions of the common good and [are] more in conformity with the dignity of the human person" (CCC §2267).

This twofold concern for the common good and the dignity of the person is highlighted in both capital punishment and the just-war theory. They are always held in tension.

Capital punishment (CCC §§2265–2267; §2306): The Roman Catholic Tradition has seen a development in its teaching on capital punishment. The movement is from a relatively uncritical acceptance of the death penalty as a legitimate means of defense by the state to a hesitance and almost absolute exclusion of it as a morally acceptable means of punishment. A tension lies within the teaching itself.

While recognizing the sacredness of human life, the Church recognizes "the right and duty of legitimate public authority to inflict punishment proportionate to the gravity of the offense" (see CCC §2266). Generally, punishment serves three purposes: "redress the disorder," "defending public order and protecting people's safety," and the "correction of the guilty party" (see CCC §2266).

Perhaps, in the past a greater emphasis was placed on the common good, captured in the first two purposes of punishment, that is, retribution and restoration of public order. In his recent reflections, as our discussion of capital punishment in Chapter Three indicated, Pope John Paul II seems to highlight the dignity of the person and, consequently, the third purpose, that is, the correction of the offender. In doing so, Church teaching is allowing for the possibility of a criminal to repent and live more in keeping with his or her dignity as a human being.

While recognizing the tragedy and ruthlessness of some crimes which civil law might judge worthy of the death penalty, Church teaching severely limits the occasions when capital punishment would be acceptable, going so far as to say that it is legitimate only when it would be an "absolute necessity: in other words, when it would not be possible otherwise to defend society. Today, however, as a result of steady improvements in the organization of the penal system, such cases are very rare, if not practically nonexistent" (*The Gospel of Life*, §56).

One sees again in this context the tension between common good and the individual good. The Church seems to have struck a balance, ensuring that the common good not be threatened by a criminal but respecting the dignity of the person and allowing for the possibility of conversion. This development in teaching has not always been received well in some societies but it appears consistent with the concerns of Catholic social teaching.

Just war (CCC §2309): The presumption against violence that is operative in the punishment of individuals who commit crimes in society is at work on the level of national and international conflicts as well. Saint Augustine, the "founder" of the just-war theory, was hardly militaristic, seeking a way to justify violence. He writes in his *City of God*: "A just war, moreover, is justified only by the injustice of an aggressor; and that injustice ought to be a source of grief to any good man, because it is human injustice" (Saint Augustine, *The City of God*, 19.7; *The Fathers of the Church*, Vol. 24; trans by Gerald Walsh, S.J., and Daniel Honan, Washington, DC: Catholic University of America Press, 1954). The purpose of reflection on a just war is not to give people a right to war but to examine a situation to see if a violent response could be morally justified.

The *Catechism of the Catholic Church* offers a summary of the conditions necessary to justify the violence of war. The legitimate authority must attend to them carefully and prudently. We include them here:

- the damage inflicted by the aggressor on the nation or community of nations must be lasting, grave, and certain;
- all other means of putting an end to it must have been shown to be impractical or ineffective;
- there must be serious prospects of success;
- the use of arms must not produce evils and disorders graver than the evil to be eliminated. The power of modern means of destruction weighs very heavily in evaluating this condition (CCC §2309).

Despite a presumption for nonviolence, then, the Roman Catholic Tradition has recognized that, in this time between the Fall in the Garden of Eden and the fullness of the kingdom of God, we will encounter paradoxes in living the life of the kingdom fully now. While not offering *carte blanche* use of violence, the Tradition allows its proportionate and restrained use both in the internal protection of the state and in its international relations.

ECONOMIC LIFE: PRIVATE PROPERTY (CCC §§2402–2414)

The Church first weighed in on the issue of private property in the encyclical letter of Pope Leo XIII *On the Condition of Labor*, 1891. Writing at a time when workers' rights were of little concern, Pope Leo affirmed the right to private property as the fruit of the laborer's toil. This right was affirmed in subsequent documents which also highlighted the communal or social aspect of private property. Pope Paul VI affirmed the right to private property but said that this was not an absolute right and that one could not be justified in keeping excess goods to oneself while others lacked basic necessities (see *On the Development of Peoples*, §23).

The current teaching is summed up in the *Catechism of the Catholic Church* which states this: "The appropriation of property is legitimate for guaranteeing the freedom and dignity of persons and for helping each of them to meet his basic needs and the needs of those in his charge" (CCC §§2402). So, one's legitimate right to private property must yield to the primary gift of the earth to all people. In this regard, goods that are produced are still seen originally belonging to all (CCC §2403).

In the treatment of this issue in social ethics, notice the ongoing attempt to balance individual autonomy and the good of the community. The themes of respect for the dignity and rights of the individual, the social nature of the person in solidarity with others, as well as the preferential option for the poor are all at work in the analysis of private property.

SOCIAL LIFE: RESISTANCE TO THE STRANGER: RACISM/MIGRATION

Our discussion of the divisions of theology began by noting that theology is not really compartmentalized; it is about the revelation of Jesus Christ. Yet it is divided up simply to note the variety within the study of theology and the distinctiveness of some areas. To lose sight of its unity, however, runs the danger of losing its richness. As our discussion of the virtue of solidarity underscored, the human family is one, even though we may distinguish ourselves according to color, gender, language, culture, geographical location, and the like. Humanity is one. Several issues arise in social ethics because we have lost sight of our common humanity. They may be summarized under the heading "resistance to the stranger."

Racism: Racism is rooted in a belief of "the biologically determined superiority of one's own race or ethnic group with respect to others" (Pontifical Council for Justice and Peace, *The Church and Racism: Toward a More Fraternal Society,* §2). Racism, as we know, may take many forms. It may be institutionalized on a grand scale by way of political practices as for example the apartheid regime in South Africa in the late twentieth century, or on a smaller scale as in a country club or organization which excludes people based on their race.

In addition to race, discrimination and resistance to the stranger may be based on religious beliefs, ethnic background, language, financial status, educational achievement, and many other factors. In all cases, however, the fundamental flaw in reasoning is the belief that some human beings are superior to others. This bias flies in the face of the respect due to all persons because of their intrinsic dignity. It also violates the common good by trampling on the rights of the individual.

The *Pastoral Constitution on the Church in the Modern World* reminds us of the theological foundation for the equality of people and the ethical foundation for a rejection of racism and unjust discrimination.

All women and men are endowed with a rational soul and are created in God's image; they have the same nature and origin and, being redeemed by Christ, they enjoy the same divine calling and destiny; there is here a basic equality between all and it must be accorded ever greater recognition....Any kind of social or cultural discrimination in basic personal rights on the grounds of sex, race, color, social conditions, language or religion, must be curbed and eradicated as incompatible with God's design (§29).

Although we include racism under the heading of social life, its ramifications for the political and economic realms should be obvious as well. Catholic social teaching, of course, condemns any denigration of the human person, for any reason. Racism is a particular manifestation of this denigration with a clear foundation. Responses to racism must focus on the dignity of the person and the oneness of the human family, seeking solidarity with one another in all things.

Migration: The interdependence of the people of the world and the reality of globalization are evident in the migration of people from one land to another. People migrate for a variety of reasons, of course. Some do so of their own free will; others do so because they feel compelled to leave their homeland for reasons of safety. The latter we call refugees. How are they to be received?

Recall the list of rights which Pope John Paul II announced to the United Nations in 1979. Among them, "the right to freedom of movement, to internal and external migration; the right to nationality and residence." Catholic social teaching presumes hospitality on the part of the nation that receives immigrants, particularly refugees. Catholic social teaching would presume virtually no restrictions on refugees by a host country precisely because the refugees are fleeing their homeland because of danger to their persons. In this case, attention to the good of the individual and his or her rights are primary.

We see a balance of the common good and the individual good in the question of immigration that is voluntary. We ought not expect unlimited access to a country simply because the authorities responsible for the common good of their particular nation must balance the needs of immigrants with the legitimate needs of their own citizens. Participation in the common good places a responsibility on the individual to consider the good of all while making claims for his own individual rights. Still, barring harm to the common good of their nation, authorities should recognize the right of people to immigrate and offer hospitality to those who wish to cross borders.

The basis for the negative moral evaluation of racism and for the call for hospitality to migrants is once again our solidarity with all humanity and our concern for the good of all human beings. Pope Paul VI wished for a future free of conflict between nations, conflicts often based on a resistance to the stranger in our midst, the fear of the other. His words touch on a hope for the future of humanity as well, a future not marked by racism or by resistance to the immigrant, particularly the refugee, the stranger. Pope Paul VI wrote: "The past has too often been characterized by relationships of violence between nations; may the day dawn when international relations will be marked with the stamp of mutual respect and friendship, of interdependence in collaboration, the betterment of all seen as the responsibility of each individual" (*On the Development of Peoples*, §65).

The issues that we have reviewed in political, economic, and social life highlight the social good that we addressed earlier: solidarity, common good, preferential option for the poor, and respect for the individual and his or her rights. As we have seen, there is an ongoing tension between, yet careful attention to, the good of the whole community and of the individual member. Achieving an appropriate balance between these goods is critical to ensure social justice.

GUIDELINES FOR CONSIDERATION OF ISSUES IN SOCIAL ETHICS

In the previous section we have been able to address only a few issues in social ethics. Many more issues arise in our daily lives as committed Christians. We offer the following questions as a type of checklist to guide the moral analysis of new issues as they arise and as a tool for the formation of conscience. We recall the four overarching goods which are always operative in moral theology, that is, the value of human life, the dignity of the human person, the social nature of the human person, and the goodness of all Creation. Focusing on the social good, we highlight solidarity among all people, the common good, a preferential option for the poor, and the good of the individual secured by human rights.

1. As I examine this issue, what am I feeling? What is in my heart? Do I have a sense of solidarity with my brothers and sisters throughout the world? How am I invited to make God's loves my own at this time?

2. Is human life itself threatened by the matter under consideration?

3. Would approval of this issue present an obstacle to the individual's exercise of freedom so as to enhance his or her dignity? Is the dignity of the human person compromised by this issue? Are the rights of the individual being denied? Are human beings used as a means or an end?

4. Does the common good require sacrifice on the part of individuals in this matter—not a sacrifice where the dignity of the individual is compromised, but a legitimate sacrifice for the good of the whole community? Would approval of this issue deprive some people of participation in the common good?

5. What impact will this matter have on the poor, those whose ability to participate in the common life is obstructed in some way?

10. Conclusion

We have offered an overview of Catholic social teaching in this chapter in order to grasp the fundamental values which are upheld and to provide principles and criteria for judgment about issues in the area of social ethics in the political, economic, and social spheres. We began with a focus on the four overarching goods of human life, the dignity of the person, the social nature of the person, and the goodness of all Creation. With these foundational goods in mind we narrowed our focus to the particular way in which the social teaching of the Church fosters and protects these goods. We highlighted the twofold focus of the social nature of the human person and his or her intrinsic dignity. Roman Catholic social teaching stresses these two hallmarks of its teaching by focusing on the virtue and practice of solidarity, the common good, a preferential option for the poor, and human rights. Whether we are addressing the political, economic, or social dimensions of life, the focus must always be on the common good, balancing the needs of the community with individual needs. We offered a brief analysis of issues in the political, economic, and social realms to show how these goods are at work and how the social teaching of the Church constantly attempts to judge prudently about moral issues while honoring both the common good and the individual good. Fundamentally, social ethics is concerned with structuring the political, economic, and social dimensions of life so that the human person may flourish in community and so that the life of the kingdom may be enjoyed in a limited way here on earth.

The American writer Henry David Thoreau captured the importance and the beauty of our moral response when he wrote in *Walden Pond*: "It is something to be able to paint a particular picture, or to carve a statue, and so to make a few objects beautiful; but it is far more glorious to carve and paint the very atmosphere and medium through which we look, which morally we can do. To affect the quality of the day, that is the highest of arts" (Thoreau, "Where I Lived and What I Lived For," *Walden Pond*, Chapter 2). Our efforts for the transformation of our world into that of the kingdom of God affect the "quality of the day" for the poor and marginalized in particular and are one more way of making God's loves our own.

11. Selected Bibliography of Church Teaching on Social Ethics

Pope Leo XIII, *On the Condition of Labor (Rerum Novarum)*, 1891.

Pope Pius XI, *Reconstructing the Social Order (Quadragesimo Anno)*, 1931.

Pope John XXIII, *Christianity and Social Progress (Mater et Magistra)*, 1961.

Pope John XXIII, *Peace on Earth (Pacem in Terris)*, 1963.

Second Vatican Council, *Pastoral Constitution on the Church in the Modern World (Gaudium et Spes)*, 1965.

Second Vatican Council, *Decree on Religious Liberty (Dignitatis Humanae)*, 1965.

Pope Paul VI, *On the Development of Peoples (Populorum Progressio)*, 1967.

Pope Paul VI, *Call to Action (Octogesima Adveniens)*, 1971.

Synod of Bishops, *Justice in the World (Justitia in Mundo)*, 1971.

Latin American Bishops' Conference, *Evangelization in Latin America's Present and Future: The Final Document*, 1979.

John Paul II, *Address to the Thirty-Fourth General Assembly of the United Nations*, 1979.

John Paul II, *On Human Work (Laborem Exercens)*, 1981.

John Paul II, *On Social Concern (Sollicitudo Rei Socialis)*, 1987.

Pontifical Council for Justice and Peace, *The Church and Racism, Toward a More Fraternal Society*, 1988.

John Paul II, *On One Hundred Years of Catholic Social Teaching (Centesimus Annus)*, 1991.

John Paul II, *The Gospel of Life (Evangelium Vitae)*, 1995.

CHAPTER TWELVE

A Catholic Approach to the Environment

(CCC §§2415–2418, §2456)

1. Introduction

The sensitive frog called Kermit in the popular television series for children, "The Muppets," once sang the song, "It's Not Easy Being Green." Obviously, this endearing amphibian was referring to his own color. Today's Christians can sympathize with Kermit's sentiments. Since the industrial revolution, it has been very hard for Christians to be green, in the sense of being aware of their responsibility to care for the environment as a part of God's gift of Creation.

Pope John Paul II was so concerned about this lack of responsibility that he delivered a message at the World Day of Peace, January 1, 1990, entitled, *The Ecological Crisis: A Common Responsibility*. Since then, he has given further instructions on this often forgotten responsibility, including an address delivered at his regular Wednesday Audience on January 17, 2001. The Holy Father's concern continues a tradition both ancient and at once dear to the faithful, echoed in the ancient covenants of Israel, alluded to in the parables of Jesus, and exemplified in the life of Saint Francis of Assisi. Perhaps this concern is illustrated in his naming of Saint Francis of Assisi as the heavenly patron of those who promote ecology in 1979.

2. What Is This Crisis?

If we even quickly scan our planet, we will immediately see that men and women have, without any hesitation, in recent centuries, devastated wooded plains and valleys, polluted the waters of rivers, lakes, seas, and oceans, made the air in certain parts of the world almost unbreathable, disturbed atmospheric systems because of the buildup of the so-called "greenhouse gases," which include carbon dioxide, methane, and chlorofluorocarbons. These gases seem to threaten to raise the earth's temperature enough to accelerate dramatic climatic change. Manufactured gases are also depleting the ozone layer, that delicate shield which protects the earth and its people from harmful ultraviolet radiation, resulting in skin cancers, cataracts, and damage to the immune system. Verdant areas of the world are continually turning into deserts (John Paul II, "Commitment to Avoid Ecological Catastrophe," The Wednesday Audience, January 17, 2001, §3). We have the problem of huge quantities of industrial waste, the ceaseless burning of fossil fuels, unrestricted deforestation, the use of deadly herbicides, damaging coolants and propellants, all causing harm to our atmosphere and environment, sometimes irreversibly (The Ecological Crisis: A Common Responsibility, 1990, §6). Species of the animal world no longer exist; some reports say that in the tropical areas of our world over one hundred biological species are destroyed each day. In addition, decades of environmental neglect by the nuclear-weapons industry have left areas of our planet polluted. The litany could go on. Perhaps, for some of us we are only conscious of this growing problem when we notice that our favorite stretch of beach is littered with plastic bottles, empty cans, and an assortment of garbage. There is no doubt that there is an ecological crisis, and this chapter hopes to explain how this crisis is linked to our faith and to our moral lives as Christians and Catholics.

3. What Is the Cause of This Crisis?

The root cause of this crisis lies in the fact that we have often forgotten the mission given to us by the Creator of the world or we have distorted that mission for our own shortsighted ends. We must return to the Book of Genesis and the Creation accounts to recapture this mission. There is a recurring theme in the early chapters of Genesis. After God created, "God saw that it was good," and behold, "it was very good" (Gen 1). God then entrusts this goodness of Creation to the man and the woman, because they have been given abilities and gifts which distinguish them from the rest of Creation. With such gifts and abilities naturally come responsibilities. They are to exercise their dominion over the earth, with its fish in the seas, the birds in the sky, and every living thing that moves, with wisdom and love (Gen 1:28). But, as Pope John Paul II reminds us, this dominion or lordship is not absolute, but rather, ministerial. We are stewards of God's Creation, made in God's image, and so we share in God's care for Creation with "holiness and righteousness" (Wis 9:3).

The Decalogue itself harkens back to the Genesis Creation account when it links the day of rest, the seventh day, with the day God rested after the work of Creation was completed. Not only are the people to rest but also the natural world, the animals who help with their labor, and the land that bears fruit (Ex 20:8–10). The people of ancient Israel even set aside every seventh year, by law, as a time of rest for the land so that it could restore itself from human use (Lev 25).

4. The Breaking of Relationships

With the first sin came selfishness and a forgetting of the original mission so that "man is no longer the Creator's steward, but an autonomous despot" ("Commitment to Avoid Ecological Catastrophe," Wednesday Audience, January 17, 2001, §4). "Therefore the land mourns, and all who live in it languish; together with the wild animals and the birds of the air, and even the fish of the sea are perishing" (Hos 4:3). In the Old Testament, there is a systematic connection between the sin of human beings and the suffering of nature. When the relationship or covenant between God and humans is broken by sin, the relationships between not only humans, but also humans and the rest of Creation is upset. The prophets, especially Hosea, Amos, and Micah, demonstrate that there is a specific link between the suffering of Creation and human sin.

"The earth dries up and withers, / the world languishes and withers; / the heavens languish together with the earth. / The earth lies polluted / under its inhabitants; / for they have transgressed laws, / violated the statutes, / broken the everlasting covenant" (Isa 24:4–5). The ancient biblical people appreciated that we are all connected in intertwining relationships, God with Creation and Creation with God, God with people and they with God, Creation with people and people with Creation. We are interdependent.

When we come to our senses and recognize this order ordained by God, as in the story of Noah, after the flood, God creates a new covenant (Gen 9:1–17). This new relationship is not only between God and humanity but also between God and the natural world, namely the animals (Gen 9:10–12) and the earth as a whole (Gen 9:13). Noah, that just man, understood the true meaning of having dominion over Creation, for he took male and female of each animal into his ark to save them from destruction (Gen 6:19).

5. Behold the Lilies of the Field

How often Jesus referred to nature as an instrument of preaching and teaching. The birds of the air and the lilies of the fields in their freedom and their beauty should inspire us to trust in the loving care of our Father (Mt 6:25–33), grace is like the wheat growing silently at night while the farmer sleeps (Mk 4:26–29). We are to be connected to Jesus as the branches are to the vine, and we will be pruned in life but just like the vine we will have greater growth and produce more fruit than before (Jn 15:1–8). One of the most powerful images of the Gospel is the comparison that Jesus draws between himself and the good shepherd who protects and loves his sheep and always goes after the lost one (Lk 15:4–7). In our simplicity, a simplicity that touches upon a truth, we always like to have the animals in the Christmas crib at the very birth of Jesus. Why? Because it gives a sense that all Creation is mysteriously linked; Jesus was close to Creation at his birth and Creation itself wanting to be part of the birth of the Savior. We have man and woman, Joseph and Mary, the God made man, the infant Jesus, the angels of the heavens with its guiding star, and the creatures of the earth united in wonder and praise.

But it is not always "O Holy Night, the Stars Are Brightly Shining." Sometimes we can no longer even see the stars. Generations continue to show a callous disregard for the harmony of Creation and the order established by our Creator. The disregard is now fed by modern consumerism in many parts of the world, a consumerism that breeds the attitude that we should all have what we want when we want it and that more is always better. In other words, modern society will find no solution to the ecological problem unless it takes a serious look at its lifestyle and it recaptures what Pope John Paul II calls the "aesthetic value of creation" (*The Ecological Crisis*, §§13–14). Let us start with this aesthetic value of Creation and, aided by the life of Saint Francis of Assisi, move towards an examination of our own individual lifestyle.

6. Brother Sun and Sister Moon

One of the most famous stories about Saint Francis takes place in front of the bishop of Assisi. Francis and his father, after their endless disputes, go before the bishop in the hope of some kind of solution. Saint Bonaventure tells us that in the heat of the moment Francis takes off all his clothes and returns them to his earthly father saying:

"Until now I have called you father here on earth. But now I can say without reservation, Our Father who art in heaven, since I have placed all my treasure and my hope in him" (Saint Bonaventure, *Legenda major*, c. 2, 4). Bonaventure is quick to explain the meaning of this radical action. Francis realizes who he really is, a creature of God. All he is and all he has is purely a gift from God. A dependence on God is also true of all other created things. We have something in common with the rest of Creation, namely, God has made us all from the earth and holds us all in existence. Not only is this a humbling realization, one that should make us want to express our gratitude to the Creator, but it should temper or order our attitude toward the rest of Creation. We are linked to all Creation, and all Creation is good, and God loves all Creation for he finds it "very good." Should we not also love Creation? Just as we thank God for making us, the rest of Creation, in a sense, gives praise to the Creator also, and reflects the beauty of God. Indeed, the Bible often refers to the goodness and beauty of Creation as the glory of God (Gen 1:4; Ps 8; Wis 13:3–5; Sir 39:16).

Saint Paul reminds us that from the greatness and beauty of created things comes a corresponding perception of the greatness and goodness of our Creator (Rom 1:20). In fact: "Our very contact with nature has a deep restorative power, contemplation of its magnificence imparts peace and serenity" (*The Ecological Crisis*, §14). Saint Thomas Aquinas taught that the diversity of Creation reflects God's glory and that in fact God created such a diverse and beautiful world so that what one creature was lacking in the representation of the divine goodness might be made up for by another. Thus, he concluded that the universe as a whole participates in the divine goodness more perfectly and represents it better than any single creature does. With such a spirituality and realization of the value of Creation, the impulse to disregard the cosmos endowed with its own internal balance and order can give way to an attitude of respect and gratefulness.

7. The Ecological Crisis and Human Ecology: A Moral Problem

It is only in recent years that we have rediscovered the delicate and intricate link that exists between all facets of Creation. We now realize that one cannot interfere in one area of the ecosystem without paying attention to the consequences of such an interference in so many other areas, and on the impact of any interference on the well-being of future generations (*The Ecological Crisis*, §6). "The dominion granted by the Creator over the mineral, vegetable, and animal resources of the universe cannot be separated from respect for moral obligations, including those toward generations to come" (CCC §2456). Disrespect for the environment reveals an underlying disrespect for life, including human life. Pope John Paul II makes this point very forcefully, calling our attention to interests in production that cause environmental damage, disregard for the dignity and health of workers, and pollution on such a scale that reveals a genuine contempt for our fellow men and women (*The Ecological Crisis*, §7). In other words, ecology is inseparably connected to justice. Right relationships with our environment mean right relationships with our fellow human beings, and respect for human life entails a respect for all of Creation. Let us illustrate this point by referring to a very useful parish resource published by the United States Conference of Catholic Bishops in 1996 called *Let the Earth Bless the Lord: God's Creation and Our Responsibility: A Catholic Approach to the Environment*. It states from the very beginning that "the Church recognizes that the web of life and the promotion of human dignity are linked to the protection and care of God's Creation" (*Let the Earth Bless the Lord*, §1).

8. A Few Sobering Facts

In his challenging publication, Kevin James Lee writes about environmental refugees in Africa (*Environmental Refugees: A New Chapter in a Familiar Story*). He states that some thirty thousand deaths occur each day because of polluted water which causes 75 percent of the world's diseases. In their poverty, many people, especially refugees, cut down trees for fuel, shelter, and for their grazing animals; the result can be devastating deforestation. Why is this devastating? Deforestation causes massive erosion of the soil, increased rates of siltation in rivers and irrigation systems, and greater potential for flooding. Land degradation, water contamination, and deforestation are serious threats to human life throughout the world, not just in Africa.

We might be tempted to offer the simple answer to this problem and to other problems like it—namely, that people in these countries should cease such harmful activities. It is only a simple answer for those of us who live in rich countries. To start with, in contrast to rich countries, nearly half the world's poorest people live in ecologically fragile areas where the land is far less productive. Such people simply struggle to stay alive each day, and in their struggle there is little time, energy, or profit gained from being concerned about the environment. The world has become a place of terrifying contrasts. Barbara Kohen, also a contributor to *Let the Earth Bless the Lord*, tells us that the combined income of the world's 358 billionaires equals the combined income of half the world's entire population of 2.5 billion (*The Flourishing of the Human Family*, §18). The world's richest 20 percent consumes 86 percent of the world's resources. The United States produces 23 percent of the world's carbon monoxide emissions while it is populated by only 4 percent of the world's peoples.

9. So What on Earth Can We Do?

Contrast some of the above figures with the Church's teaching that the earth is ultimately a common heritage where its fruits are for the benefit of all. "God destined the earth and all its contains for all people and nations" (*Pastoral Constitution on the Church in the Mod-*

ern World, §69). Created things, therefore, belong not to the few, but to the entire human family. There is an injustice if the privileged continue to accumulate excess goods and squander the world's resources which forces those living in conditions of misery to scratch out an existence, regardless of the consequences for the environment and future generations. "Today, the dramatic threat of ecological breakdown is teaching us the extent to which greed and selfishness—both individual and collective—are contrary to the order of Creation, an order which is characterized by mutual interdependence" (*The Ecological Crisis,* §8).

A NEW SOLIDARITY AMONG THE NATIONS

The management of the earth's goods and the earth's health transcends the borders of separate countries and states. There is a need for an internationally coordinated approach. The relationship between the highly industrialized nations and the developing nations becomes pivotal. It would be unjust for the former to impose restrictive environmental standards on the developing countries but to ignore the same standards within their own borders. World leaders carry so much responsibility in this area of international solidarity and justice. "The ecological crisis reveals the urgent moral need for a new solidarity, especially in relations between the developing nations and those that are highly industrialized. States must increasingly share responsibility, in complementary ways, for the promotion of a natural and social environment that is both peaceful and healthy" (*The Ecological Crisis,* §10).

AN OPTION FOR THE POOR

Both the heart of the problem and the key to the solution are linked to structural forms of poverty in our world. In the Old Testament, the "anawim," those on the margins, the poor, the widows, the orphans, and the stranger were special to God. This option for the poor, or special regard and concern for them, is also central to the ministry and message of Jesus in the gospels. It is the poor who suffer most from environmental hardships and disasters. It would be unjust to strive to improve the environment while making the poor bear the brunt of the burden—for example, if we clean up a particular area or district, but in the process leave the poor in that district without jobs, shelter, or food. "Nature will truly enjoy its second spring only when humanity has compassion for its own weakest members" (United States Conference of Catholic Bishops, *Renewing the Earth: An Invitation to Reflection and Action on Environment in Light of Catholic Social Teaching*, §48).

What are these structural forms of poverty towards which human compassion must turn? Unjust land distribution in many countries leads to subsistence farming, which in turn leads to the exhaustion of the land. There is urgent need for land distribution reform. Heavily indebted developing countries believe they have to destroy their natural heritage so as to survive. The repaying of international debts and the developing of exports in many of these countries comes at the price of irreparable ecological damage. During his lifetime, Pope Paul VI had hoped for an era when "developing countries will thus no longer risk being overwhelmed by debts whose payment swallows up the greater part of their gains" (*On the Development of Peoples,* §54). Pope John Paul II has the same hope. "The poor, to whom the earth is entrusted no less than to others, must find a way out of their poverty. This will require a courageous reform of structures, as well as new ways of relating among peoples and states" (*The Ecological Crisis*, §11).

SUSTAINABLE DEVELOPMENT?

The phrase "sustainable development" really poses a question: How can we on the one hand meet the economic and social needs of people today throughout the world and on the other hand keep in mind the needs of future generations after us without doing irreparable damage to our environment? The word "sustainable" is significant because it does not refer to some quick-fix solution that will offer employment to poor people just for the moment or the immediate future. For example, a large chemical factory is to be built in a poor part of Asia by a multinational company; this project will bring large profits to a First World country because of the cheap labor found in the Third World country and also give employment to the locals. But it also pollutes the atmosphere, the rivers, and the soil with toxic waste and damages the long-term health of the workers. This picture is not one of sustainable development.

Sustainable development will take greater planning, greater honesty, and greater generosity on the part of both the developed country and the developing country. Powerful nations that have a huge influence over international economic forces have a special role and responsibility, while developing nations need national policies that consider the poor and the local environment. All nations will have to work together for this sustainable development. This is why Pope John Paul II argues that "No plan or organization, however, will be able to effect the necessary changes unless world leaders are truly convinced of the absolute need for this new solidarity, which is demanded of them by the ecological crisis and which is essential for peace" (*The Ecological Crisis*, §10).

AN END TO WAR

Recent history has demonstrated that despite international agreements, chemical, bacteriological, and biological warfare and experimentation continues. We have weapons that can radically alter the balance of nature. Even conventional warfare destroys human life and social structures, damages the land, poisons the water and soil, destroys forests and vegetation, and often forces huge numbers of refugees to move into areas that cannot sustain or cope with their basic human needs. War is the scourge of the environment as well as its peoples. Working together for peace is at the same time working together to protect a fragile environment.

A CHANGE OF ATTITUDE AND LIFESTYLE

Perhaps many Catholics once dismissed ecological issues as being only the concern of radical "green" groups. Unless we opt to be very selective regarding Church teaching, those dismissive days are over. The Church is calling us all to a genuine conversion in thought and behavior in this matter. "We need a change of heart to save the planet for our children and generations yet unborn" (*Renewing the Earth*, §417). We also need a sense of moderation, simplicity, and self-discipline, as is called for by Pope John Paul II, and a rejection of instant gratification, consumerism, and indifference to the damage we cause to the environment. Inspired by these sentiments, the Italian bishops went so far as to state that ecological awareness correctly understood is no less than a dimension of Christian asceticism. The ecological crisis is truly a moral issue, for it involves conversion, justice, and God's right order. That is why we treat it as a special issue in this book.

EDUCATION

Many of us are simply not aware of the state of our own environment or the ecological crisis that is taking place in other parts of the world. An education in ecological facts and responsibilities is a good starting point for most Catholics. *Let the Earth Bless the Lord* suggests that parishes launch an environmental justice initiative for the purpose of education and action. *Renewing the Earth* invites "teachers and educators to emphasize in their classrooms and curricula a respect for nature, and a commitment to practices and behavior that bring these attitudes into the daily lives of their students and themselves" (§415). Pope John Paul II reminds us that such education begins in the home. "The first educator, however, is the family, where the child learns to respect his neighbor and to love nature" (*The Ecological Crisis*, §13).

INFLUENCING POLICY

While the small things we do all make a difference, such as purchasing and using recyclable goods, choosing to reduce our use of disposable plastics, and purchasing non-toxic cleaning products, it is national and international policies that have a huge influence on the future of our environment. We should be aware of our country's commitment to humanitarian assistance, to research, and our government's involvement in various international protocols that are aimed at protecting our earth. Not only should we be aware of our country's stance, but we should use our influence to further ecologically sound policy.

> We urge policy makers and public officials to focus more directly on the ethical dimensions of environmental policy and on its relation to development, to seek the common good, and to resist short-term pressures in order to meet our long-term responsibility to future generations....We need to use our voices and votes to shape a nation more committed to the universal good and an ethic of environmental solidarity (*Renewing the Earth*, §416).

10. Hopeful Signs for Renewing the Face of the Earth

Christians must approach any crisis with the virtue of hope, and there are reasons to be hopeful. Theologians, ethicists, and scripture scholars are rediscovering and enriching the insights of our Catholic tradition on the relationship between the dignity of the human person and the care of God's Creation. One only needs to walk into a Christian bookshop or library to be overwhelmed by the volume of writing and reflection dedicated to this concern. We have noticed this renewed interest in the environment during our visits to the classroom or discussions with youth in the parishes. Scientists, experts in the environment, and economists continue to make predictions and suggestions in order to move the world and its leaders to action. The teaching Church continues to place the challenge and the call to conversion regarding the environment and justice before the faithful. Citizens throughout the world are making their voices heard and their votes count when it comes to the choice of leaders who will protect our ecological heritage and show concern for the poor and vulnerable.

As Pope John Paul II reminds us, Christians have a special responsibility in this area and should be leaders. We believe that God is the Creator, that his Creation is good, that we are called to be stewards, that we are called to love our brothers and sisters, especially those most in need. After all we are called to make God's loves our own. "The commitment of believers to a healthy environment for everyone stems directly from their belief in God the Creator, from their recognition of the effects of original and personal sin, and from the certainty of having been redeemed in Christ" (*The Ecological Crisis*, §16).

11. Let All the Earth Praise the Lord: Guidelines for Consideration

When you have a little free time, look again at the blue of the ocean and the incredible beauty and variety of the plants and flowers in your region, smell the fresh air if you visit the mountains, and hear the birds in the countryside. As the saying goes: "Stop and smell the flowers" for all of creation—day and night, fire and wind, sea and land—reveals the glory of God and his closeness to his people (CCC §1147). To be aware of the wonder of God's Creation enables us to be in touch with the crime of its destruction. Let us not forget that people are the apex of Creation and that they suffer when the earth is abused.

The following questions may help us to be more attentive to the ecological issues and more critical of the abuse of the environment.

1. In a world often obsessed with owning, controlling, and consuming, do governments and business enterprises give enough attention to the delicate nature of the environment, the struggles of the poor, and the responsibility to preserve the world's natural heritage and resources for future generations?

2. What priorities and lifestyles need to change in order to improve the lives of those who are victims of an abused environment? How can one observe the admonishment of the *Catechism of the Catholic Church* to consume goods in moderation so that the better part of them should be given to the sick and the poor (CCC §2405).

3. Do the products people use, the companies they invest in, and the political votes they cast help to restore our environment or contribute to the present ecological crisis?

4. Is it possible that people are simply uninformed and make decisions out of ignorance or the assumption that they are masters over God's Creation rather than stewards?

Acknowledging the solidarity among all creatures arising from the fact that all have the same Creator and all are ordered to his glory (CCC §344), we can pray the prayer of Azariah:

Bless the Lord, you heavens; sing praise to him and
　　highly exalt him forever,
Bless the Lord, you angels of the Lord;
Bless the Lord, all you waters;
Bless the Lord, sun and moon;
Bless the Lord, stars of heaven;
Bless the Lord, all rain and dew;
Bless the Lord, mountains and hills,

Bless the Lord, all that grows in the ground;

Bless the Lord, you whales and all that swim in the waters;

Bless the Lord, all birds of the air;

Bless the Lord, all wild animals and cattle;

Bless the Lord, spirits and souls of the righteous;

Bless the Lord, you who are holy and humble of heart;

All who worship the Lord, bless the God of gods,

sing praise to him and give thanks to him,

for his mercy endures forever.

The Prayer of Azariah, from the Book of Daniel

12. Selected Bibliography of Church Teaching on the Environment

Paul VI, *On the Development of Peoples (Populorum Progressio),* 1967.

Paul VI, *Call to Action (Octogesima Adveniens),* 1971.

John Paul II, *The Ecological Crisis: A Common Responsibility,* 1990.

United States Conference of Catholic Bishops, *Renewing the Earth: An Invitation to Reflection and Action on Environment in Light of Catholic Social Teaching,* 1991.

United States Conference of Catholic Bishops, *Let the Earth Bless the Lord: God's Creation and Our Responsibility, A Catholic Approach to the Environment,* 1996.

John Paul II, *"Commitment to Avoid Ecological Catastrophe,"* The Wednesday Audience, January 17, 2001.

Afterword

Saint Alphonsus introduced his moral theology with the following words to his readers:

> My intention in writing this *Moral Theology*, which has a strictly practical goal, was not to present you with a thick scholastic treatise on "human actions." Rather, wanting to help with the salvation of souls, I believed myself obliged to choose solely those questions which, in this area, we deem the most necessary and useful to know for the conduct of life. Had I acted otherwise in my studies I would have wasted both my lamp oil and my efforts; and you, dear reader, would be wasting your time in reading such useless writings (Alphonsus, *Gaudé*, II, 689).

Our goals were not different from Saint Alphonsus. We set out to present the essentials of moral theology within the Roman Catholic Tradition. We began with a recognition that the moral life and moral theology are lived and studied under the impulse of God's grace. Creating us for love, God graces us to respond in love, to find our way home. Our hope for the reader is that this work has contributed to a greater understanding of the relationship between faith and who we are called to be as people made in the image of God, that it has helped to grasp more completely the fullness of life to which we are called.

We pray that we have not wasted both our lamp oil and efforts and that you, dear reader, have not found here useless writings.

Glossary of Terms

Abortion   Abortion is "the deliberate and direct killing, by whatever means it is carried out, of a human being in the initial phase of his or her existence, extending from conception to birth (John Paul II, *The Gospel of Life*, §58)

Act, Human   A human act is one which requires freedom and knowledge on the part of the moral agent. When these requirements are not present, due to ignorance or passion, one's culpability is lessened.

Artificial Insemination   In this process, the male spermatozoa is inserted into a woman to bring about conception.

Beatitudes   The promise of Christ concerning happiness or blessedness as proclaimed in the Sermon on the Mount (Mt 5:3–12; Lk 6:20–23). They are considered basic qualities of Christian holiness (CCC §§1716–1719).

Bioethics   Bioethics is that branch of moral theology which deals with questions of life, its protection, and enhancement.

Birth Control/Responsible Parenthood   Parents may wish to space the birth of their children or, for serious reasons, choose not to have children at a particular time. In doing so, they should use means consistent with Church teaching. Parents also have the duty to make sure that their decision in regard to the spacing of children is made responsibly and unselfishly (CCC §2368).

Chastity Chastity is the virtue associated with sexuality. The chaste person successfully integrates sexuality within himself or herself as a body/soul unity (CCC §2337). Chastity "consists in self-control, in the capacity of guiding the sexual instinct to the service of love and of integrating it in the development of the person" (*Educational Guidance in Human Love*, §18).

Common Good The common good is "the sum total of social conditions which allow people, either as groups or as individuals, to reach their fulfillment more fully and more easily" (*Pastoral Constitution on the Church in the Modern World*, §26).

Conscience Conscience refers to the secret core and sanctuary where a person is alone with God (*Pastoral Constitution on the Church in the Modern World*, §16). In exercising conscience, persons are able to perceive principles of morality, apply them in given circumstances, and make a judgment about acts they are going to perform or have already done.

Conscience, Correct A correct conscience judges as good that which is truly good and as evil that which is truly evil.

Conscience, Erroneous An erroneous conscience judges as good that which is evil or as evil that which is good. An erroneous conscience may be vincibly erroneous or invincibly erroneous.

Conversion Conversion is a change of heart, a turn away from sin, and a return to God's embrace.

Definitive Dogma Definitive dogma refers to teachings "proposed by the church—whether in solemn judgment or in the ordinary and universal magisterium—as divinely revealed and calling for faith" (Congregation for the Doctrine of the Faith, *Profession of Faith*).

Deposit of Faith   The deposit of faith is a term used to describe the sum of revelation and tradition entrusted to the Church and its teaching office to be safeguarded and passed on from one generation to the next within the Christian community.

Desire   God creates us with a longing for himself and for the good. Desire is the emotion which moves us to love what is good. Desires are properly ordered when we love and are drawn to that which is really good. They are disordered when we perceive and pursue as good that which is really harmful to ourselves or others.

Dignity, Human   Human dignity refers to the stature that human beings possess as people created in the image and likeness of God. Human dignity is not conferred on people based on their reputation, their productivity, or their self-sufficiency.

Dissent   Dissent refers primarily to a public acknowledgment of one's inability to accept the teaching of the Church, whether definitive or non-definitive, infallibly defined or not. Official Church documents refer to dissent as "carefully orchestrated protests and polemics carried on in the media" (*The Splendor of Truth*, §113), which are opposed to unity in the Church.

Doctrine   Doctrine refers to all teachings of the Church, some presumed to be divinely revealed, others less directly connected to divine revelation but still important for the faithful.

Doctrine, Definitive   The truths of definitive doctrine are a "deeper understanding of some truth concerning faith or morals" (Pope John Paul II, *Ad Tuendam Fidem*, §3). They are "required for the sacred preservation and faithful explanation of the...deposit of faith" (*Code of Canon Law*, canon 750, §2).

Doctrine, Authoritative Non-definitive   Authoritative non-definitive doctrine is teaching which is related to the more fundamental truths of the faith but not in a way in which the teaching is "required for the sacred preservation and faithful explanation of the...deposit of the faith" (*Code of Canon Law*, canon 750, §2). These teachings are the moral wisdom offered by the magisterium to the Church community as its best understanding of the truth of the matter under consideration, whether that be a theological opinion or a particular moral issue.

Dogma   Dogma refers to the basic tenets or creeds of the faith. They are presumed to be divinely revealed.

Embryo   The human being in the first six weeks of development. The embryo and all human life must be treated as a person from conception (CCC §2274).

Environmental Ethics   Environmental ethics is a relatively new area of reflection in moral theology. It begins with a recognition that human beings are stewards of God's Creation, even while being the crown of Creation. Environmental ethics attempts to guide sustainable development in a way which respects the needs of humanity as well as the goodness of Creation, recognizing that our environment is a heritage to be handed on to future generations.

Euthanasia   Euthanasia is "an action or omission which of itself and by intention causes death, with the purpose of eliminating all suffering. Euthanasia's terms of reference, therefore, are to be found in the intention of the will and in the methods used" (*The Gospel of Life*, §65; see also *Declaration on Euthanasia*).

Freedom, Human   Human freedom is a gift of the Creator unique to humanity. Made in the image and likeness of God, human beings are not predetermined but invited to respond to God's love by shaping themselves as people of love. Freedom is characterized not so much as liberty from constraints as capacity to choose for excellence.

Habit   A habit is a disposition to some thought or act facilitated by repetition.

Health   Health refers to physical, psychological, and spiritual well-being. One suffers and experiences poor health when disequilibrium is present in any of these areas.

Human (Moral) Virtues   Prudence, justice, fortitude, and temperance are called the human or moral virtues. They are the fruit of God's grace and human freedom, shaping people in the image of God. These virtues are also the cardinal (from the Latin word *cardo* meaning "hinge") virtues because all the other virtues are related to them (CCC §§1805–1809).

Infallibility   Infallibility means that something is without error. In the Church, infallibility refers to a charism possessed by the pope, as head of the college of bishops, and the bishops themselves, in union with the pope. It refers to the authority with which a teaching is proclaimed and affirms that the teaching office of the Church cannot err when it teaches infallibly in the area of faith and morals.

Killing and Letting Die   The Church accepts the distinction between killing and letting die, regarding innocent human life. Killing means taking deliberate steps to bring about death while one may let someone die through inaction. All killing of innocent human life is wrong. All letting die is not wrong, depending on the circumstances and intention of the person acting.

Magisterium   The magisterium is comprised of the bishops of the Church and is the authentic interpreter of Scripture and Tradition for the Catholic community. There are various expressions of this teaching office. The extraordinary magisterium refers to the pope speaking in union with the college of bishops or speaking alone as head of the college of bishops. The ordinary magisterium takes different forms: a national episcopal conference, a region of bishops, or the teaching of a single bishop (including the pope).

Moral Act, Components   Every moral act has three components: the object, the intention, and the circumstances. The object is what is done; the intention points to the desired goal; and the circumstances are all the relevant factors which contribute to the moral dilemma.

Moral Life   The moral life is the response to the initiative of love that God has taken on our behalf (*The Splendor of Truth*, §10). Called to the fullness of life, our free response is evident in virtuous moral lives and virtuous actions or in abuses of freedom evidenced in vice and sin.

Moral Theology   Moral Theology is that branch of theology which studies the implications of our faith for the type of persons we become and the kinds of actions that we do. It is a systematic presentation of the development of the Catholic Tradition in this area of theology.

Natural Family Planning   Through natural family planning, couples exercise responsible parenthood by restricting their expressions of love through the conjugal act to infertile periods of the woman. This method of contraception is consistent with Church teaching (CCC §2370).

Natural Law   Through natural law, human beings attempt to grasp the mind of God and his will for humanity and the world. Natural law presumes that the Creator ordered the world for the good of all creatures and placed within the hearts of human beings an ability to understand that order to some degree and to exercise their freedom consistent with it. The Tradition has always suggested that natural law is based primarily on human reason.

Norms   A norm is an action guide that describes conduct to be avoided as morally wrong (proscribed) or to be done as morally right (prescribed). Formal norms relate to our character ("Be charitable"); material norms are particular, behavioral, specific, and concrete ("Do not steal").

Reason   Reason is a distinctive mark of humanity. It is the power of the intellect to distinguish the truth. Reason is often placed in opposition to emotion and passion, but mature human reason will draw on the emotions in its discernment of the truth. Thus, the truly reasonable person is characterized by properly ordered feeling, thinking, willing, and acting.

Right Moral Action   Actions are judged morally right when they contribute to the authentic human good of a person. When they do so, they are also directed toward God who is the ultimate goal of human life. In God is our "full and perfect happiness" (*The Splendor of Truth*, §72).

Sensus Fidei   The *sensus fidei* refers to a kind of intuition that believers have as to what pertains to the faith and what does not. The Second Vatican Council says that because of this *sensus fidei* the faithful recognize the Word of God for what it is, cling to the faith, penetrate its depths, and apply it to life (*Dogmatic Constitution on Divine Revelation*, §12).

Sensus Fidelium   The *sensus fidelium* refers to the thought of the faithful on a particular matter. Founded on the *sensus fidei*, the *sensus fidelium* asks what the faith community believes about a particular issue in light of their faith.

Sexual Ethics   Sexual ethics is that branch of moral theology which deals primarily with the relational nature of the human person. Accepting sexuality and sexual energy as a gift from God, sexual ethics offers guidance in the proper channeling of one's sexual energy, particularly through the virtue of chastity.

Sexuality   Sexuality is "a dimension of one's restless heart, which continually yearns for interpersonal communion, glimpsed and experienced to varying degrees in this life, ultimately finding full oneness only in God, here and hereafter....[A] fundamental component of personality in and through which we, as male or female, experience our relatedness to self, others, the world, and even God" (*Human Sexuality: A Catholic Perspective for Education and Lifelong Learning*, §9).

Sin   Sin is a break in relationship with God which is the result of a free choice for evil on the part of a person. Sin also breaks relationships with others, with ourselves, and with all of Creation.

Sin, Mortal   Mortal sin destroys love in our hearts, referred to in the *Catechism* as sanctifying grace (CCC §1861). It turns us away from God, who is our ultimate end, and consequently eternal happiness (CCC §1855). For such a radical disorder to occur, three conditions must be met: the object or the concern of our action must be grave, we must choose with full knowledge what we are doing, and do so with deliberate consent (CCC §§1873–1874).

Sin, Social   All sin is social in that it affects our relationship with God and others. Social sin, a term coined in the late 1960s, refers to sinful structures which are systemically dehumanizing and encourage personal sin.

Sin, Venial   A venial sin is a less serious choice for evil. It does not constitute a complete turning away from God's love.

Sin, Original   Original sin occurred at the origins of the human race; the personal sin of Adam, as described in Genesis 2:8—3:24, passed on to all persons (with the certain exception of Jesus Christ and the Blessed Virgin Mary) as a privation of grace; original sin is not a personal sin committed by each individual but, rather, in the words of Pope Paul VI, "it is human nature so fallen, stripped of the grace that clothed it, injured in its natural powers and subjected to the dominion of death, that is transmitted to all men, and it is in this sense that every man is born in sin" (*Credo of the People of God*).

Social Teaching of the Church   Social ethics is concerned with structuring the political, economic, and social dimensions of life in the light of the gospel so that the human person may flourish in community and so that the life of the kingdom of God may be enjoyed in a limited way here on earth.

Theological Virtues   The theological virtues are faith, hope, and charity. These are given to humanity to find its way home to God more easily. These virtues are divine precisely because they come from God and move us toward God.

Tradition   A tradition is a fundamental structure of human and social life, based on the long history of various cultures throughout the world. Tradition is about the transmission or the handing on of the meaning of life. It is a guide to living, a map for the difficult terrain of living, surviving, and even flourishing with meaning and purpose.

Tradition, Roman Catholic   The Roman Catholic Tradition, along with Sacred Scripture but always as its servant, is one of the sources of revelation in the Catholic Church. "Tradition and scripture make up a single sacred deposit of the word of God, which is entrusted to the church" (*Dogmatic Constitution on Divine Revelation*, §10).

Virtue   A virtue is a habitual and determined tending toward the good which disposes a person to do the right thing (CCC §1803). See human virtues and theological virtues.

Wrong Moral Action   Actions are judged to be morally wrong when they do harm to the human person. Unlike right moral actions, these actions are not directed to God who is the ultimate goal of human life. Rather they are choices for a short-term goal which is harmful to the person.

Index